The Complete Guide to Selling on

The Complete Guide to Selling on eBay for Beginners 2025

Building Your Online Business from Scratch

Camila Goda

The Complete Guide to Selling on eBay for Beginners 2025

DISCLAIMER

While every precaution has been taken in the preparation of this book, the publisher assumes no responsibility for errors or omissions, or for damages resulting from the use of the information contained herein.

The Complete Guide to Selling on eBay for Beginners 2025: Building Your Online Business from Scratch

First edition.

The Complete Guide to Selling on eBay for Beginners 2025

COPYRIGHT © CAMILA GODA 2025. ALL RIGHTS RESERVED

Before this document can be legally duplicated or reproduced in any manner, the publisher's consent must be gained. Therefore, the contents within this document can neither be stored electronically, transferred, nor kept in a database. Neither in part, nor in full can this document be copied, scanned, faxed, or retained without approval from the publisher or creator.

The Complete Guide to Selling on eBay for Beginners 2025

TABLE OF CONTENTS

Disclaimer 2
Copyright © Camila Goda 2025. All Rights Reserved 3
Table of Contents 4
Introduction 10
    Welcome to the World of eBay Selling 10
        What Makes eBay a Great Platform for Beginners? 10
        Understanding the eBay Marketplace in 2025: Trends and Opportunities 12
        Setting Realistic Expectations and Goals 16
        Essential Terminology You Need to Know 18
        Navigating the eBay Platform: A Beginner's Tour 22
Chapter 1 25
    Setting Up Your eBay Seller Account for Success 25
        Creating a New eBay Account: Step-by-Step 25
        Choosing the Right Account Type: Personal vs. Business 28
        Verifying Your Account and Payment Information 31
        Understanding eBay's Seller Fees and Structures (2025 Updates). 34
        Exploring eBay Managed Payments: How It Works 36
Chapter 2 40
    Crafting Your Seller Profile and Building Trust 40
        Choosing a Professional and Memorable Username 40
        Writing a Compelling "About Me" Section 42
        Setting Up Your Return Policy and Shipping Preferences 45
        Understanding and Utilizing eBay's Feedback System 48
        Building a Positive Seller Reputation from Day One 51
Chapter 3 55
    Discovering Profitable Items to Sell on eBay 55
        Identifying Your Niche: Passion, Knowledge, and Market Demand 55

The Complete Guide to Selling on eBay for Beginners 2025

    Researching Product Ideas: Trends, Best-Sellers, and Underserved Markets 58

    Sourcing Your Inventory 61

    Understanding Product Regulations and Restrictions on eBay 64

Chapter 4 67

    Creating High-Converting eBay Listings: The Essentials 67

    Writing Compelling and Keyword-Rich Titles 67

    Crafting Detailed and Persuasive Product Descriptions 69

    Utilizing eBay's Item Specifics for Maximum Visibility.................... 72

    Understanding Condition Guidelines and Being Honest 75

    Setting Competitive Pricing Strategies 77

Chapter 5 81

    The Power of Visuals: Taking and Optimizing Product Photos 81

    Essential Equipment for Great Product Photography (Even on a Budget) 81

    Lighting Techniques for Clear and Appealing Images 83

    Composition and Angles to Showcase Your Items 86

    Editing and Optimizing Photos for eBay's Requirements 89

    Using Multiple Images to Increase Buyer Confidence 92

Chapter 6 96

    Mastering eBay's Listing Formats and Options 96

    Auction vs. Fixed-Price Listings: Choosing the Right Approach 96

    Understanding "Buy It Now" and "Best Offer" Options 98

    Scheduling Listings for Optimal Visibility..................................... 101

    Utilizing eBay's Promoted Listings for Increased Exposure (Introduction).. 104

    Exploring eBay's International Selling Options (Introduction) 106

Chapter 7 111

    Managing Your Sales and Orders Effectively 111

    Understanding eBay's Seller Hub: Your Central Command Center 111

    Tracking Sales and Monitoring Your Inventory 114

    Communicating with Buyers Professionally and Promptly 116

Handling Payments and Understanding eBay's Payment Processes 119

Dealing with Cancellations and Returns 122

Chapter 8 125

Streamlining Your Shipping Process for Success 125

Understanding eBay's Shipping Options and Policies 125

Calculating Shipping Costs Accurately 128

Choosing the Right Packaging Materials 131

Printing Shipping Labels Through eBay and Other Services 134

Tracking Shipments and Keeping Buyers Informed 136

Exploring Different Shipping Carriers and Their Advantages 139

Chapter 9 142

Providing Excellent Customer Service: Building Loyalty 142

The Importance of Positive Customer Interactions 142

Responding to Inquiries and Resolving Issues Effectively 145

Handling Negative Feedback Professionally 147

Encouraging Positive Feedback and Reviews 150

Building Long-Term Relationships with Your Customers 153

Chapter 10 158

Optimizing Your Listings for Maximum Visibility 158

Deep Dive into eBay SEO: Understanding Search Algorithms 158

Utilizing Keywords Effectively in Titles and Descriptions 160

Leveraging Item Specifics and Categories 163

Understanding eBay's Best Match Algorithm 166

Keeping Up with eBay's Search Updates (2025 Considerations).. 168

Chapter 11 172

Leveraging eBay's Marketing and Promotional Tools 172

Mastering Promoted Listings: Advanced Strategies 172

Creating and Managing eBay Store Subscriptions (If Applicable) . 175

Utilizing eBay's Sales Events and Promotions 178

Exploring External Marketing Strategies to Drive Traffic 181

The Complete Guide to Selling on eBay for Beginners 2025

  Understanding eBay's Advertising Options 184
Chapter 12 187
  Managing Your Finances and Tracking Your Performance................187
    Setting Up Effective Financial Tracking Systems.......................187
    Understanding eBay Fees and Calculating Profit Margins............190
    Managing Taxes and Record-Keeping for Your Business................193
    Analyzing Your Sales Data and Identifying Areas for Improvement
   195
    Reinvesting Profits for Growth.. 198
Chapter 13 202
  Expanding Your Business: Scaling and Automation.......................... 202
    Exploring Dropshipping and Other Fulfillment Methods in More
    Detail... 202
    Considering Hiring Help or Outsourcing Tasks............................. 205
    Utilizing eBay Automation Tools for Efficiency 207
    Expanding Your Product Line and Exploring New Niches............ 210
    Understanding eBay's Business Policies for Larger Sellers 213
Chapter 14 218
  Navigating eBay's Policies and Seller Standards (2025 Updates)......218
    Understanding and Adhering to eBay's Rules and Regulations.....218
    Maintaining High Seller Standards and Avoiding Penalties 221
    Staying Informed About Policy Changes and Updates 224
    Protecting Yourself from Scams and Fraud...................................... 226
Chapter 15 230
  The Future of Selling on eBay: Trends and Predictions for 2025 and
  Beyond 230
    Emerging Technologies and Their Impact on eBay 230
    Shifting Consumer Behaviors and Expectations 233
    Adapting Your Strategies for Long-Term Success 236
    Resources for Staying Updated on eBay Trends 239
Conclusion 243
Appendices.. 246

Appendix A: Essential Tools and Resources for eBay Sellers 246

Appendix B: Glossary of eBay Terms 249

Appendix C: Common Mistakes to Avoid as a New eBay Seller 251

The Complete Guide to Selling on eBay for Beginners 2025

PART 1

Getting Started with Your eBay Journey

The Complete Guide to Selling on eBay for Beginners 2025

INTRODUCTION

WELCOME TO THE WORLD OF EBAY SELLING

WHAT MAKES EBAY A GREAT PLATFORM FOR BEGINNERS?

When someone first sets out to make money online, the number of platforms and options can be overwhelming. But few platforms offer the same blend of simplicity, reach, flexibility, and opportunity for growth as eBay. There's something uniquely approachable about it—an online marketplace that feels both familiar and vast, where nearly anyone with an internet connection and something to sell can get started with little more than a camera phone and some curiosity. For beginners, this is not just a matter of convenience; it's an invitation into the world of entrepreneurship without the barriers that typically stand in the way.

One of the first reasons eBay stands out for newcomers is the sheer ease of entry. There's no need to build a website, learn complex coding, or even design an online storefront. With just a few guided steps, a person can set up an account, list an item, and start accepting bids or purchases within the hour. The platform handles the backend—the hosting, the payment processing, the visibility—so the seller can focus on the product and the customer. This simplicity allows new users to jump in, experiment, and learn by doing. Mistakes are part of the process, and on eBay, they don't cost thousands of dollars or months of work. The platform is forgiving and user-friendly, offering helpful prompts, seller protections, and an intuitive layout that takes the stress out of the technical side of selling.

The second great advantage for beginners lies in eBay's massive, built-in customer base. Unlike starting an independent eCommerce website, where one must figure out how to generate traffic from scratch, eBay offers exposure to millions of active buyers from around the world. These buyers aren't just browsing passively—they're actively searching for products, often with clear intent to purchase. This level of buyer readiness means that even a completely unknown seller has a chance to make a sale quickly, without needing to invest in advertising or social media marketing. The audience is already there. All a beginner has to do is show up and offer something of value.

Another reason the platform is so welcoming to newcomers is the variety of items that can be sold. From used books and vintage collectibles to new electronics and handmade crafts, eBay allows for an incredible range of product types. This flexibility empowers beginners to start with what they already have, without needing to buy inventory upfront. A seller can look around their home, find unused or unwanted items, and turn them into cash. This not only minimizes risk but also allows for real-time learning. By observing what sells quickly and what lingers, beginners get a free education in market demand, pricing strategies, and customer preferences. It's business school by doing—except the lessons are practical, fast, and sometimes even profitable.

eBay also supports gradual scaling in a way that suits the natural rhythm of beginners. Some platforms demand immediate volume, large investments, or fulfillment logistics that can overwhelm someone just starting out. eBay, in contrast, lets sellers grow at their own pace. You can begin by selling one or two items a week, and over time, build up to a full-fledged business. There's no requirement to open a store right away, and there's room for experimentation. You can test different categories, adjust descriptions and images, shift pricing, and find your niche organically. Because the platform is flexible and responsive, sellers are free to evolve their approach without penalty or judgment.

Trust also plays a crucial role. eBay has been around since the mid-1990s and has earned a reputation for being a secure and reliable marketplace. Buyers know and trust the brand, and this built-in credibility extends to new sellers. Even if someone is listing an item for the first time, the trust buyers have in the eBay system helps overcome the natural skepticism they might have toward lesser-known sellers. The platform's feedback system, buyer protection policies, and secure payment options (primarily handled through PayPal or direct bank payments) all contribute to a sense of safety for both parties. For beginners, this trust cushion means they don't need to spend time convincing people to give them a chance. The platform's infrastructure does a lot of that work.

Another underrated benefit is the supportive seller community. From forums and tutorials to third-party YouTube guides and seller groups, there is a vast reservoir of knowledge available to anyone willing to learn. The eBay community is filled with experienced sellers who remember what it was like to be new, and they're often generous with their advice. Beginners don't have to feel alone in the process. Whether they're struggling to calculate shipping costs or wondering how to deal with an unresponsive buyer, there's usually someone who's been there and is willing to help. In a digital age where isolation is often the norm, this sense of connection can make a world of difference.

For those who value flexibility, eBay offers unmatched freedom. A person can sell from anywhere, at any time. There's no obligation to keep regular hours, rent a space, or hire a team. This freedom allows beginners to build their online business around their existing life rather than upending everything to pursue a new career. Parents can sell during naptime, students between classes, or full-time workers on weekends. The platform adjusts to your schedule—not the other way around. This makes it especially attractive to those who want to test the waters of entrepreneurship before diving in fully.

In terms of analytics and data, eBay offers valuable insights to help beginners grow smarter. Every listing comes with data about views, watchers, and performance. This means that even small-scale sellers can start to understand trends and buyer behavior. Over time, these insights become invaluable for making better decisions about inventory, timing, and pricing. While other platforms may lock these kinds of metrics behind premium plans or advanced tools, eBay provides them freely and in a digestible format. This empowers beginners to act like seasoned professionals—even before they feel like one.

There's also something deeply motivating about the real-time nature of eBay sales. Unlike platforms that may take weeks or months to deliver results, eBay has the potential to reward effort quickly. Listing an item in the morning and getting a sale by evening is not uncommon. That kind of instant feedback is powerful for new sellers. It validates the work, builds confidence, and creates momentum. Every sale is a signal that you're doing something right—and that you can keep building on it.

Finally, eBay encourages a mindset of resourcefulness and creativity. Beginners learn not just how to sell, but how to think like a seller. They start noticing value in things they once ignored, like old electronics, vintage clothes, or discontinued toys. They begin to see trends in buyer interest, recognize seasonal patterns, and develop instincts for spotting undervalued items at thrift stores, garage sales, or wholesale websites. In essence, the platform teaches the fundamentals of business—supply, demand, negotiation, customer service—not through textbooks, but through experience.

The beauty of this platform is not just that it's easy to use or that it reaches millions of buyers. It's that it turns everyday people into entrepreneurs. It opens the door to opportunity without requiring perfect knowledge, capital, or a polished business plan. It simply asks that you start where you are, use what you have, and learn as you go. For those at the beginning of their online business journey, that invitation is not just generous—it's transformative.

UNDERSTANDING THE EBAY MARKETPLACE IN 2025: TRENDS AND OPPORTUNITIES

The eBay marketplace in 2025 is more dynamic, competitive, and opportunity-rich than ever before. It's no longer just a place to auction off used goods or stumble upon rare collectibles—though those elements still thrive. Today, it is a refined ecosystem shaped by global buying trends, evolving technology, and consumer expectations that demand speed, authenticity, and reliability. For those entering the space now, understanding what this marketplace looks like—and more importantly, what it rewards—is essential. It is not enough to simply list an item and wait. Success comes to those who understand the pulse of the platform and can adapt to its rhythms.

One of the most significant shifts shaping eBay in 2025 is the steady blending of new and used goods within the same digital aisles. In previous years, eBay leaned more heavily toward secondhand items, collectibles, and hard-to-find treasures. While that market remains strong, the demand for brand-new products—especially in categories like electronics, fashion, health and wellness, and home essentials—has surged. Buyers now come to eBay expecting the same kind of shopping experience they would find on major retail sites. They want professional photos, same-day or next-day shipping options, and hassle-free returns. This trend has created a golden opportunity for sellers who can source or create new products, package them well, and fulfill orders quickly. It also opens the door for partnerships with wholesalers, dropshippers, or liquidation suppliers who can help beginners tap into new-in-box inventory without heavy upfront investment.

At the same time, the appreciation for pre-owned items has not diminished—in fact, it has evolved. The modern consumer is more environmentally conscious and value-driven, which fuels demand for quality secondhand goods in areas like refurbished tech, designer fashion, vintage home décor, and sustainable lifestyle items. eBay continues to serve as one of the world's leading platforms for circular commerce, meaning it enables products to be reused, recycled, and resold, contributing to a more sustainable global economy. This offers a compelling opportunity for sellers to position themselves not just as merchants, but as contributors to a movement. Sellers who can offer gently used or refurbished items with full transparency and competitive pricing often find an eager and appreciative audience.

Another defining trait of the marketplace this year is the explosion of niche markets. As buyers become more specific in what they're searching for—whether it's retro gaming consoles, K-pop memorabilia, rare LEGO sets, or handcrafted herbal skincare—the platform increasingly rewards sellers who specialize. These micro-markets allow individuals to become known for a certain category or style, building repeat customers and even brand identity over time. In many cases, it's not the broad, general stores that win but the small shops that offer a deep, focused inventory in a specific category. Specialization builds trust. It shows buyers that the seller knows their niche and can curate a collection worth exploring.

Technology continues to reshape how transactions take place. Artificial intelligence and machine learning now play a stronger role in listing optimization, search results, and customer service interactions. eBay's own algorithm, called Cassini, has grown more intelligent and nuanced, rewarding not just keyword use, but the entire buyer experience. Factors such as fast shipping, responsive communication, clear return policies, competitive pricing, and high-resolution photos influence visibility in search rankings. For new sellers, this means success is not just about what you sell, but how you sell it. Listings that are accurate, visually appealing, and supported by excellent service rise faster in the algorithm and are more likely to close sales.

Mobile shopping has also reached a new level of dominance in 2025. The majority of eBay users now browse, compare, and buy through their smartphones or tablets. This has led to the platform emphasizing mobile-optimized listings, where concise titles, clean image formatting, and easily digestible descriptions make a substantial difference. Sellers who consider how their listings look on a mobile screen—versus a desktop computer—are better positioned to attract and convert these modern buyers. In essence, sellers must think like marketers, not just merchants. Every element of a listing must now function like an ad: it needs to grab attention, deliver key information fast, and make a compelling case for purchase within seconds.

Trust and transparency have never been more important. Today's buyers, bombarded by options, want to feel confident in every transaction. That means seller reputation carries enormous weight. Feedback scores, detailed seller ratings, and consistent positive experiences are more than just badges—they're lifelines. New sellers must be deliberate in cultivating trust from the beginning, even if it means sacrificing a bit of profit at first to provide stellar customer service. Fast shipping, clear communication, careful packaging, and an easy return policy build the kind of reputation that the algorithm and customers alike reward. This isn't a space where shortcuts pay off; long-term success is built one great transaction at a time.

Global commerce is also more accessible than ever through the platform's expanded international shipping options. In 2025, cross-border selling has become smoother, more affordable, and more rewarding. With features like eBay's Global Shipping Program and international fulfillment partnerships, sellers in the U.S. can easily reach customers in the UK, Canada, Australia, and other parts of the world without the stress of managing complex logistics. This opens enormous opportunity for those who carry unique items or products in high global demand. While domestic sales will always be important, tapping into international interest can dramatically expand one's customer base and income potential.

The platform is also leaning into video content and live selling events, which have become significant tools for engagement and conversion. Sellers who incorporate short videos into their listings—such as product demos, condition overviews, or behind-the-scenes packaging videos—often see higher buyer interest. These videos humanize the transaction, reduce uncertainty, and increase conversion rates. Additionally, live-streaming sales events hosted through eBay's app or external platforms have started to mirror the popularity of home shopping networks, allowing sellers to present items in real time, answer questions, and drive urgency. This kind of direct-to-buyer interaction is becoming a powerful sales driver, especially for those who enjoy being on camera or telling the story behind their products.

The growing importance of branding can't be ignored either. Even within a marketplace like eBay—historically known for one-off listings—sellers are finding success in building recognizable, repeatable brand identities. From custom packaging and thank-you notes to consistent photo styles and logo watermarks, small details set top-performing sellers apart. A buyer who recognizes a seller's "look" or voice is more likely to return, refer others, and leave glowing reviews. In this way, every sale becomes a stepping stone toward something bigger: not just a successful listing, but a thriving online presence.

Looking ahead, artificial intelligence integration is expected to continue expanding. Tools that assist with product sourcing, price comparison, automated messaging, and even listing generation are helping level the playing field for beginners. You no longer need a business degree to analyze what's working or decide how to price your inventory. The data is at your fingertips, and smart tools can turn insights into action. Those who embrace these tools—not to replace their effort, but to amplify it—will be better equipped to grow efficiently and make smarter choices.

At its heart, the marketplace remains an equalizer. It does not care about age, background, or previous business experience. What it rewards is consistency, care, and creativity. The trends of 2025 show that there is space for new voices, fresh perspectives, and untapped product categories. Whether someone is reselling thrift store finds, dropshipping trending gadgets, or curating a line of handmade goods, the door is open. But walking through it requires awareness. Not just of how the marketplace works, but of how buyers behave, what they value, and what earns their trust.

Understanding the marketplace today means seeing it as a living, breathing environment. It evolves every month, shaped by global shifts, platform changes, and cultural moods. But it also holds timeless truths: treat people well, deliver on your promises, and take pride in what you sell. Those principles, coupled with the trends defining 2025, form the foundation for success. This is not just a space to make money—it's a place to build something real, sustainable, and even joyful.

SETTING REALISTIC EXPECTATIONS AND GOALS

Starting any business—online or offline—requires more than just ambition. It demands patience, discipline, and a clear understanding of what's truly achievable in the beginning stages. When selling on eBay, especially as a beginner, setting realistic expectations and goals isn't just a good idea; it's a necessary foundation for sustainable growth. The early days can be exciting, even exhilarating, but without a measured mindset, that initial rush can quickly turn into frustration. Success in this space is entirely possible, but it doesn't come overnight. Understanding the terrain before rushing into it helps ensure that every step taken is purposeful and rewarding.

One of the most common misconceptions among new sellers is the belief that profits will be immediate and substantial. It's easy to fall into this trap, especially when browsing through success stories of seasoned sellers making thousands of dollars each month. What those stories often skip over is the long path it took to reach that point—months, sometimes years, of trial and error, learning, and reinvestment. The truth is, most beginners start slowly. Their first few sales might only bring in modest earnings, and that's completely normal. It's not a failure—it's the starting line. In fact, these early sales are less about profit and more about learning the system, understanding customer behavior, and establishing a seller reputation.

One of the first goals any beginner should focus on is building credibility. In the eBay ecosystem, feedback matters. It's one of the primary ways buyers determine whether they can trust a seller, especially in a marketplace flooded with options. Gaining those initial positive reviews often requires putting customer experience above profit. That might mean underpricing a few items to encourage sales or going the extra mile with packaging and communication. The short-term gains may not be impressive in terms of money, but what's being built is far more valuable: trust and visibility. Once positive feedback starts accumulating, it has a compounding effect. Future buyers are more likely to purchase, and eBay's algorithm is more likely to show your listings in search results.

Expectations also need to account for the time and effort required in the beginning. Listing an item isn't just a matter of uploading a photo and typing a few words. It involves market research, writing a clear and accurate description, taking high-quality photos, determining the right pricing strategy, and selecting shipping options. For someone new to the platform, this can be a time-consuming process. But like any skill, it becomes faster and more intuitive with practice. The key is to be patient with yourself and understand that efficiency grows with experience. Every listing teaches something—whether it's how to write a better title, how to price more competitively, or how to pack items more securely. These lessons don't always come with immediate financial rewards, but they build a strong foundation for future success.

Financial goals in the early stages should be approached with a long-term mindset. Expecting to replace a full-time income within the first month is unrealistic and often leads to burnout or discouragement. A more grounded approach is to start small and scale intentionally. Perhaps the initial goal is simply to make enough to cover a few personal expenses, build a cushion for reinvestment, or generate capital to acquire better inventory. Each time a goal is met, a new one can be set—slightly higher, slightly more challenging, but always achievable. This ladder approach not only builds confidence but keeps the journey manageable and enjoyable.

Another important consideration is the concept of reinvestment. It's tempting to withdraw every dollar earned from early sales, especially when those first profits feel hard-won. But one of the most effective strategies for growth is to view early earnings as seed money for future listings. Buying better inventory, upgrading equipment, or investing in tools like photo lighting or shipping supplies can significantly elevate the quality of your store. These aren't frivolous expenses—they're strategic moves that pave the way for long-term growth. Understanding this from the beginning can reshape how success is measured. It's not about how much you keep in your pocket today, but how much you're setting yourself up to earn tomorrow.

Expectations should also take into account the unpredictable nature of sales cycles. There will be days or even weeks when sales slow down without a clear explanation. This is normal. Buyer behavior fluctuates due to seasons, economic factors, holidays, and trends. What sold like wildfire in November might barely move in February. Instead of seeing these slow periods as failures, it's more useful to view them as opportunities to analyze, refine, and plan. Sellers who weather these quiet times with curiosity rather than panic often emerge stronger, having learned how to adapt and improve rather than abandon ship.

Managing expectations also involves preparing for occasional negative experiences. Not every buyer will be pleasant. Some might complain, demand refunds, or leave unfair feedback. There might be issues with shipping, lost packages, or unexpected costs. These challenges are part of the journey, not signs that the path is wrong. The key is to develop resilience and professionalism. Learning how to handle conflict gracefully, respond to complaints promptly, and protect your account through proper documentation are essential skills that strengthen your presence on the platform. The best sellers aren't the ones who never make mistakes—they're the ones who know how to bounce back.

A significant goal that new sellers often overlook is creating a system. Selling randomly, without structure, can become chaotic as your inventory and order volume grows. Taking the time early on to develop a workflow—how you store inventory, track expenses, print shipping labels, and communicate with buyers—pays enormous dividends later. A good system frees up mental energy, reduces errors, and allows you to focus on strategy rather than stress. Setting the goal of developing a reliable routine is just as important as chasing revenue targets.

Another important mindset shift for beginners is recognizing that growth is not always linear. There will be plateaus. Some goals will take longer than expected. A new product line might flop. A brilliant marketing idea might fall flat. But each of these setbacks is also a feedback mechanism. They help you recalibrate, innovate, and improve. The most successful eBay sellers aren't lucky—they're persistent. They keep showing up, listing new items, learning from analytics, and listening to customer feedback. They don't get discouraged by a slow week or a disappointing month because they understand the long view. They know that consistency builds momentum, and momentum builds businesses.

It's also helpful to periodically pause and reflect on your "why." Goals become more powerful when they are tied to a deeper purpose. Maybe the aim is to gain financial independence, pay off debt, or transition into self-employment. Maybe it's about having more flexibility to spend time with family or explore creative passions. Whatever the reason, revisiting that deeper motivation can reignite energy during challenging times. When expectations feel misaligned or progress feels slow, reconnecting with your why brings clarity and perspective.

Ultimately, success on eBay in 2025 is deeply personal. There's no single measure that applies to everyone. Some will be thrilled with an extra few hundred dollars a month; others will aim to build full-scale stores with employees and warehouses. What matters is defining success on your own terms and measuring it against your own goals—not someone else's highlight reel. Realistic expectations don't limit ambition—they sharpen it. They provide the guardrails that keep you focused, balanced, and moving forward.

In the end, setting expectations and goals isn't about playing small—it's about playing smart. It's about approaching the process with humility, grit, and a willingness to grow. With the right mindset, every sale becomes more than a transaction. It becomes a step toward something greater—something built with intention, patience, and purpose. That's the kind of success that lasts.

ESSENTIAL TERMINOLOGY YOU NEED TO KNOW

Entering the world of eBay in 2025 can feel like stepping into a new country where everyone speaks a slightly different language. While the platform has worked hard over the years to be beginner-friendly, it still operates with a set of unique terms and concepts that, at first glance, may feel overwhelming or even intimidating. However, learning this language is less about memorization and more about immersion—understanding what these terms mean in context, how they relate to your activity as a seller, and how mastering them can make you a more confident and successful participant in the marketplace.

One of the first terms you'll encounter is "listing." A listing refers to the page you create when you want to sell an item. It's your digital storefront for that particular product, and it includes the title, description, photos, pricing, shipping options, and return policy. Every element of a listing matters because it affects whether a buyer clicks, purchases, or passes. Listings are not static; they can be revised, optimized, and relisted. Getting comfortable with the anatomy of a good listing is one of the most important early steps in your selling journey.

Closely tied to your listings is the concept of "Buy It Now" versus "Auction." eBay was originally built on the auction model, where items are listed with a starting price, and buyers bid over a fixed period, typically 1 to 10 days. The highest bidder wins. This format still exists and can be useful for rare or collectible items, but in recent years, "Buy It Now" has become the preferred format for most transactions. It allows sellers to set a fixed price, and buyers can purchase instantly without waiting. Understanding when to use each format strategically is part of your evolution as a seller. Auctions can generate excitement and competition, while Buy It Now offers predictability and speed.

Another key term is "Best Offer." This feature, when enabled on a fixed-price listing, lets buyers propose a lower price than what you're asking. As a seller, you can accept, decline, or counteroffer. While it might seem like inviting negotiation slows down the sales process, it can actually encourage engagement and allow you to move inventory while maintaining some pricing control. It's especially effective for items with flexible margins or when you're willing to compromise on price to gain feedback or visibility.

You'll also hear a lot about "feedback." On eBay, feedback is the public rating system that both buyers and sellers use to evaluate each other after a transaction. Feedback includes a star rating and optional written comments. For sellers, positive feedback is essential—it builds credibility, improves visibility in search results, and reassures potential buyers. Neutral or negative feedback can affect your reputation and standing on the platform. That's why professional communication, fast shipping, accurate descriptions, and excellent customer service aren't optional— they're part of your brand. Your feedback score is visible to every buyer, and in many ways, it serves as your business card.

Then there's "DSR," or Detailed Seller Ratings. These are additional star ratings that buyers give across four categories: item as described, communication, shipping time, and shipping charges. These ratings, though not always publicly visible in full, contribute to your overall seller performance and can influence your eligibility for certain programs, including eBay's Top Rated Seller status. While a perfect DSR isn't required, consistently low scores can trigger account reviews or restrictions. These metrics are meant to encourage consistency and transparency in the selling process.

You'll also want to become familiar with the "Final Value Fee." This is the percentage eBay takes from the total amount of a sale—including the item price, shipping, and tax. It's how eBay makes money, and it varies by category. For most sellers, this fee hovers around 12% to 15%. Understanding this fee structure is crucial for pricing your items in a way that maintains profitability. Some sellers make the mistake of listing items without factoring in eBay's cut, only to discover later that they've barely broken even—or worse, lost money.

A related term is the "Insertion Fee." This is the charge eBay may apply just to list an item, whether it sells or not. However, eBay provides a number of free listings per month (often 250 or more) for most sellers, especially those with personal or starter accounts. Going beyond the free limit triggers a small fee, which is generally nominal. For most beginners, these insertion fees won't be a major concern unless you're listing in high volume or in categories that carry premium fees. Even so, knowing they exist helps avoid surprise charges.

When your item sells, you'll need to handle "shipping." This term might seem straightforward, but on eBay, shipping involves several important choices. You'll decide whether to offer "free shipping" (which usually means you include the cost in the item price) or "calculated shipping" (where the buyer pays based on their location). You'll choose between shipping services—USPS, UPS, FedEx, or eBay's discounted shipping labels—and decide whether to offer international shipping through programs like eBay International Standard Delivery. The term "handling time" refers to how long it takes you to ship the item after the buyer pays. Meeting or beating your stated handling time contributes to positive feedback and seller performance metrics.

A useful feature in the shipping process is "tracking," which is the number assigned by the shipping carrier to monitor a package's journey. Uploading tracking numbers to eBay is strongly encouraged, and in some cases, required. Buyers appreciate being able to follow their order, and eBay uses tracking data to confirm that orders were shipped and delivered on time. If an order goes missing or is delayed, tracking is your first line of defense and can protect you during a dispute.

The term "returns" refers to whether or not you accept items being sent back. eBay gives sellers flexibility in crafting return policies—30-day free returns, buyer-pays-return-shipping, or no returns at all. While accepting returns may seem risky, eBay tends to favor listings with more generous return policies in search placement. Buyers also feel more confident purchasing when they know they have options. For high-volume sellers or those operating in competitive categories, offering returns can be a smart strategic move. Regardless of your policy, clear communication about returns is critical to avoiding misunderstandings.

You'll also hear about "eBay Stores." This term refers to a subscription-based selling model where you pay a monthly fee for additional tools, branding options, and increased listing allowances. Stores range in size—from a basic starter store to an advanced enterprise store—and are suited to different seller levels. For new sellers, an eBay Store may not be necessary right away, but as your inventory grows and you become more consistent in your operations, the added features and discounts can justify the cost.

When managing multiple listings, the term "inventory" becomes central. On eBay, managing your inventory means more than keeping items on a shelf. It means knowing what you have, what's listed, what's sold, and what's in transit. Tools such as eBay's Seller Hub offer inventory management features that track stock levels, sales history, and pricing trends. For larger-scale operations, integration with third-party software can streamline these tasks. Understanding your inventory allows for better forecasting, avoids overselling, and helps identify which products are your best performers.

One of the most empowering terms you'll encounter is "Seller Hub." This is your command center as an eBay seller. It consolidates your orders, listings, messages, performance metrics, and marketing tools in one dashboard. Mastering Seller Hub is like learning how to read a map—it helps you navigate your day-to-day operations and plan strategically. Whether you want to analyze sales trends, track customer behavior, or run promotions, the Seller Hub offers the data and tools needed to make informed decisions.

Becoming fluent in the terminology of eBay is not just about avoiding confusion—it's about empowerment. Every term unlocks a new layer of understanding and control. It helps you ask better questions, solve problems faster, and interact with confidence in a platform filled with opportunities. Like any new vocabulary, it might feel foreign at first. But with continued use, these words become second nature, and with them comes the knowledge to operate your business with clarity, precision, and purpose.

NAVIGATING THE EBAY PLATFORM: A BEGINNER'S TOUR

Navigating eBay for the first time can feel like stepping into a massive marketplace with countless stalls, each one offering different types of goods, strategies, and experiences. The sheer volume of options can be overwhelming to the untrained eye, but the beauty of eBay is that it was built to be intuitive once you understand the flow. For beginners, the platform is not just a place to sell—it's a carefully structured system where every click, tab, and link has a specific purpose designed to support your success as a seller. Familiarity with the platform's structure, functions, and pathways will not only increase your confidence but also allow you to maximize efficiency and results.

When you first log in to eBay, you're greeted with the homepage—a clean interface that feels like a blend between a digital storefront and a search engine. At the very top of the page is the universal search bar. This is the tool buyers and sellers alike use to find specific products or categories. For sellers, this feature is also crucial when researching what items are trending or checking out the competition. Right beside the search bar, you'll notice links to your account, messages, and cart. These are persistent features, meaning no matter where you navigate on eBay, they remain accessible for ease of use.

The next critical area to become comfortable with is the navigation menu. Hovering over the "My eBay" tab will reveal options such as Summary, Selling, Buying, Watchlist, and Saved Searches. The Summary page is your control panel. It gives you a broad overview of your activity—items you're selling, bids you're winning or watching, messages you've received, and any recent account notifications. This is where you can quickly take stock of your status and prioritize what to tackle next.

Clicking on "Selling" brings you to one of the most important spaces on the entire platform. Here, eBay provides you with a detailed breakdown of all your current selling activity. You can view your active listings, sold items, unsold items, and drafts. You can also access reports about your performance and see how your listings are doing in terms of views, watchers, and sales. Each listing is clickable, allowing you to revise, relist, or end it altogether. This area becomes your daily workspace, especially once you begin listing multiple items.

Central to this experience is the "Seller Hub." This powerful toolset is available to every seller and acts like a mission control dashboard. It offers detailed insights into your orders, returns, performance metrics, and marketing tools. While Seller Hub may look complex at first, each section is designed to help you make informed decisions. The Orders tab, for instance, is where you manage your sales: print shipping labels, update tracking information, or send messages to buyers. The Performance tab lets you see how well you're meeting eBay's standards in areas like shipping time, customer service, and transaction defects.

In the Listings tab of the Seller Hub, you gain access to powerful listing management tools. You can filter your listings by status—whether they're active, scheduled, or ended—and make bulk edits, which saves significant time. Want to adjust prices for a group of similar items or update shipping policies across the board? The Listings tab makes that easy. For beginners who start small, this feature may not be essential on day one, but as your store grows, it will become indispensable.

Another area to understand early on is the eBay listing creation process. When you're ready to sell an item, clicking "Create Listing" leads you to a form where you input the details of what you're offering. This is where your title, category, item specifics, photos, description, price, and shipping details come together to form a compelling and optimized listing. eBay offers category suggestions based on your title and even provides pricing guidance based on similar sold items. Every section in this form is important—not only for attracting buyers but also for protecting you during disputes. Being specific, accurate, and detailed is the golden rule when it comes to creating listings that convert.

Once your items are listed and selling begins, you'll also need to get familiar with the messaging system. Buyers often reach out with questions about your listings—sometimes asking for additional details, photos, or requesting bundle deals. These communications show up in your eBay Messages inbox, accessible via "My eBay" or Seller Hub. Prompt, professional responses build trust and can turn curious browsers into committed buyers. The messaging system is also where you'll resolve potential issues such as returns, shipping concerns, or post-sale questions. eBay favors sellers who engage respectfully and solve problems swiftly, so learning to manage these communications efficiently is vital.

The Payments tab is another critical feature. In 2025, eBay manages payments directly through its Managed Payments system, eliminating the need for third-party processors like PayPal for most transactions. Here, you'll see a clear record of your incoming payments, pending payouts, and completed transactions. You can set how frequently your funds are transferred to your bank account—daily, weekly, or on-demand. This area also gives you transparency about fees deducted from each sale, including final value fees, shipping label costs, and taxes. Monitoring this section helps you maintain financial control and ensures you're operating profitably.

Shipping tools are built right into the platform to streamline order fulfillment. After an item sells, you can click "Print Shipping Label" directly from the order screen. eBay provides discounted shipping rates from major carriers like USPS, FedEx, and UPS. You enter the package weight and dimensions, select a service, and print the label—all without leaving the platform. eBay automatically updates the tracking number and notifies the buyer. This smooth process reduces errors, saves time, and meets eBay's expectations for prompt shipping. Within this shipping workflow, you also have access to features like bulk label printing, shipping presets, and pickup scheduling.

As you become more active, the "Marketing" section in Seller Hub becomes valuable. It allows you to promote listings through various tools, such as Promoted Listings and markdown sales. Promoted Listings increase your item's visibility in search results, which can be a powerful boost in competitive categories. You can set a custom ad rate or let eBay adjust it dynamically to maximize exposure. Markdown sales let you temporarily reduce prices or offer deals like "Buy One, Get One" to entice buyers. The Marketing section includes performance analytics that tell you which campaigns are converting and how to improve them.

The final piece of the platform to get comfortable with is your Account Settings. These are found in the top right corner under your profile icon. Here, you can manage your contact information, payment preferences, shipping addresses, return policies, and business information. This area might not require daily attention, but it's essential to visit regularly to ensure everything is accurate and aligned with your goals. It's also where you can customize your notifications, adjust site preferences, and manage user permissions if you're running your store with help from others.

At first, it's perfectly natural to feel like you're just trying to keep up. The key is to explore the platform one layer at a time. Begin with the basics—creating listings, managing orders, and communicating with buyers. Gradually, as you gain confidence, expand into Seller Hub tools, promotional strategies, and advanced shipping options. eBay is designed to reward learning by giving sellers increasingly powerful tools as they grow. The more time you spend inside the platform, the more familiar its features become. What once looked like a complex labyrinth soon transforms into a logical, empowering system—one that supports your success not through luck or guesswork, but through structure, insight, and control.

CHAPTER 1
SETTING UP YOUR EBAY SELLER ACCOUNT FOR SUCCESS

CREATING A NEW EBAY ACCOUNT: STEP-BY-STEP

Creating a new eBay account is the very first milestone on your path to becoming a successful online seller. It's more than just entering your name and email address—it's about building a foundation for your business. While the process is fairly simple and accessible to anyone, it's important to walk through each step deliberately. Every detail you enter and every decision you make during setup will influence how smooth and secure your selling experience becomes. In 2025, eBay has optimized its user onboarding process to be faster, more intuitive, and better integrated with other tools—but understanding each step is still essential for setting up your business the right way.

Step 1: Visit the eBay Homepage
To begin, open your internet browser and go to www.ebay.com. Whether you're using a desktop, tablet, or smartphone, the layout adjusts automatically for a smooth experience. At the top left or right corner of the homepage, depending on your region, you'll see a link that says "Register." Click this to start the sign-up process. You don't need to download any software—everything is web-based, though eBay does offer a mobile app that you can explore once your account is created.

Step 2: Choose the Right Account Type
eBay offers two main types of accounts: personal and business. If you're starting out casually—perhaps selling used items from around the house—a personal account will work just fine. However, if you're planning to build a brand, purchase inventory, and operate like a store, it's best to start with a business account from day one. This allows you to enter your business name, register under your company (if applicable), and access business-level selling tools. Selecting the correct account type early on prevents the hassle of switching later, although eBay does allow you to upgrade your account when needed.

Step 3: Enter Your Basic Information
Once you've selected your account type, you'll be asked to provide some key information. For personal accounts, this includes your full name, email address, and a password. For business accounts, you'll need to provide your business name, business email, and a contact person's details. eBay places high importance on accurate information, especially for seller verification purposes. Make sure to use a professional email

address—preferably one tied to your business brand. Once entered, click "Create account" to move forward.

Step 4: Verify Your Email Address
eBay will send a verification email to the address you entered. Open your inbox and look for a message from eBay. Click the verification link inside to activate your account. This step helps prevent fraud and ensures your email is legitimate and able to receive important notifications. If you don't see the email right away, check your spam or promotions folder.

Step 5: Add a Phone Number for Verification and Security
After email verification, eBay will prompt you to add a phone number. This is a vital step for two reasons: account recovery and identity verification. eBay may send you security codes or alerts when unusual activity occurs, so it's important to use a number that you actively monitor. Once entered, you'll receive a one-time verification code via SMS. Input the code into the form to proceed. This also strengthens your account's security and allows you to activate two-step authentication later on, which is highly recommended.

Step 6: Set Up Your Payment Information
To sell on eBay, you need to connect your account to a bank account where your earnings can be deposited. Since eBay uses a managed payments system, all buyer payments go through eBay first, then get deposited into your linked bank account. You'll be asked to enter your banking information, including your account number and routing number (or IBAN and SWIFT code for international sellers). Be sure to use a business bank account if you're setting up a business profile. After this is completed, eBay may take 1–2 business days to verify the banking information, although this is often instant.

Step 7: Set Up Your Selling Preferences
Next, you'll configure the preferences for your selling activities. This includes selecting how you want to handle returns, shipping, and communications with buyers. eBay offers default settings, but it's wise to personalize them. Choose a return policy that aligns with your product type and comfort level—many buyers prefer sellers who accept returns within 30 days. Set up shipping policies that define your handling time (how quickly you ship after a sale), your shipping carriers, and whether you offer free or paid shipping. You can always revise these later in your "Account Settings," but getting it right from the start provides consistency and avoids confusion.

Step 8: Choose Your Username and Customize Your Profile
Your eBay username is how the community will identify you. Choose something professional, memorable, and relevant to your niche or brand. Avoid overly complicated names or anything that looks untrustworthy. If

your business has a name, try to align your eBay username with it for branding consistency. After choosing your username, you can upload a profile picture, write a short bio, and add a location. These small touches help humanize your seller profile and build trust with potential buyers.

Step 9: Explore the Seller Hub

Once your account is verified and your preferences are set, go to eBay's Seller Hub—a powerful dashboard that organizes everything about your selling activities. You can access this from the "My eBay" dropdown menu under "Selling." The Seller Hub lets you create new listings, manage inventory, track orders, respond to messages, and analyze performance. Familiarizing yourself with this dashboard early on makes managing your business more streamlined and less overwhelming.

Step 10: List Your First Item

Now that your account is fully set up, you're ready to list your first item. Click "List an Item" from your dashboard or Seller Hub. eBay will guide you through the process by prompting you to enter the item's title, choose a category, upload photos, and write a description. You'll also set your price, decide on auction or fixed-price format, and select your shipping preferences. Once everything is in place, hit "List It" and your item will go live. This is where your selling journey officially begins.

Step 11: Link to the eBay Mobile App

To manage your account on the go, download the eBay app from the App Store or Google Play. Log in with your new account credentials. The app is fully equipped to let you list items, respond to buyers, track shipping, and receive alerts. This helps you stay responsive and engaged even when you're away from your computer.

Step 12: Monitor Your Messages and Notifications

After listing items, stay vigilant. Buyers may send questions, offers, or requests via eBay's messaging system. You'll be notified via email or the eBay app when messages come in. Prompt, courteous communication improves your chances of making sales and builds a reputation for excellent customer service. Also, monitor notifications for updates on policy changes, seller tips, and promotions from eBay itself.

Step 13: Review eBay's Selling Policies and Community Standards

Before you ramp up your listings, it's a good idea to read through eBay's seller policies. These outline your responsibilities, including the standards for item accuracy, shipping times, return management, and prohibited items. Violations can result in penalties or account restrictions, so staying compliant ensures your business runs smoothly.

Step 14: Enable Two-Factor Authentication (2FA)

To protect your account, enable 2FA under your security settings. This adds an extra layer of security by requiring a one-time code sent to your phone whenever you log in from a new device. In today's digital environment, protecting your business from fraud and unauthorized access is non-negotiable.

Step 15: Begin Tracking Your Performance
As sales come in, eBay will provide performance analytics showing your transaction history, feedback score, shipping speed, and customer satisfaction. These metrics influence your visibility and seller rating. Understanding them early helps you identify what's working and what needs improvement.

By following these fifteen essential steps, you create a stable, secure, and professional eBay seller account ready for growth. Each action builds on the last, shaping the experience buyers will have with you. And with every listing, message, or shipping label you print, you're not just learning a platform—you're building a business from the ground up.

CHOOSING THE RIGHT ACCOUNT TYPE: PERSONAL VS. BUSINESS

When stepping into the world of eBay selling, one of the first significant decisions you'll face is whether to register with a personal account or a business account. This choice isn't just a formality. It's the framework on which the rest of your eBay selling experience will be built. Understanding the difference between these account types and the implications of each choice is key to setting yourself up for sustainable success. In 2025, eBay has continued refining its platform to support both casual sellers and established businesses, offering unique features and tools for each type of account. But to use those tools effectively, you need to understand what they unlock, what they limit, and how each aligns with your long-term goals.

A personal account is often the default starting point for many users. It's designed for individuals who plan to sell occasionally or in a more relaxed, less formal way. Maybe you're looking to declutter your home, flip a few items here and there, or dip your toes into online sales without a big commitment. A personal account supports this kind of use. It's quick to set up, requires minimal information to verify your identity, and doesn't require a business name or formal structure. It allows you to create listings, communicate with buyers, receive payments, and manage shipping and returns with most of the basic tools available on eBay. For someone who's unsure of their long-term intentions with online selling, or who simply wants to offload a few items occasionally, this account type offers flexibility and low pressure.

However, the advantages of a personal account begin to diminish when you start thinking about consistency, volume, branding, or growth. That's where the business account comes into play. A business account is tailored for sellers who treat eBay as a commercial platform rather than a garage sale. It is designed for those who have a product line, want to establish a presence, and potentially scale operations. Setting up a business account requires a few more steps. You'll need to register with your business name, provide tax information depending on your region, and often include a registered business address. But the investment in time pays off in terms of access to advanced tools, better analytics, and a more professional storefront.

What distinguishes a business account isn't just the structure, but the perception it creates in the eyes of your customers. Shoppers on eBay are becoming increasingly savvy. When they see a seller listed as a business, it communicates stability, reliability, and credibility. It sets a tone that can encourage confidence and trust—two essential ingredients in online commerce. A business account allows you to use your store name on your listings, which means you can build brand recognition and encourage repeat buyers. You can even design a custom storefront with logos, banners, categories, and policies that reflect your brand identity. This level of customization simply isn't possible with a personal account.

Functionally, the business account also unlocks more robust reporting features. You can access deeper insights into your sales trends, buyer behavior, and product performance. These tools are invaluable for anyone who wants to grow strategically, make data-driven decisions, and adjust listings based on performance. You also gain access to promotional tools, such as the ability to run markdown sales, offer multi-buy discounts, and create coupon codes. These features can significantly improve your ability to attract buyers and stay competitive in a crowded marketplace.

Another benefit is that with a business account, you can register for eBay's volume discounts and special shipping rates. If you sell regularly or plan to scale, the savings on shipping alone can make a measurable difference in your bottom line. eBay's partnerships with major carriers offer advantages that casual sellers rarely tap into. Additionally, having a business account often speeds up the process of getting support from eBay. You may find that your requests are prioritized, and the level of service may be slightly more responsive, especially when your account activity shows you're operating professionally.

There's also the matter of taxes. In many jurisdictions, the IRS or local tax authorities expect you to report income from online selling. When using a business account, you are more transparently positioned to handle tax matters. eBay will send tax documents such as Form 1099-K if your sales pass the reporting threshold. Having your business bank account and eBay transactions separate from your personal finances simplifies the accounting process. With a personal account, it's easier for expenses and revenue to blur together, which can cause complications at tax time.

That said, starting with a business account is not always the best choice for everyone. If you're brand new to online selling, unsure about your product direction, or just exploring the platform to get a feel for how it works, you might benefit from beginning with a personal account. It allows you to experiment with listings, shipping methods, and buyer interactions without overcommitting. Some sellers start this way and then switch to a business account once they have more clarity and momentum. eBay makes the transition relatively straightforward, though it does require re-entering some business details and possibly re-verifying your account identity.

There are also legal and regulatory differences to consider depending on your location. In some countries, operating under a business account means adhering to consumer protection laws more rigorously. For instance, you may be required to clearly post return policies, include business contact details, and comply with specific refund rules. This may seem daunting at first, but it actually works in your favor in the long run. Buyers are more likely to purchase from sellers who are transparent and compliant, and a strong policy foundation reduces the chance of disputes or misunderstandings.

In terms of flexibility, both account types allow you to access the full spectrum of product categories, shipping methods, and payment systems. However, a business account allows multiple users to help manage listings, fulfill orders, and handle customer service, which is important if you plan to grow into a team or need administrative help. Personal accounts are single-user only, meaning if you're handling more volume or more complexity, things can get bottlenecked quickly.

One final consideration is longevity. A business account gives you a structure that can evolve as your brand does. You can build an eBay store, link it with external websites, drive social media traffic, and even expand into multi-channel selling. All of these things are more difficult to accomplish with a personal account, which isn't designed for scalability or brand building. The infrastructure of a business account, from analytics to customer support tools, is there to support growth. That foundation becomes even more valuable as eBay continues to evolve in 2025, offering integrations with automation tools, inventory syncing, and enhanced mobile capabilities.

In the end, the choice between a personal and business account should align with your vision. If you're here to sell the occasional item and test the waters, personal may suit you just fine. But if you've got a product line in mind, a niche to serve, or a goal to grow your presence and profits, there's little question that a business account is the right step. It's more than just a registration type—it's a signal of intention, a framework for professionalism, and the beginning of building a reliable, recognizable brand in one of the world's most active digital marketplaces.

The Complete Guide to Selling on eBay for Beginners 2025

VERIFYING YOUR ACCOUNT AND PAYMENT INFORMATION

Before any seller can truly begin transacting on eBay with confidence and legitimacy, one crucial step must be completed: verifying both the account and the payment information. In 2025, eBay has continued to evolve its verification process to reflect the growing importance of online security, trust, and seamless financial integration. For beginners, this step may feel procedural, but it's actually foundational—it's what transitions you from being just a registered user to being a trusted participant in eBay's global commerce ecosystem. Without verification, many of the platform's features remain locked or restricted, and buyers may be hesitant to engage with a seller who hasn't completed these basic requirements.

When an account is first created, whether personal or business, eBay initiates a baseline identity verification process. This typically includes email verification, mobile number authentication, and, depending on your region, possibly identity document checks. The platform's algorithms and security systems are designed to prevent fraud, ensure accountability, and comply with financial regulations. For sellers, this verification is not only about legitimacy—it's about unlocking the tools needed to grow. Verifying your identity gives eBay confidence in your intentions, and in return, it gives you access to a wide range of seller tools, dashboard analytics, listing capabilities, and customer support services.

The email verification step is straightforward but vital. After registering, eBay sends an automated message to the email address provided during sign-up. The email contains a verification link that must be clicked within a limited timeframe. This step confirms that the email address belongs to the user and allows eBay to deliver important notifications about account activity, buyer messages, and transaction updates. Failing to complete this step means the account remains incomplete and functionally limited. Sellers may miss important buyer inquiries, be unable to recover their account if access is lost, or be flagged for suspicious activity if multiple notifications bounce back.

Mobile verification is the next layer. eBay requests a valid mobile phone number to send a one-time code via SMS. This serves as a two-factor authentication mechanism that helps protect your account against unauthorized access. It also functions as an additional contact method for time-sensitive updates and security alerts. More importantly, eBay uses mobile verification to filter out bots and duplicate accounts. For a seller, this extra layer of verification increases the perceived trustworthiness of the account in the eyes of both the platform and potential buyers.

Identity verification may also be required, especially when registering as a business or when hitting certain sales thresholds. In 2025, eBay's identity checks often involve uploading a government-issued ID, such as a passport, driver's license, or national identification card. These documents are cross-checked using automated systems and sometimes manually reviewed for authenticity. This process protects the platform from identity fraud and financial misconduct. For sellers, completing identity verification is a gateway to higher transaction limits and eligibility for payment disbursement without delays. It also ensures compliance with global anti-money laundering (AML) and know-your-customer (KYC) laws.

Alongside identity checks, verifying your payment information is equally essential. eBay has moved away from PayPal-centric payments and now uses its own payment infrastructure, which requires sellers to link a valid bank account to receive funds from sales. This system, called eBay Payments, centralizes all transactions directly on the platform, allowing buyers to pay using various methods—credit and debit cards, Apple Pay, Google Pay, and even gift cards—while eBay distributes the funds to sellers after deducting any fees.

To verify your payment details, you must provide a bank account under your legal name or your business's legal name, depending on your account type. eBay will initiate a small deposit—usually just a few cents—into the provided account. You will be required to confirm the exact deposit amount, proving that the account is accessible and under your control. This simple action is critical in preventing fraudulent actors from linking accounts they do not own. Once the bank account is confirmed, you'll be eligible to receive payouts from completed sales, usually within one to three business days depending on your settings and transaction history.

In addition to verifying the payout method, sellers are also asked to provide a preferred payment method for covering seller fees. This could be the same bank account or a separate credit or debit card. eBay charges fees based on final sale values, listing enhancements, and optional features like promoted listings. By linking a payment method for these fees, you ensure uninterrupted service and avoid account restrictions. Failing to do so may result in listings being paused or removed, especially if fees are left unpaid.

eBay has also implemented additional safeguards in recent years, including address verification. This step may involve submitting utility bills, lease agreements, or bank statements that match the name and address on file. While not always required, this level of verification may be triggered if eBay's systems detect inconsistencies or if a seller begins to scale rapidly. For example, a seller who jumps from listing ten items to one hundred in a short period may be asked to reconfirm their address and identity to ensure that growth is legitimate and not part of fraudulent activity.

In 2025, with the increasing sophistication of digital fraud, eBay's layered verification process is not a hurdle—it's a protective measure for everyone involved. As a seller, going through each step carefully and completely sets you up with a reputation of legitimacy and dependability from day one. Buyers are far more likely to complete purchases when they feel secure, and eBay prominently displays trusted seller badges or indicators for verified sellers. These badges don't just offer visual reassurance—they influence purchasing behavior, leading to higher conversion rates and repeat customers.

Verifying your account and payment details also has implications for dispute resolution. Should any transaction dispute arise—be it a return request, chargeback, or item not received claim—eBay's decision-making process often leans more favorably toward verified sellers who have demonstrated transparency and accountability. It allows the platform to mediate with confidence and access the necessary transaction records and payment trail quickly.

Completing all verification steps also prepares you for future opportunities within the eBay seller ecosystem. Verified sellers are eligible for programs like eBay Top Rated Seller status, exclusive promotions, advanced listing tools, and integrations with third-party platforms like shipping services and inventory software. These advantages are only accessible once your account is fully verified, meaning the verification process is not just a security measure—it's a door to growth.

Sellers should also be aware that verification is not necessarily a one-time event. eBay may periodically request updates or re-verification, especially if your business grows significantly, if you change your bank or personal details, or if any suspicious activity is detected. Keeping your contact information, identity documentation, and payment methods up to date is essential for maintaining a good standing and avoiding interruptions.

In the early stages of selling, it might be tempting to bypass or delay these steps in an effort to list products quickly and start generating income. But skipping verification only leads to future delays, limitations, and complications. Completing verification immediately not only fast-tracks your access to eBay's full suite of selling tools—it instills discipline, professionalism, and security from the very beginning. It allows you to operate with confidence, knowing that your transactions are protected, your payouts are secure, and your reputation is backed by one of the most trusted online marketplaces in the world.

UNDERSTANDING EBAY'S SELLER FEES AND STRUCTURES (2025 UPDATES)

Understanding how eBay structures its seller fees is one of the most important parts of running a successful store on the platform. In 2025, these fees have evolved to reflect the increasingly sophisticated nature of online selling, with more tailored pricing options depending on the seller's niche, business model, and volume of transactions. For any beginner looking to build a sustainable online business, knowing how much it costs to list, sell, and promote items is essential. These fees are not hidden or arbitrary—they are predictable, transparent, and, if managed wisely, entirely manageable. They shape the way sellers price their items, plan their profit margins, and scale their operations.

At the heart of eBay's fee structure are two main categories: the insertion fee and the final value fee. The insertion fee is the amount charged to list an item on the platform, while the final value fee is a percentage of the total sale price, including shipping and any applicable taxes, that eBay charges once an item is sold. In 2025, eBay has continued its policy of offering the first 250 listings per month for free for most sellers, under what's known as zero insertion fee listings. This allowance resets every month and gives beginners a generous amount of breathing room to experiment with listings, refine product descriptions, and test pricing strategies without upfront financial pressure.

However, once a seller exceeds the free listing threshold, insertion fees begin to apply. These fees are generally modest—usually a flat rate per listing—but they can add up quickly if a seller operates at high volume without strategic planning. Additionally, certain listing upgrades such as adding subtitles, using bold fonts, or placing an item in multiple categories incur extra insertion charges. These enhancements are optional but are designed to boost visibility in a crowded marketplace. Sellers must weigh whether the potential increase in sales justifies the additional cost of these enhancements.

The final value fee is the most significant component of eBay's fee structure. This is where eBay earns the majority of its revenue from sellers. In 2025, this fee continues to be calculated as a percentage of the total transaction value, and the exact percentage varies depending on the item category. For most standard categories, such as clothing, electronics, home goods, and collectibles, the fee ranges from 10% to 15%. However, there are exceptions—categories like heavy equipment, industrial tools, or vehicles may have different fee structures altogether, often with capped maximum charges or tiered pricing systems.

It's important to understand that eBay calculates the final value fee based on the full amount the buyer pays—including shipping costs. This means that inflating shipping prices as a way to lower the sale price and reduce fees no longer works, and in fact, it can hurt the seller's reputation. Buyers expect fair and transparent pricing, and eBay's algorithms penalize listings that appear to be manipulating costs. As such, sellers are encouraged to offer reasonable shipping rates and build the cost of doing business—including fees—into their item prices in a clear and honest way.

In addition to these core fees, eBay also offers promotional tools that come with associated costs. One of the most commonly used tools is Promoted Listings. This feature allows sellers to pay for enhanced visibility by having their listings appear in sponsored positions across eBay's search results and browsing pages. In 2025, eBay has made significant improvements to its Promoted Listings system, offering more advanced targeting options and better analytics. The fee for using Promoted Listings is performance-based—meaning the seller only pays when the promoted listing results in a sale, and the fee is calculated as a percentage of the sale price. Sellers can choose their ad rate, which gives them control over how aggressively they want to promote an item. Setting a higher ad rate increases the chances of visibility but also reduces the overall profit margin.

eBay has also introduced Promoted Listings Advanced, a cost-per-click model aimed at more experienced sellers or those in highly competitive categories. This model charges sellers every time a shopper clicks on a promoted listing, regardless of whether the item is ultimately purchased. While this strategy can bring a flood of traffic, it requires careful keyword targeting, budgeting, and monitoring to ensure a return on investment. Beginners are encouraged to start with standard Promoted Listings before moving into more advanced advertising models once they understand buyer behavior and conversion rates.

Another fee that new sellers must be aware of is the payment processing fee. With eBay managing payments directly instead of relying on third-party processors like PayPal, this fee is built into the final value fee and no longer appears as a separate charge. The benefit of this consolidation is simplified accounting and streamlined financial reporting. However, sellers still need to remember that this fee is not waived; it is just bundled into the total transaction cost.

eBay's fee structure also includes optional store subscriptions, which become relevant as sellers grow their operations. There are different tiers of store subscriptions—Starter, Basic, Premium, Anchor, and Enterprise—each offering increasing benefits in terms of free listings, advanced tools, branding options, and lower final value fees. For example, sellers with a Basic Store get more zero insertion listings and lower per-item fees than those without a store. The subscription fee is charged monthly and ranges depending on the tier selected. This model benefits serious sellers who need more tools and inventory space than the standard account provides, and it becomes cost-effective when a seller consistently exceeds the limits of the free tools provided in a non-subscription account.

To ensure transparency, eBay provides detailed fee breakdowns in the Seller Hub. This centralized dashboard shows fees per transaction, aggregated monthly charges, and promotional spending. Sellers can download these summaries to analyze their costs, adjust strategies, and prepare for tax season. It also allows them to pinpoint high-fee areas and determine whether adjustments in pricing or promotion strategy might improve their profitability.

International fees are also worth mentioning. If a seller chooses to offer international shipping or list on eBay's global sites, additional fees may apply. These fees account for currency conversions, cross-border transaction costs, and increased logistical complexity. While eBay provides international shipping tools to simplify the process, it's important for sellers to read the fine print and consider whether the profit margins justify global expansion early in the journey.

There are also some penalties that appear in the form of additional charges if sellers don't follow eBay's policies. For instance, excessive cancellations, late shipments, or poor customer service ratings can result in account downgrades, which may come with higher final value fees. eBay uses performance metrics to determine a seller's standing, and those who maintain high standards are rewarded not just with more visibility, but also more favorable fees and access to premium programs. Conversely, sellers with a record of policy violations or unresolved disputes may see higher fees and limited account privileges.

Understanding eBay's seller fees and structures in 2025 isn't just about knowing what you'll be charged—it's about knowing how to work within that structure strategically. Each fee has a purpose, and when used with intention, it can become a tool rather than a burden. Sellers who price intelligently, monitor performance, and take advantage of bundled features can keep their costs low and their profits healthy. Selling on eBay is no longer about guessing how much you'll earn after fees; it's about mastering the system so you can predict, plan, and grow with confidence.

EXPLORING EBAY MANAGED PAYMENTS: HOW IT WORKS

In 2025, eBay's move to Managed Payments continues to be one of the most significant changes to the platform's payment structure. This system was introduced to provide a more streamlined and integrated experience for both buyers and sellers. Prior to Managed Payments, eBay relied on PayPal as its primary payment processor, but with the shift to Managed Payments, eBay now handles all transactions directly, allowing for faster, more flexible payment options. For beginners looking to understand how this system works and how it affects their eBay business, it's essential to dive into the details of Managed Payments, how it operates, and the benefits it brings to sellers.

Managed Payments is designed to simplify the entire payment process. Before this system, eBay sellers had to deal with multiple accounts, including PayPal for payment processing and a separate bank account for managing funds. With Managed Payments, eBay consolidates this system into one cohesive platform. This means that sellers no longer need to have a separate PayPal account or worry about withdrawing funds from PayPal to their bank account. Instead, eBay handles all payments within its own ecosystem, making the process more efficient and predictable.

The primary benefit of eBay Managed Payments is that it gives sellers access to a broader range of payment options. Buyers can pay using various methods, including credit cards, debit cards, Apple Pay, Google Pay, and even eBay gift cards, in addition to PayPal. This flexibility is essential for accommodating a global customer base that uses different payment methods. By offering more payment options, sellers can increase their potential pool of customers and ultimately boost sales. For buyers, this system creates a more convenient, one-stop-shop for making payments across the platform.

When a buyer makes a purchase, the payment is processed directly through eBay's payment system, and funds are typically deposited into the seller's account within two to three business days. The deposit is automatically transferred to the seller's linked bank account, making it simple to track and manage. This payment flow removes the complexity of dealing with multiple payment processors, giving sellers a clearer picture of their cash flow. Additionally, eBay ensures that payments are protected through its own payment security systems, reducing the risk of fraud or chargebacks that were previously more common with PayPal.

Sellers who are enrolled in Managed Payments enjoy the added convenience of a single payment platform. All transaction-related activities, such as issuing refunds, tracking payments, and managing financial records, are handled through the seller dashboard. This integration eliminates the need to log into multiple platforms or keep track of separate fees. Sellers can easily access transaction histories, download reports, and handle any customer service issues directly within the eBay Seller Hub, streamlining the management of their eBay business.

A key advantage of eBay's Managed Payments is the simplified fee structure. Under this system, eBay combines the fees for payment processing, listing fees, and final value fees into one unified charge. While the final value fee percentage remains relatively consistent, with slight variations depending on the category of the item, the payment processing fee is automatically factored into the overall cost of selling on the platform.

This consolidation makes it easier for sellers to calculate their profit margins and track expenses without having to juggle multiple fees from different providers.

One of the most important aspects of Managed Payments is that it eliminates the need for third-party payment processors, such as PayPal, which used to be the go-to platform for eBay sellers. Prior to the introduction of Managed Payments, sellers were required to integrate PayPal into their listings, making it a mandatory part of the selling process. This often led to confusion and frustration, especially when PayPal would flag accounts or hold funds due to suspected fraudulent activity or customer disputes. Managed Payments eliminates this third-party dependency, and with eBay controlling the payment process, the platform can more easily resolve any issues that may arise.

For beginners, this means fewer steps to set up and manage payments. Sellers can link their bank accounts directly to eBay, which simplifies the process of receiving funds. Since eBay now processes all payments, there's no need to wait for PayPal to transfer funds into the seller's bank account. Payments are deposited directly into the seller's linked account, and the entire process is automated. This ensures that funds are available quickly and consistently, reducing the time spent managing payments.

In addition to the convenience of processing payments directly, eBay also integrates tax management within the Managed Payments system. In 2025, this is particularly important as eBay takes on the responsibility of collecting and remitting sales tax for orders shipped to U.S. buyers, in accordance with state regulations. This eliminates the burden for sellers who may not be familiar with the complex tax laws that vary by state. eBay's system automatically calculates the appropriate tax rate based on the buyer's location and ensures that taxes are paid correctly. This removes the administrative headache for sellers, particularly those who sell across multiple states or countries, and ensures compliance with tax regulations.

With the new payment structure, eBay also provides sellers with more transparency regarding transaction fees. While the final value fees have remained consistent, eBay now provides detailed breakdowns of the fees charged on each transaction, including the payment processing fee, in the seller dashboard. This transparency makes it easier for sellers to understand exactly where their money is going and to optimize their listings to account for fees. Additionally, sellers can track their earnings and understand the impact of promotions, returns, and shipping costs on their profits in a single dashboard.

One of the key challenges for sellers under the old system was dealing with disputes and chargebacks, particularly those that arose from PayPal transactions. With Managed Payments, eBay now handles chargebacks and disputes directly, which streamlines the process and removes the need for sellers to interact with third-party payment processors. If a buyer initiates a chargeback or reports an issue with a transaction, eBay's customer service team works directly with the seller to resolve the matter. The platform's dispute resolution system ensures that sellers are not left in the dark, and it offers guidance on how to protect themselves from chargebacks by providing tracking information, clear refund policies, and other best practices.

As beneficial as Managed Payments is, it's important to understand the payment cycle and how it can impact sellers. Payments are not processed instantaneously but typically take two to three business days after the transaction is completed. This is important for beginners to consider when planning for cash flow. In the case of a seller who operates with a large inventory and relies on frequent payouts, understanding this payment cycle is crucial for maintaining a healthy cash flow. While payments are deposited quickly, it's wise for new sellers to have a buffer to avoid disruptions in inventory purchases or shipping expenses.

To get started with Managed Payments, beginners simply need to sign up for eBay's program when setting up their account or when migrating from a previous PayPal-based setup. The process involves linking a valid bank account, verifying the seller's identity, and agreeing to eBay's terms and conditions. Once enrolled, the seller's payment settings will be automatically adjusted, and future transactions will be processed through eBay's Managed Payments system.

Overall, eBay's Managed Payments system has streamlined the payment process for both sellers and buyers, making transactions smoother, faster, and more transparent. For sellers, it offers a simplified, all-in-one solution for handling payments, disputes, taxes, and fees. By cutting out third-party payment processors like PayPal and integrating everything within the eBay ecosystem, the platform has created a more efficient, secure, and reliable system for online selling. While the system may take some time to adjust to, especially for those who are used to PayPal, the benefits far outweigh the transition challenges, and Managed Payments is a key part of building a successful online business on eBay.

CHAPTER 2
CRAFTING YOUR SELLER PROFILE AND BUILDING TRUST

CHOOSING A PROFESSIONAL AND MEMORABLE USERNAME

Choosing a professional and memorable username for your eBay account is one of the most important decisions you will make as you begin your online selling journey. While it may seem like a trivial detail, your username plays a significant role in shaping how buyers perceive you and your business. It's your first impression, and it can have a lasting impact on your sales, credibility, and customer engagement. As such, it's essential to think carefully about what you want your username to represent and how it can support your long-term goals as a seller on eBay.

The username you choose will be more than just an identifier; it will be the cornerstone of your brand on eBay. When potential buyers search for products or browse categories, your username is the first thing they'll see. A strong, memorable username can help set you apart from the competition, while a poorly chosen one can make it harder for buyers to find you or feel confident in purchasing from you. A professional username gives the impression that you are serious about your business and can help establish trust with buyers from the moment they see it.

One of the key factors to keep in mind when selecting your username is that it should be easy to remember. Think about how a potential buyer might find you in search results. If your username is complex, difficult to spell, or full of random numbers and symbols, it will be harder for customers to recall. In contrast, a simple, clear, and easy-to-type name will increase the chances of buyers finding your listings and remembering your brand in the future. This is especially important in the crowded eBay marketplace, where there are millions of sellers competing for attention. Your username should make you stand out for the right reasons.

In addition to being memorable, your username should reflect your business or niche. If you're selling a specific type of product, such as vintage clothing, home decor, or electronics, consider incorporating that into your username. This helps to immediately communicate to buyers what your store is all about. For example, if you sell eco-friendly products, a username like "GreenGoods" or "EcoEssentials" not only describes what you sell but also helps you build a brand identity around your niche. A relevant username can make it easier for customers to identify your store as the go-to place for specific items, making your offerings feel more specialized and appealing.

While creativity is important, it's also essential to keep your username professional. Avoid using slang, cutesy phrases, or anything that could come across as unprofessional or overly gimmicky. Even if you're running a fun or quirky store, your username should still maintain a level of professionalism to establish credibility. A username that's too playful or offbeat might lead customers to question the legitimacy of your business or the quality of your products. On the other hand, a professional username signals that you are running a serious operation and can be trusted to deliver high-quality products and customer service.

When choosing a username, it's also essential to consider its longevity. While you might be starting out with a small selection of products, think about the future of your business. Choose a name that won't limit you as your business grows. For example, if you plan to expand your product offerings or enter new categories in the future, avoid using a name that's too specific to one type of product. A more general name, such as "ShopSavvy" or "PrimePicks," allows you to branch out and diversify your inventory without being restricted by your username. A versatile name also allows you to build a broader brand identity that can evolve over time, rather than being tied to a single product category.

In addition to considering your business's growth potential, you should also make sure that your username is available on other platforms. Building a brand across multiple channels is essential for growing your online business, and having a consistent username across eBay, social media platforms, and your website can help reinforce your brand identity. If you plan to market your products through platforms like Instagram, Facebook, or Twitter, ensure that the username you choose is available across these sites as well. This creates a cohesive online presence that makes it easier for customers to find and engage with your business across different platforms.

Another important aspect to think about is the length of your username. While eBay allows you to choose a username up to 50 characters long, it's generally best to keep it shorter and more concise. A shorter username is easier for buyers to remember, type, and share. It's also less likely to get truncated in search results or in your store's URL. Ideally, aim for a username that's between 10 to 20 characters, as this strikes a balance between being descriptive and easily memorable. If you find that your desired username is already taken, try using variations or adding numbers and symbols, but only if they don't make the name difficult to remember or type.

Avoid using special characters, punctuation marks, or spaces in your username. While eBay allows some special characters, using them can create confusion for buyers who may not know how to type them correctly. Stick to letters and numbers to ensure that your username is as easy to remember and type as possible. Additionally, avoid using overly complicated combinations of numbers or letters, which can appear spammy or untrustworthy to potential buyers. Simplicity and clarity should always be your priority.

It's also a good idea to check for trademark issues when choosing your username. Avoid using brand names or logos that are trademarked, as this could lead to legal complications. eBay has strict policies regarding intellectual property rights, and using a name that infringes on someone else's trademark can result in your account being suspended or your listings being removed. Do a quick search to see if the username you're considering is already in use by another business, and make sure that it doesn't violate any trademarks. A unique, original name will help you avoid potential legal issues down the road and allow you to establish a distinct brand identity.

Lastly, test your username before finalizing it. Share it with friends, family, or colleagues and get their feedback on how it sounds and how easy it is to remember. Sometimes, a name that seems perfect in theory might not work as well in practice. It's always a good idea to get input from others to make sure that your username resonates with your target audience and accurately reflects your business.

Ultimately, your username is an essential part of building your eBay presence and reputation. By selecting a professional, memorable, and relevant name, you're setting the foundation for a strong brand that can grow with your business. Whether you're just starting out or looking to rebrand, take the time to choose a username that reflects your vision, is easy for customers to recall, and helps you stand out in a competitive marketplace. A well-chosen username is more than just an identifier – it's a critical element of your eBay business strategy that can have a lasting impact on your success.

WRITING A COMPELLING "ABOUT ME" SECTION

When starting an eBay business, one of the most essential components of your store is the "About Me" section. This section is more than just a few lines about who you are—it's an opportunity to connect with potential buyers, build trust, and showcase what makes your store unique. The "About Me" section is often one of the first things a customer will read when they visit your store, so it's important to make it count. A compelling "About Me" page can help set the tone for your entire business, encouraging customers to make purchases while ensuring that they feel confident and comfortable buying from you.

To craft a truly engaging "About Me" section, start by thinking about what you want your potential customers to know about you and your business. Buyers on eBay want to feel a personal connection to the sellers they're buying from. This connection is crucial, as it can give them peace of mind that they are purchasing from someone who is trustworthy, reliable, and committed to delivering high-quality products. Start by introducing yourself. Your name, a brief background, and why you started selling on eBay can help humanize your store and create a relationship with your audience. Let your personality shine through, but keep in mind that the goal is to establish credibility and trust, so maintain a tone that reflects professionalism and friendliness.

As you dive deeper into the content of your "About Me" section, think about the story behind your business. Every business has a story, and sharing yours can be an effective way to engage potential customers. Perhaps you've been collecting vintage items for years, or maybe your passion for a specific product led you to start selling. Whatever the story may be, don't hesitate to share it. Storytelling can create an emotional connection with your audience, which is essential for building loyalty and encouraging repeat customers. If you have a personal or inspiring reason for starting your business, be sure to include it, as it can resonate with buyers who share similar interests or values.

Another key component to a strong "About Me" section is emphasizing your commitment to customer service. Customers want to know that they can trust you to deliver excellent service and resolve any issues that may arise. Be sure to mention your dedication to providing great customer experiences. Highlight the steps you take to ensure satisfaction, such as offering easy returns or responding promptly to customer inquiries. Reassure your buyers that you are there to support them throughout the entire buying process, from answering questions about products to resolving issues after a purchase. When customers feel supported, they are more likely to leave positive feedback and return for future purchases, which is crucial for long-term success on eBay.

Your "About Me" section should also reflect your business's values and mission. What sets you apart from the competition? Whether it's your commitment to sustainability, your expertise in a particular niche, or your exceptional attention to detail, make sure to communicate what makes your business unique. For example, if you specialize in eco-friendly products, let buyers know that your business is committed to sustainable practices. If you pride yourself on offering rare or hard-to-find items, mention that as well. The goal is to convey what differentiates your store from others, giving customers a reason to choose you over other sellers in the marketplace.

While it's important to tell your story and highlight your values, your "About Me" section should also be practical. Buyers are ultimately on eBay to make purchases, so you want to provide them with the information they need to feel confident about their decision. Be clear about what your store offers, what types of products you sell, and what customers can expect when they purchase from you. If you have specific policies regarding shipping, returns, or payment methods, include these details so that customers can make informed decisions before making a purchase. This transparency helps to build trust and ensures that buyers have a positive shopping experience.

Additionally, including a call to action (CTA) at the end of your "About Me" section can be a powerful way to encourage engagement and drive sales. A well-crafted CTA invites potential buyers to take the next step, whether it's browsing your product listings, following your store for updates, or contacting you with any questions. For example, you could say something like, "Browse my listings to find unique, high-quality items you won't find anywhere else" or "Feel free to reach out with any questions—I'm always happy to help!" A CTA not only encourages interaction but also reinforces your commitment to customer service, showing that you're accessible and ready to assist.

In addition to the content itself, the format and presentation of your "About Me" section matter as well. Keep it easy to read and visually appealing by breaking up long paragraphs into smaller, digestible chunks. Use a conversational yet professional tone that reflects your brand's personality, and make sure the layout is clean and easy to navigate. You don't want your buyers to feel overwhelmed by a wall of text, so make sure to structure your writing in a way that guides them through your story, values, and policies without overwhelming them with too much information at once.

To further enhance the impact of your "About Me" section, consider adding a personal touch in the form of a photo or logo. A photo of yourself or your workspace can help buyers feel more connected to you as a person, and a logo can help reinforce your brand identity. Visual elements can help make your "About Me" page more memorable and can help build a stronger relationship with your audience. Keep in mind that the visuals you choose should align with your brand's aesthetic, whether it's minimalist, vintage, or modern, to ensure consistency throughout your eBay store.

It's also worth noting that your "About Me" section is not set in stone. As your business grows and evolves, so too can the story you tell about it. Don't be afraid to revisit your "About Me" page periodically to ensure that it still accurately reflects your business and your values. As you expand your product offerings or introduce new services, update your page to reflect these changes. Regularly refreshing your content can also help keep your store feeling dynamic and engaging, which is crucial for maintaining long-term success on eBay.

Writing a compelling "About Me" section is an essential part of creating a successful eBay business. It's not just a place to tell your story—it's an opportunity to connect with customers, build trust, and showcase what makes your business unique. By sharing your background, your commitment to customer service, and your business's values, you can create a page that resonates with potential buyers and sets you up for success. Take the time to craft an engaging, professional, and memorable "About Me" section, and watch it work to establish a lasting relationship with your customers.

SETTING UP YOUR RETURN POLICY AND SHIPPING PREFERENCES

Setting up your return policy and shipping preferences on eBay is one of the most critical steps in ensuring a smooth and successful selling experience. These two components not only help you maintain customer satisfaction but also protect your reputation as a seller. A well-defined return policy and clear shipping preferences can significantly impact buyer trust, influence purchasing decisions, and contribute to your overall success on the platform. Understanding how to set up these policies correctly is vital for ensuring that your eBay store runs efficiently and that both you and your customers have a positive experience.

When it comes to setting your return policy, clarity and transparency are paramount. Buyers want to know exactly what they can expect if they need to return an item, and having a solid return policy in place reassures them that their purchase is protected. The first thing to consider is the length of your return period. eBay allows sellers to choose from a range of return periods, such as 30 days, 60 days, or even 14 days. While offering a longer return period can be attractive to potential buyers, it's essential to balance flexibility with practicality. A 30-day return policy is often a good starting point for most sellers, but depending on the nature of your products, you may choose a shorter or longer period. Remember, the goal is to ensure that customers have enough time to evaluate their purchases and feel confident in their decision to buy from you.

Another important aspect of your return policy is whether you will accept returns for all reasons or only under specific conditions. Most sellers opt to accept returns for any reason, as it provides the highest level of customer satisfaction. This approach aligns with eBay's buyer protection policies, which encourage sellers to maintain a positive buyer experience. However, some sellers may choose to limit returns to cases where the item is damaged or not as described. In this case, it's crucial to clearly state in your return policy that returns are only accepted under specific circumstances, such as defective or misrepresented items. Be transparent about the conditions under which a return will be accepted to avoid any confusion or dissatisfaction from buyers.

The next consideration is who will cover the return shipping costs. Many sellers choose to have the buyer pay for return shipping, particularly for items that are being returned due to buyer's remorse. On the other hand, sellers who want to provide a more customer-friendly return experience may choose to cover return shipping, especially if the item is defective or not as described. It's important to clearly communicate who will be responsible for return shipping in your policy. If you decide to offer free return shipping, keep in mind that eBay has a "free returns" program that can help boost the visibility of your listings. Buyers often feel more confident purchasing from a seller who offers free returns, as it signals trust and a commitment to customer satisfaction.

Your return policy should also address how refunds will be processed. Once a return is accepted, how quickly will the buyer receive their money back? A fast and efficient refund process is crucial for maintaining positive feedback and keeping customers satisfied. Most sellers offer full refunds for returned items, but it's important to ensure that the refund is processed promptly once the item is returned. eBay offers an automated refund system, which can make this process easier and faster for both you and the buyer. However, if you prefer a more manual approach, be sure to communicate the expected time frame for issuing a refund so that customers know when they can expect to see their money returned.

When it comes to setting your shipping preferences, there are several factors to consider to ensure that your shipping policies are clear and efficient. The first decision you'll need to make is whether to offer domestic shipping only or include international shipping in your offerings. Offering international shipping can open up your business to a larger market, potentially increasing your sales. However, international shipping can be more complex and costly. If you decide to ship internationally, be sure to familiarize yourself with eBay's Global Shipping Program (GSP), which simplifies the process by handling customs, duties, and international shipping fees on your behalf. If you choose to only offer domestic shipping, make sure to clearly communicate the countries you ship to and any restrictions you may have.

One of the most important aspects of setting up your shipping preferences is determining the shipping methods you will use. eBay offers a range of options, including standard shipping, expedited shipping, and overnight shipping. The method you choose will depend on the type of product you're selling, your target customer, and the cost of shipping. Standard shipping is the most affordable option, but it can take longer for customers to receive their items. If you're selling time-sensitive products or catering to customers who want faster delivery, expedited or overnight shipping may be more appropriate. However, these shipping methods come with higher fees, so you'll need to weigh the cost against the benefit of offering faster delivery.

Another important consideration is whether to offer free shipping. Free shipping is a popular option among buyers and can help make your listings more attractive. However, it's essential to factor the cost of shipping into your overall pricing strategy. Offering free shipping doesn't necessarily mean you're losing money, but it does mean that you will need to adjust the price of your item accordingly. Some sellers include the cost of shipping in the item price, while others offer free shipping as part of a promotional strategy or as an added benefit for higher-priced items. Regardless of your approach, it's important to be transparent about your shipping costs, so buyers understand the value they're receiving.

In addition to deciding on shipping methods and costs, you'll also need to determine your handling time. Handling time refers to the number of business days it takes for you to prepare and ship an item after a purchase is made. Buyers are often keen on fast shipping, so offering a short handling time can make your listings more appealing. However, it's crucial to set a realistic handling time based on your capabilities. If you're selling high-volume items or managing your store on your own, it may take longer to ship products, so you'll want to factor that into your handling time. Setting an accurate handling time not only helps manage customer expectations but also prevents you from receiving negative feedback due to shipping delays.

Lastly, you'll need to decide on shipping carriers. eBay partners with major carriers such as USPS, UPS, and FedEx, offering a range of services that vary in speed and cost. The carrier you choose will depend on the size and weight of your items, as well as your desired delivery time frame. For smaller items, USPS is often the most affordable option, while larger, heavier items may require UPS or FedEx services. Be sure to offer a range of shipping options to suit different customer preferences, and consider using eBay's shipping calculator to determine the most cost-effective options for your listings.

Ultimately, your return policy and shipping preferences are critical elements of your eBay business. By setting clear, fair, and customer-friendly policies, you create an environment where buyers feel confident and supported throughout their purchasing experience. Offering a transparent return policy that includes clear guidelines on returns, shipping responsibilities, and refunds helps to manage customer expectations and reduce potential disputes. Meanwhile, defining your shipping preferences ensures that customers know exactly how their items will be delivered, which can help boost your sales and improve your seller reputation. When both of these aspects are handled with care and attention to detail, you'll be well on your way to running a successful eBay business.

UNDERSTANDING AND UTILIZING EBAY'S FEEDBACK SYSTEM

The eBay feedback system plays a central role in building trust between buyers and sellers, especially in an online marketplace where physical interaction is absent. Feedback, which can be left by buyers and sellers after a transaction is completed, is an essential tool that reflects the reputation of sellers and provides insight into the reliability and quality of their products and services. In 2025, the eBay feedback system remains a cornerstone of the platform's marketplace, with buyers using feedback to make informed purchasing decisions and sellers leveraging it to attract more customers and grow their businesses. Understanding how this system works, and how to effectively utilize it, is crucial for anyone starting their eBay journey, as it directly influences both sales and customer satisfaction.

At its core, eBay's feedback system operates on a simple premise: buyers and sellers rate their transaction experiences with each other. Feedback is given in the form of positive, neutral, or negative ratings, along with written comments that provide additional context or detail about the transaction. While the feedback score is important, the written feedback provides deeper insight into a seller's service quality, including their communication, shipping speed, product accuracy, and overall customer service.

The feedback score itself is composed of the number of positive, neutral, and negative feedback ratings a seller receives over time. A higher score, particularly one with a greater percentage of positive feedback, increases a seller's credibility. For new sellers, starting with a strong feedback profile is essential to establish trust in the competitive eBay marketplace. Sellers with consistent positive feedback are more likely to gain the confidence of potential buyers, who tend to favor well-reviewed sellers when making purchasing decisions. Even a small number of negative or neutral feedback ratings can tarnish a seller's reputation and impact sales.

When navigating the eBay feedback system, it's important to understand the different types of feedback and how they impact a seller's overall profile. Positive feedback is the most desirable and signals a successful transaction where both the buyer and seller are satisfied. Neutral feedback is typically given when the buyer is neither completely satisfied nor dissatisfied but feels that there was room for improvement. Negative feedback, while less common, can be a major red flag for both current and potential buyers. Negative feedback usually indicates issues with the product, service, shipping delays, or communication failures, and it can significantly hurt a seller's reputation if not addressed promptly and professionally.

For sellers, receiving feedback can be a double-edged sword. Positive feedback boosts reputation and attracts more buyers, while negative feedback can deter future sales and negatively impact the seller's standing in eBay's search results. However, sellers can mitigate the impact of negative feedback by addressing the issues promptly and professionally. If a buyer leaves negative feedback, it's crucial to respond in a courteous and solution-oriented manner. Offering an apology, explaining the issue, and offering a resolution can sometimes help turn a negative situation around. eBay also allows sellers to respond publicly to feedback, which gives them the opportunity to clarify their side of the story. However, it's important to remain professional in these responses and avoid sounding defensive, as this could further harm the seller's reputation.

One of the most effective ways to avoid negative feedback is to provide excellent customer service throughout the entire transaction process. This includes clear and honest communication, accurate product descriptions, fast shipping, and effective problem resolution. By ensuring that buyers are satisfied with their experience, sellers can encourage positive feedback and reduce the likelihood of receiving neutral or negative ratings. Even when a mistake occurs, addressing it swiftly and professionally can prevent dissatisfaction and mitigate the impact of the mistake on the seller's feedback score.

While feedback is important, eBay's feedback system includes a couple of features that sellers can use to their advantage. The first is the ability to leave feedback for buyers. This is an opportunity for sellers to rate the buyer's behavior and communication, which can help create a more balanced feedback profile. However, sellers should be aware that feedback for buyers is less impactful than feedback for sellers and should be used appropriately. For example, leaving positive feedback for buyers who promptly pay and communicate well is a great way to build rapport and encourage repeat business. On the other hand, leaving negative feedback for buyers who engage in fraudulent activity or fail to pay for items is a necessary step to maintain a fair and safe marketplace.

Another tool that sellers can use to help manage their feedback profile is eBay's Feedback Removal policy. eBay provides guidelines for when negative or neutral feedback may be removed. For instance, if a buyer leaves feedback that violates eBay's policies—such as using inappropriate language or leaving feedback based on issues that were beyond the seller's control—sellers can request feedback removal. Additionally, feedback can be removed if the buyer opened a case that was resolved in the seller's favor, such as in cases of item not received or item not as described. Sellers must demonstrate that the feedback violates eBay's policies to have it removed, but this process can help sellers protect their reputation when unjust negative feedback is left.

In 2025, eBay has also introduced tools to help sellers manage and maintain their feedback scores. One such tool is the Seller Dashboard, which provides sellers with a snapshot of their feedback ratings, allowing them to see trends, analyze areas of improvement, and track their performance over time. This tool also provides sellers with alerts if their feedback score drops below a certain threshold, allowing them to take action before it affects their standing. By regularly monitoring their feedback and addressing any issues early on, sellers can maintain a strong reputation and avoid long-term negative consequences.

Another feature that helps sellers is the "Top Rated Seller" program, which recognizes high-performing sellers who maintain exceptional feedback ratings. To qualify for this status, sellers must meet specific criteria, including a high percentage of positive feedback, timely shipping, and low levels of returns and customer complaints. Becoming a Top Rated Seller brings numerous benefits, including increased visibility in search results, eligibility for discounted fees, and a badge on listings that signals reliability to potential buyers. Achieving and maintaining Top Rated Seller status is an excellent way to build trust and credibility with buyers, which can lead to increased sales.

In addition to monitoring and responding to feedback, sellers can also use feedback as a valuable source of information to improve their business. By analyzing feedback comments, sellers can identify patterns and recurring issues that may need to be addressed. For example, if several buyers mention slow shipping times, a seller might consider investing in faster shipping options or improving processing times. If multiple buyers comment on a product's quality, the seller might need to revisit product sourcing or revise the product description to better manage expectations. Feedback, in this way, can serve as a mirror, reflecting areas where a seller can improve their business and customer experience.

The feedback system is also tied to eBay's seller protection policies. If a buyer leaves negative feedback and the seller resolves the issue, the seller may be able to request that eBay remove the feedback. Additionally, if a seller complies with eBay's policies and provides excellent customer service, they can protect themselves from retaliatory negative feedback, which can sometimes occur in contentious transactions. Sellers who are proactive about maintaining good communication and resolving disputes effectively can prevent most negative feedback scenarios from escalating.

Ultimately, feedback is one of the most powerful tools a seller can use on eBay to build a successful business. By understanding how the feedback system works and actively managing it, sellers can create a positive, trustworthy reputation that encourages more buyers to choose their products. Regularly monitoring feedback, responding professionally to any concerns, and using feedback to continuously improve operations are all key strategies for leveraging the feedback system to its fullest potential. A strong feedback profile not only enhances buyer trust but also helps sellers gain a competitive edge in the ever-evolving eBay marketplace.

BUILDING A POSITIVE SELLER REPUTATION FROM DAY ONE

Building a positive seller reputation on eBay is one of the most critical steps to achieving success in the marketplace. From the moment a new seller sets up their account, they are in the process of creating an impression that will affect their ability to attract customers and close sales. Reputation is everything on eBay, and while it takes time to build a solid one, there are steps that can be taken from day one to set the foundation for a strong, trustworthy profile.

The reputation a seller builds on eBay is reflected in their feedback score. This score, accumulated over time, directly influences the trust that buyers place in a seller. A high feedback rating signals that the seller has provided a satisfactory experience for previous buyers, while negative feedback can undermine a seller's standing. However, it's not just about the score—it's about the overall experience a seller creates for their customers, which includes communication, product accuracy, shipping times, and customer service. These elements come together to form a seller's reputation, and the more positive experiences a seller can create, the stronger their reputation will become.

One of the first and most important things a seller can do is to ensure they are listing quality products that match their descriptions. Misleading or inaccurate product descriptions are a quick way to damage a reputation and lead to negative feedback. Sellers should aim to be as honest and thorough as possible in their product listings. This includes clearly stating the condition of the item, providing accurate measurements, highlighting any flaws or imperfections, and using high-quality images. If an item is pre-owned, this should be communicated clearly, and if it is new, the seller should specify any packaging or manufacturer details that would help the buyer make an informed decision. When buyers know exactly what they are getting, they are more likely to leave positive feedback and return for future purchases.

Communication is another critical factor in building a positive reputation. Sellers should respond to buyer inquiries promptly and professionally. Buyers may have questions about the product, shipping times, or payment methods, and timely, helpful responses show that the seller values customer service. Clear communication before, during, and after the transaction helps to build trust. For example, if there is a delay in shipping due to an unforeseen circumstance, the seller should reach out to the buyer and inform them of the situation. Proactive communication can prevent misunderstandings and give the impression that the seller is attentive and reliable. Moreover, addressing concerns or resolving issues quickly can prevent negative feedback, which would otherwise harm the seller's reputation.

Shipping speed and accuracy are equally essential components of a positive seller reputation. Buyers expect fast and reliable shipping, and any delay can cause frustration. To build a strong reputation from the start, sellers should offer prompt shipping and update tracking information as soon as it becomes available. One way to stand out as a seller is by offering same-day or next-day shipping, which can be a significant draw for buyers looking for speedy delivery. Additionally, providing accurate shipping costs and reliable shipping options ensures that the buyer knows exactly what to expect. For high-value or fragile items, consider using insured or expedited shipping services to protect both the product and the transaction.

Offering excellent post-sale support is another way to create a lasting positive reputation. If a buyer has an issue with a product after receiving it, the seller should be open to resolving the matter in a fair and amicable way. Offering refunds, exchanges, or even partial refunds in situations where a buyer isn't satisfied with their purchase can go a long way in preserving the seller's reputation. Being flexible and accommodating in these situations can even turn an initially negative experience into a positive one, with buyers often returning to leave glowing reviews about how the situation was handled. Customers remember great service, and word of mouth—whether through feedback on eBay or outside the platform—can have a lasting impact on a seller's business.

Another way to build a positive reputation from day one is by keeping a consistent and reliable selling schedule. Sellers who list new items regularly and consistently can create an impression of professionalism and reliability. Having an active presence on eBay, with regular updates to their inventory, helps sellers stay top-of-mind for potential buyers. Regular activity also improves visibility within eBay's search algorithms, meaning that sellers who consistently list and sell products are more likely to show up in search results when buyers are looking for their items. By keeping an updated inventory, maintaining a steady flow of products, and responding to customer queries quickly, sellers can build trust and encourage buyers to return for repeat purchases.

In addition to these strategies, it's also essential for sellers to monitor their eBay account for any negative feedback and address any issues that arise promptly. Negative feedback is inevitable, especially when starting out, but how a seller handles it can make all the difference. If negative feedback is left, the seller should reach out to the buyer to understand their concerns and see if the issue can be resolved. Often, buyers are willing to update or retract their feedback if the situation is handled professionally and the issue is addressed to their satisfaction. Sellers should remain calm and respectful in their responses and avoid getting defensive, as this can escalate the situation. If the issue cannot be resolved and the feedback remains negative, it's important to continue providing excellent service to future buyers and let the feedback system work over time.

Another important consideration for sellers looking to build a strong reputation is eBay's "Top Rated Seller" program, which offers several advantages to sellers who meet specific criteria. This program rewards sellers who consistently provide excellent customer service, accurate descriptions, and on-time delivery. To qualify for Top Rated Seller status, sellers must meet certain performance standards, including having a high percentage of positive feedback, providing fast shipping, and offering excellent communication. Sellers who achieve Top Rated Seller status enjoy increased visibility in search results, lower fees, and the prestigious badge that signals to buyers that they are trustworthy and reliable. This status not only boosts a seller's credibility but also provides a competitive edge in a crowded marketplace.

Building a positive reputation is not just about avoiding negative feedback—it's about creating an experience that goes above and beyond what buyers expect. Exceptional service, transparent listings, fast shipping, and excellent communication are the pillars upon which a strong seller reputation is built. Sellers who consistently provide these aspects of service will find themselves with loyal customers, repeat business, and a positive feedback profile. Over time, this reputation will grow, and as it does, so will the opportunities for the seller's business to flourish. The effort put into building a positive reputation from day one will pay dividends in the form of customer trust, repeat sales, and long-term success.

PART 2

Finding Your Products and Mastering Listings

CHAPTER 3
DISCOVERING PROFITABLE ITEMS TO SELL ON EBAY

IDENTIFYING YOUR NICHE: PASSION, KNOWLEDGE, AND MARKET DEMAND

When embarking on a journey as an eBay seller, one of the most crucial decisions you'll make is selecting your niche. This choice will shape the direction of your business, determine the types of products you sell, and influence your success in the marketplace. Identifying the right niche is a balancing act between your passion and knowledge, and the demands of the market. It's about finding that sweet spot where what you love and know intersects with what buyers are actively seeking.

The first element to consider when choosing your niche is passion. This is arguably the most important factor. Selling on eBay requires dedication, and when you're passionate about the products you're offering, it makes the entire process more enjoyable and sustainable. Passion fuels your motivation, helps you weather the inevitable challenges, and keeps you engaged over the long term. If you're passionate about a specific area—whether it's vintage items, electronics, fashion, or collectibles—you'll likely be more eager to research products, refine your listings, and engage with potential buyers. This enthusiasm can be contagious, as buyers are often drawn to sellers who exhibit genuine interest and expertise in their products.

However, passion alone isn't enough. While it's true that selling what you love can be incredibly fulfilling, it's important to ensure that your niche is one that has real market demand. This is where knowledge of the market becomes essential. To succeed as an eBay seller, you need to understand not only what you love, but also what buyers are actively searching for and willing to purchase. The ideal niche should have a healthy balance of personal interest and commercial potential. This is where research comes into play.

The first step in identifying a profitable niche is to conduct thorough market research. Begin by exploring eBay itself, looking at the categories and subcategories of products that are being sold. Take note of what's trending, what's popular, and what seems to have a steady flow of transactions. Pay attention to how many items are listed, how many have been sold, and what kind of feedback these sellers are receiving. This information will give you an idea of what is in demand, what has competition, and what products might be underserved. Use tools like eBay's trending list or Google Trends to gain insights into current market interests. These tools can reveal patterns, seasonality, and consumer behavior that will help guide your decisions.

It's also important to assess your own expertise and experience in the niche you are considering. Selling on eBay isn't just about offering products; it's about offering value through knowledge. Buyers are more likely to trust and purchase from a seller who can demonstrate expertise, whether it's through detailed product descriptions, answering questions about the product, or offering recommendations based on experience. For example, if you have a deep understanding of camera equipment, you might be able to sell not only cameras but also accessories, parts, and guides. If you're passionate about vintage clothing, your ability to discern the condition, value, and authenticity of items can help you stand out in a crowded market. Your knowledge will set you apart and help build trust with potential buyers.

While passion and knowledge are key, they must be paired with an understanding of market demand. To identify a niche with genuine demand, you need to find a market that is large enough to support ongoing sales but not so oversaturated that it's difficult to stand out. This is a delicate balance, as a niche that is too narrow might not have enough buyers, while a niche that is too broad might leave you competing with thousands of other sellers. For example, the general category of "electronics" might seem promising, but it's a highly competitive market with countless sellers offering the same products. On the other hand, a niche such as "vintage stereo equipment from the 1980s" may be more specific, but it's also likely to have a smaller, yet passionate, customer base that's willing to pay a premium for well-maintained, rare items.

To assess market demand, consider both the volume and quality of listings. Tools like Terapeak, which is integrated into eBay, can provide data on product trends, sales volume, and average prices. This information is valuable for understanding not only how many people are selling similar items but also how much they are able to sell them for. It's important to strike a balance between choosing a niche with enough demand and avoiding a niche where the competition is too fierce. You can also conduct surveys, ask for feedback from potential customers, or use social media to gauge interest in the niche you're considering. Engaging directly with your target audience can help you determine whether your products will appeal to them.

Once you've identified a potential niche, take the time to evaluate the pricing dynamics within that space. Sellers within your chosen niche may offer products at varying price points, from low-cost, high-volume items to rare, high-value pieces. Assessing pricing trends will help you understand whether you should position yourself as a budget-friendly seller or as someone offering premium products. Understanding the price points that work within your niche will also help you plan your inventory, determine your profit margins, and set competitive pricing strategies.

Another factor to consider when selecting your niche is scalability. Is your niche one that allows you to grow your business over time? Ideally, you'll want to choose a niche that offers opportunities to expand and diversify your offerings. For example, if you start with a niche in vintage toy cars, you might eventually expand into related categories like model trains, action figures, or even vintage advertising materials. Diversifying your product offerings can help you reach a wider audience and reduce the risk of relying too heavily on one product category. Moreover, as your reputation and visibility grow, you'll be able to attract more customers, which will allow you to reinvest in your business and grow your inventory.

Another consideration is the level of competition in the niche. While a certain level of competition is healthy and signals that there's demand, too much competition can make it difficult to get noticed. When evaluating competition, look for areas where you can differentiate yourself. For example, if you're selling in a popular category, you might focus on a specific product feature or offer superior customer service to stand out. By adding a unique element to your business, whether it's through the products you offer or the way you present them, you can carve out a space for yourself in the market.

As you identify your niche, think about the long-term sustainability of the products you're selling. Some niches are cyclical, with demand fluctuating based on seasons, trends, or economic conditions. Others are evergreen, with steady, ongoing demand regardless of external factors. Ideally, you want to choose a niche that provides long-term opportunities rather than one that's reliant on short-lived trends. Understanding the sustainability of your niche will help you plan for the future, make smarter investments in inventory, and avoid unnecessary risks.

Identifying the right niche for your eBay business is a combination of passion, knowledge, and market demand. Your passion for a particular product category will help fuel your drive, while your knowledge will allow you to offer genuine value to customers. At the same time, understanding the demand for those products is crucial to ensure that your business will thrive. By conducting thorough market research, understanding pricing trends, and evaluating competition, you can find a niche that not only aligns with your interests but also has the potential for long-term success. With a well-chosen niche, you'll be on your way to building a thriving eBay business.

RESEARCHING PRODUCT IDEAS: TRENDS, BEST-SELLERS, AND UNDERSERVED MARKETS

When it comes to building a successful eBay business, one of the most critical steps is identifying the right products to sell. The process of researching product ideas is not only about picking something that interests you but also about finding items that will appeal to buyers and generate consistent sales. To do this effectively, you need to tap into current trends, understand what is already a best-seller, and identify underserved markets that present opportunities for growth. By combining your knowledge with thorough research, you can pinpoint the products that will resonate with buyers and set the foundation for your eBay business.

The first step in researching product ideas is understanding the current trends in the marketplace. Trends are fluid and can change rapidly, influenced by seasonality, cultural shifts, technological advancements, and consumer behavior. Tracking trends allows you to anticipate what buyers are looking for before it becomes mainstream, giving you a competitive edge. One of the most effective ways to research trends is by monitoring the platforms where products are frequently sold or discussed. Websites like eBay itself, Amazon, Google Trends, and social media platforms provide a wealth of data regarding what is hot at any given moment.

On eBay, you can look at trending categories and top-selling items within those categories. The platform has a section dedicated to trending items, which can give you an instant snapshot of products that are seeing an uptick in sales. From electronics and fashion to collectibles and home goods, these trends often reflect what buyers are actively searching for. Additionally, eBay's Terapeak tool, which is integrated into the platform, allows you to explore sales data in more detail. Terapeak provides insights into sales trends, including the number of items sold, average selling prices, and competition levels. It's an invaluable resource for understanding which products are currently in demand and which ones might be worth pursuing.

Google Trends is another essential tool in identifying trending products. By entering specific keywords related to products or categories, you can see how interest in those items has changed over time. This tool gives you a sense of whether a product is in a temporary surge or if it's likely to sustain long-term interest. For example, if you notice that interest in eco-friendly products is steadily increasing, this could be an indication of a larger movement toward sustainability that you can capitalize on. By recognizing these shifts in consumer interest, you can position your eBay store to meet the growing demand.

Social media platforms like Instagram, Pinterest, and TikTok have also become powerful sources for spotting trends. Influencers, brands, and everyday consumers often share what they're using or buying, and these posts can generate viral interest in particular products. By paying attention to what's gaining traction on these platforms, you can identify product ideas before they become mainstream, giving you an opportunity to ride the wave of demand. Hashtags related to certain products or themes can help you find the products that are resonating with specific communities. For instance, if you're interested in fashion, checking hashtags like #sustainablefashion or #vintageclothing could point you toward popular styles that buyers are excited about.

While trends provide an excellent starting point for your research, identifying best-sellers is also essential. Best-selling products are items that have already proven to have market demand and consistent sales. On eBay, you can search for popular items in specific categories to get a sense of what's moving well. For instance, if you're considering selling tech gadgets, you might search for the most popular smartphones, accessories, or computer peripherals. By analyzing these best-sellers, you can learn about the types of products that consistently attract buyers and generate substantial revenue.

It's important to look beyond just eBay's best-sellers and explore broader marketplaces, such as Amazon, Etsy, and Walmart. These platforms often have lists of best-selling products, organized by category, which can offer you additional insights into what buyers are interested in. In particular, Amazon's "Best Sellers" list is updated frequently and reflects what products are currently being sold in large volumes. By comparing the best-sellers on eBay with those on other platforms, you can identify overlap or discover products that may not be as competitive on eBay but still have strong demand elsewhere.

However, simply focusing on trends and best-sellers can lead to an over-saturated market. One way to differentiate yourself and avoid fierce competition is by identifying underserved markets. These are niches where there is demand for certain products, but the competition is still relatively low. Underserved markets represent a golden opportunity because they allow you to target buyers who are looking for specific products that aren't being widely offered. The key to identifying these markets is to look for gaps or underserved categories within popular trends and best-selling products.

To find underserved markets, start by exploring niche categories on eBay. While some categories like electronics and fashion may seem saturated, others, such as vintage collectibles, specialized hobby items, or eco-friendly products, may still have room for new sellers. You can also use eBay's search filters to narrow down categories and look for products with fewer listings but steady sales. This can indicate a market that is growing but hasn't yet attracted a flood of competitors.

Another approach to identifying underserved markets is by conducting customer research. Look at forums, social media groups, and online communities related to specific product interests. By engaging with these communities, you can learn about their needs and pain points. Are there products they want but can't easily find? Are there common complaints about existing products in the market? By addressing these gaps, you can offer solutions that other sellers haven't thought of. Additionally, consider reaching out to people who are already part of these communities to get feedback on product ideas. This direct connection can provide invaluable insight into the preferences and desires of your target audience.

It's also important to assess the scalability of underserved markets. While they may offer lower competition, they also may have a smaller customer base. It's important to consider whether the niche has room to grow over time or if it's limited in size. For example, a niche focused on vintage typewriters might be popular among collectors but may not have the same scalability as a niche for eco-friendly home products, which could appeal to a wider audience. As you research underserved markets, try to gauge whether the demand for certain products is growing or if it's a static market that may plateau over time.

After identifying potential product ideas based on trends, best-sellers, and underserved markets, it's time to validate these ideas further. One of the most effective ways to test the viability of a product is by starting small. You can begin by listing a few items in your chosen niche to see how they perform. This will give you real-world data on how buyers respond to your listings and allow you to tweak your approach accordingly. It also gives you the opportunity to refine your listings, adjust your pricing strategy, and improve your customer service before scaling up.

At the same time, continually monitor the market and adjust your product offerings based on feedback and sales data. Trends evolve, and what is popular today may not be as in-demand tomorrow. By staying flexible and keeping an eye on changing market conditions, you can ensure that your eBay business remains relevant and competitive in the long term.

Researching product ideas is a vital step in building a successful eBay business. By understanding trends, analyzing best-sellers, and identifying underserved markets, you can find products that meet the needs of buyers and offer strong sales potential. With careful research, a commitment to providing value, and the ability to adapt to changing market conditions, you can identify products that will allow your eBay business to thrive. This research will serve as the foundation for your product selection and give you the tools to create an inventory that resonates with your target audience, leading to long-term success on the platform.

SOURCING YOUR INVENTORY

One of the key factors in running a successful eBay business is sourcing your inventory. Without the right products to sell, you simply won't be able to make sales or grow your business. For beginners, the process of finding products to sell can feel daunting, but the reality is there are multiple methods available to source inventory, many of which don't require a huge upfront investment. Whether you're looking for items in your own home, browsing thrift stores and garage sales, connecting with wholesalers, or exploring online marketplaces, there are many paths to acquiring inventory. Each method has its own set of advantages and challenges, but with a little research and persistence, you can build a profitable product portfolio.

One of the easiest and most cost-effective ways to start sourcing inventory is by looking around your own home. This approach requires minimal effort and virtually no upfront costs. Many people have unused or unwanted items lying around their house, from clothing and books to electronics, toys, or even collectibles. These items can often be sold for a profit, especially if they're in good condition and meet the demands of eBay buyers. Starting with items you already own is a fantastic way to test the waters and get a feel for how eBay works without making a financial commitment.

The benefit of sourcing around your home is not only the low cost but also the speed with which you can begin selling. You can start listing items almost immediately, which is a great way to begin learning the nuances of creating listings, setting prices, and shipping items without the pressure of having to source products from other places. As you go through your home, think about the things you haven't used in a while. Could a collection of old books be sold as a set? Are there vintage toys that might interest collectors? Could your old camera equipment or electronics find a new home with someone looking for these items?

Once you've exhausted what's available in your home, thrift stores and garage sales offer an excellent opportunity to source unique, in-demand products. Thrift stores are often packed with hidden gems—items that are undervalued or overlooked by the general public. With a keen eye, you can find high-quality or rare items such as clothing, vintage items, home decor, and electronics that can be resold at a significant markup on eBay. Garage sales, estate sales, and flea markets are also great places to look for inventory, as they often feature second-hand goods that sellers are looking to offload at bargain prices. In both cases, you'll have the opportunity to buy products in bulk or for a fraction of their retail price, allowing you to profit when reselling them online.

One key advantage of thrift stores and garage sales is that you can often negotiate the price, especially if you're purchasing multiple items. If you've been to these types of sales enough, you'll learn which sellers are more open to bargaining. Don't be afraid to make offers below the asking price, especially if you can justify it with comparable items or if you plan to buy in bulk. Some experienced eBay sellers make a habit of visiting thrift stores regularly to find items that are undervalued or rare and can be sold at a higher price on the platform.

Another advantage of sourcing from thrift stores and garage sales is the variety of products available. From vintage clothing to antique furniture or electronics, you'll encounter a range of items that appeal to specific buyer niches. This gives you the opportunity to focus on niche markets and build a product offering that aligns with the interests and preferences of your target audience. However, it's essential to keep in mind that not every item you find will be profitable. It's important to learn how to identify items with a high resale value and avoid products that will have limited appeal or lower demand.

For those who want to scale their eBay business and have more consistent access to inventory, wholesalers and dropshipping can be a viable option. Wholesalers are businesses that sell products in bulk at a discounted price to retailers, and in this case, eBay sellers. Purchasing from wholesalers allows you to buy larger quantities of products at lower costs, which enables you to make a higher profit margin when selling on eBay. Many wholesalers also offer products across a variety of categories, giving you flexibility when it comes to curating your product offering.

However, working with wholesalers comes with some upfront costs, as you'll need to invest in bulk orders. It's important to carefully research wholesalers before making a commitment. Look for reputable suppliers who offer quality products, fair pricing, and reliable shipping. You'll also want to ensure that the products you're purchasing from wholesalers have strong demand on eBay, as purchasing large quantities of items that don't sell quickly can quickly tie up your capital.

Dropshipping is another model that's closely related to wholesaling but works differently. In a dropshipping business, you don't purchase inventory upfront. Instead, when a buyer purchases an item from your eBay store, you place an order with a supplier who ships the product directly to the customer. The key advantage of dropshipping is that you don't have to worry about storing or managing inventory, and you don't need to make an upfront investment in bulk purchases. However, because you're relying on third-party suppliers to fulfill orders, your profit margins may be lower, and you may have less control over shipping times and product availability.

To get started with dropshipping, you can partner with suppliers who specialize in eBay dropshipping or find suppliers through platforms like AliExpress, Oberlo, or SaleHoo. These platforms connect sellers with suppliers who are willing to dropship products directly to customers. While dropshipping reduces your initial investment and inventory management responsibilities, it also comes with potential challenges, such as longer shipping times or issues with product quality. It's important to carefully vet your suppliers and set realistic expectations with your customers about shipping timelines.

In addition to these traditional methods, online marketplaces are another option for sourcing inventory. Platforms like Alibaba, Amazon, and even eBay itself offer a vast range of products at wholesale prices that can be resold on eBay. By browsing online marketplaces, you can find products in bulk or from third-party sellers who specialize in offering lower-cost items for resale. Similar to dropshipping, online marketplaces provide access to a wide selection of products that can be sold without managing your own inventory. However, like with dropshipping, you must carefully vet the sellers and ensure that you're purchasing from reputable sources.

One of the advantages of sourcing from online marketplaces is the sheer volume of available products. You can find nearly anything you want, from electronics to clothing, home goods, and accessories. Online marketplaces also allow you to compare prices, find trending products, and explore niche categories that might not be as readily available through traditional suppliers.

The main disadvantage, however, is that you're competing with many other sellers who are also sourcing products from these platforms. This means you'll need to find ways to differentiate yourself, such as offering better customer service, creating compelling product listings, or focusing on specific niches that attract dedicated buyers.

Sourcing inventory for your eBay business is a process that requires careful consideration of your budget, your target market, and your business goals. Whether you start by searching around your home, shopping at thrift stores and garage sales, working with wholesalers, dropshipping, or exploring online marketplaces, there are plenty of options available to help you find products that will resonate with eBay buyers. By understanding the pros and cons of each sourcing method, you can make informed decisions and build a diverse inventory that supports your long-term success on eBay. With time and research, you'll be able to identify the most profitable products, streamline your sourcing process, and grow your business to new heights.

UNDERSTANDING PRODUCT REGULATIONS AND RESTRICTIONS ON EBAY

Understanding product regulations and restrictions on eBay is crucial for any seller looking to build a successful online business. Compliance with eBay's rules not only ensures that your listings stay live but also helps you avoid penalties, account suspension, or legal complications. While eBay provides an extensive marketplace where sellers can list and sell a wide range of products, it also maintains strict guidelines on what can and cannot be sold. Understanding these regulations and restrictions is an essential part of your seller journey, and failing to adhere to these rules can result in unwanted consequences.

The first step in understanding product regulations is recognizing that eBay operates within a global marketplace. This means that while eBay offers opportunities for sellers from different regions and countries to connect with buyers, there are also laws and regulations in various jurisdictions that govern what can and cannot be sold. For instance, certain products may be legal to sell in one country but prohibited in another. It is your responsibility as a seller to be aware of the rules that apply not only to the platform but also to the regions where your buyers reside.

One of the most common types of regulated products includes items that are considered hazardous or unsafe. These products often fall under government regulations that are designed to protect consumers from health or safety risks. eBay has specific restrictions on items such as chemicals, weapons, explosives, and certain electronics that may pose a danger if misused. For example, you cannot sell items that contain hazardous materials like asbestos or lead, nor can you list dangerous weapons like firearms or knives unless you comply with strict legal guidelines.

Similarly, any products related to tobacco, alcohol, and drugs are heavily regulated and typically prohibited on eBay. While you may be allowed to sell items such as cigars or cigarette lighters, eBay strictly prohibits the sale of cigarettes, e-cigarettes, and tobacco-related products. Selling prescription drugs or controlled substances is also not allowed on eBay, as this would violate both eBay's rules and the law. These types of products require strict regulatory control, and selling them without the appropriate permits or licenses could lead to serious legal consequences.

Another category of items subject to strict regulations is counterfeit or replica products. eBay has a zero-tolerance policy for counterfeit goods, and the sale of counterfeit products can result in immediate account suspension. This includes any goods that are designed to look like branded products, such as fake luxury handbags, electronics, or clothing. To prevent the sale of counterfeit items, eBay uses various authentication systems and works closely with brands to identify and remove fake listings. As a seller, it is your responsibility to ensure that the products you're listing are genuine and accurately described. If you sell counterfeit items—whether knowingly or unknowingly—you risk losing your seller account and facing legal action.

In addition to counterfeit goods, there are certain restrictions on the sale of used items. While selling pre-owned products is a popular practice on eBay, certain categories of used items, such as used cosmetics, personal hygiene products, or items that come into contact with the body, have strict regulations. For example, eBay restricts the sale of used items like open bottles of shampoo, used toothbrushes, or second-hand makeup because these items could pose a risk to health or hygiene. Before listing used items, it is important to check eBay's policies for each product category to determine whether or not it is allowed to be sold in its pre-owned condition.

Another area to be aware of is the sale of items related to endangered species or protected wildlife. eBay has restrictions on products made from or containing parts of animals that are endangered or protected under international law. This includes items made from ivory, certain types of coral, and animal skins. These regulations are designed to protect wildlife and prevent illegal trafficking of protected species. As a seller, it is important to ensure that any products you list do not fall into these categories and that you are not inadvertently violating animal protection laws.

eBay also restricts the sale of certain types of digital content, such as software and media. While selling digital goods like eBooks, music, or videos is permitted, there are limitations on what can be sold and how it can be distributed. For example, selling pirated software or unlicensed media files is strictly prohibited on eBay. Additionally, if you are selling digital content that is copyrighted, you must ensure that you have the right to distribute it, or you may face legal repercussions. Sellers must also follow the rules surrounding digital delivery, such as ensuring that buyers receive their purchases in the proper format and that the content complies with copyright laws.

It's also important to be aware of restrictions related to the sale of medical devices and health-related products. Certain medical items, such as surgical instruments, diagnostic equipment, and medical devices, are regulated by health authorities and can only be sold by authorized sellers. For example, selling prescription medical devices or drugs is prohibited unless you have the appropriate certifications or licenses. Similarly, eBay has policies that govern the sale of over-the-counter medications, supplements, and health products. Sellers should be familiar with local laws related to health products and ensure that they are complying with all relevant regulations before listing such items.

As a seller, you also need to be aware of eBay's rules around intellectual property rights. Intellectual property infringement occurs when you sell products that violate the copyrights, trademarks, or patents of other entities. This could include selling unauthorized copies of branded goods, or products that infringe on patents or protected logos. eBay works diligently to enforce intellectual property laws, and violating these can lead to your listings being removed and your account being suspended. Therefore, it is important to verify that the products you list do not infringe on the intellectual property rights of others, and you should be prepared to provide documentation if requested by eBay to prove authenticity.

To ensure that you are fully compliant with eBay's regulations and restrictions, it is advisable to regularly review the platform's seller policies, which are frequently updated. eBay provides detailed guidelines on what products can be sold, as well as any restrictions or requirements for specific categories. These guidelines are easily accessible in the Seller Hub, and they outline the dos and don'ts for every product category you might consider selling. Familiarizing yourself with these policies will help you avoid mistakes that could jeopardize your ability to sell on the platform.

In addition to following eBay's rules, sellers are also responsible for complying with local, state, and federal regulations regarding product safety, labeling, and sales. If you are unsure whether a product falls within eBay's restrictions or legal requirements, it's a good idea to consult with a legal expert or reach out to eBay's support team for guidance.

By understanding eBay's product regulations and restrictions, you can avoid common pitfalls and build a sustainable, legal, and profitable business. Sellers who follow the rules not only help protect consumers but also enhance their reputation, build trust, and increase the likelihood of success in the eBay marketplace.

CHAPTER 4
CREATING HIGH-CONVERTING EBAY LISTINGS: THE ESSENTIALS

WRITING COMPELLING AND KEYWORD-RICH TITLES

Writing compelling and keyword-rich titles is one of the most essential skills for any seller on eBay. In a marketplace crowded with millions of listings, it is critical to capture the attention of potential buyers while ensuring your products are easy to find. An effective title is the first step in creating a listing that not only stands out but also drives traffic to your store and improves your visibility in eBay search results.

The title of your listing serves multiple functions. First, it gives potential buyers a snapshot of what the product is. Second, it must be optimized for eBay's search algorithm, known as Cassini, which determines which products are shown to buyers based on keywords. An optimized, compelling title can increase your visibility and click-through rate, leading to higher sales. Third, a good title sets the tone for your brand, conveying professionalism and trustworthiness.

To craft an effective eBay title, start by focusing on clarity and accuracy. Misleading or overly vague titles might draw initial attention, but they won't help you build trust with your customers. It's crucial that your title accurately reflects the product you're selling. For example, if you're listing a vintage leather jacket, you'll want to be specific about the material, style, and other relevant details in the title. A generic title such as "Leather Jacket" is not likely to capture the buyer's interest. Instead, a title like "Vintage Brown Leather Jacket, Men's XL, Made in USA, Soft Distressed" is far more informative and appealing. Buyers know exactly what they're looking at and can make an informed decision more easily.

When constructing your title, always remember that eBay has a character limit for product titles—80 characters. This limitation means that every word counts, and you need to make each one work for you. While it might be tempting to add as many keywords as possible, overcrowding your title with irrelevant or excessive words can reduce its effectiveness. Keep it concise and to the point, while ensuring it accurately describes your product and its most important features.

To make sure your title is both compelling and discoverable, it's vital to understand the power of keywords. Keywords are the terms buyers are most likely to type into the search bar when looking for products similar to yours. The goal is to find the balance between the words that accurately describe your product and the words that potential buyers are actually using to find products like it. By including these keywords in your title, you increase the chances that your listing will appear when buyers conduct searches on eBay.

Keyword research is an essential part of this process. To identify which keywords are most relevant for your product, start by looking at similar listings on eBay. Check out the top-selling items in your category and pay attention to the common terms and phrases used in their titles. Also, use eBay's search suggestions, which will show you common searches based on the words you begin typing. Another useful tool is eBay's search analytics tool, which helps you assess the popularity of certain keywords.

Once you have gathered a list of relevant keywords, prioritize them in your title. Place the most important keywords at the beginning, as eBay's algorithm tends to give more weight to the first few words in a title. For example, if you are selling a "Samsung Galaxy S21 128GB" phone, the title should begin with those words since they are the most searched terms by buyers. Adding descriptors like "Unlocked" or "Brand New" can help further qualify the product, but they should follow the primary keywords. You want your title to match what buyers are searching for, but you also want it to make sense and remain attractive.

One of the biggest mistakes new sellers make is stuffing their titles with keywords, often known as "keyword spamming." This occurs when sellers add multiple irrelevant keywords in an attempt to rank higher in search results. For example, a title like "Samsung Galaxy S21 128GB Unlocked, New, Smartphone, Android, Mobile" can seem overwhelming to buyers and feels unnatural. While all these words may technically be relevant, the title is not as appealing or user-friendly. It's important to keep the flow of the title natural and readable. Your primary objective is to make sure that a buyer can quickly understand what you're selling.

Including relevant details in your title is another key aspect of creating a compelling listing. For example, mention the brand, model, size, color, and condition of the item. If it's an item that has multiple variations, such as a clothing piece available in different sizes or colors, make sure to highlight the specific details of the variant you're offering. If you're selling a rare item or limited edition, mention that in the title as well. Details like "Limited Edition," "Vintage," "Rare," or "New With Tags" can help capture the interest of buyers who are looking for something special.

However, be careful not to overcomplicate your title with excessive details. While it's important to provide enough information for buyers to know what they're looking at, too many adjectives or descriptors can confuse the search algorithm. Stay focused on the product's main attributes and ensure they're clearly conveyed. When writing your title, aim for a balance between including enough details to be informative and not overwhelming the buyer.

The language you use in your title also plays a crucial role in making it compelling. Try to use words that evoke a sense of urgency or exclusivity. Phrases like "New," "Limited Edition," or "Buy Now" can make your listing more attractive. Similarly, words that convey high quality or rarity, such as "Authentic," "Luxury," or "Premium," can enhance the appeal of your product. If your item is particularly sought-after or has a unique feature, emphasizing this in the title can help differentiate it from the competition.

Additionally, it's important to remember that eBay uses both the title and the description to match listings with search queries. While your title needs to include the most relevant keywords, you should also optimize your product description with the same care and attention. A strong description, along with a compelling title, will ensure that your listing ranks higher in search results and provides the information potential buyers need to make a decision.

After you've created your title, be sure to review it before posting. This step allows you to check for any spelling or grammatical errors that could make your listing look unprofessional. A clean, error-free title not only looks better but also enhances your credibility as a seller.

Writing a compelling and keyword-rich title requires a balance between creativity, accuracy, and search engine optimization. By incorporating relevant keywords, providing clear and accurate descriptions, and using language that entices buyers, you'll increase your chances of standing out in eBay's crowded marketplace. A great title doesn't just describe a product; it captures attention, builds trust, and drives potential buyers to click on your listing. With practice and attention to detail, your titles will help boost visibility, drive sales, and grow your online business.

CRAFTING DETAILED AND PERSUASIVE PRODUCT DESCRIPTIONS

Crafting detailed and persuasive product descriptions is a critical component of successfully selling on eBay. In the vast online marketplace, where consumers can't physically touch or examine products before making a purchase, your product description becomes the primary way to communicate the value and quality of the item. A well-written description provides potential buyers with the necessary information to make informed purchasing decisions, while also helping to differentiate your listing from the millions of others that buyers can choose from. A compelling description not only conveys the features and benefits of your product but also helps to build trust and rapport with your audience.

The first step in creating a strong product description is to be clear and accurate. Misleading descriptions can lead to negative feedback, disputes, and even returns, all of which can harm your seller reputation.

When you write your description, ensure that it matches the product's actual condition, features, and specifications. Be as transparent as possible. For instance, if the item is pre-owned, it's important to mention any signs of wear and tear or imperfections. Being upfront about any flaws builds trust with potential buyers, who are more likely to appreciate your honesty and make a purchase knowing exactly what to expect.

In addition to accuracy, your description should be as detailed as necessary. Buyers want to know everything about a product before committing to a purchase. This includes key details such as brand, size, color, material, weight, and any other specifications that make the item unique. The more information you can provide, the easier it is for buyers to assess whether the product meets their needs. For example, if you're selling a piece of furniture, include details about its dimensions, the material it's made from, whether it's easy to assemble, and any other important characteristics. Buyers of clothing will likely want to know the fabric content, measurements, and care instructions. Electronics might require technical specifications, compatibility information, or details about the warranty. Every type of product has its own set of important details, so ensure that your descriptions are tailored to the specific items you're selling.

While being informative is important, making your description persuasive is equally essential. A good product description not only tells the buyer what the item is, but it also communicates why they should buy it. This is where the art of persuasive writing comes in. Persuasive descriptions are written in a way that highlights the value of the product and creates a sense of desire. Use language that emphasizes the benefits of the item, as well as how it can solve the buyer's problems or fulfill their needs. Instead of merely stating what the item is, explain how it can enhance the buyer's life. For example, if you're selling a kitchen blender, it's not enough to say it has a powerful motor and multiple settings. Instead, you could emphasize how it will save the buyer time in the kitchen, help them create healthy meals with ease, or even mention how it can blend ingredients into silky-smooth textures perfect for family meals.

One effective strategy is to describe how the product solves a problem or improves a situation for the buyer. For example, "This high-quality, durable pair of running shoes will help you achieve your fitness goals by providing maximum comfort and support, preventing injury, and improving your overall running experience." Such a description does not simply highlight features; it also emphasizes the benefits that resonate with the buyer's goals.

Using sensory language can also help make your descriptions more engaging. Instead of merely listing features, describe the way the product feels, looks, smells, or sounds. For instance, a description of a pair of leather shoes might include words like "luxuriously soft" or "richly textured." A description of a scented candle could evoke the scent, such as "warm, soothing vanilla with a hint of spice, perfect for creating a cozy atmosphere in your home." By helping potential buyers envision the experience of using the product, you create a stronger emotional connection.

Another important aspect of persuasive writing is to focus on the value of the product rather than just the cost. While buyers are always looking for good deals, they are also looking for value. Instead of only emphasizing the price, describe the long-term benefits the product offers. A high-quality kitchen appliance, for example, may be more expensive than a cheaper version, but its durability, energy efficiency, and superior performance make it a worthwhile investment. Highlighting the longevity, quality, or exclusivity of your product can justify its price and convince buyers that they are making a smart purchase.

In addition to providing the necessary information, you also want to consider the tone of your description. A friendly, conversational tone can go a long way in building rapport with buyers. While it's important to remain professional, writing in a way that feels approachable and engaging can make your description stand out. Imagine that you're having a conversation with a potential buyer. How would you describe the product in a way that's clear, helpful, and compelling? Write as though you're providing an excellent customer service experience, with the goal of answering questions before they're asked.

When crafting your product descriptions, it's essential to optimize them for search engines, including eBay's search algorithm. This involves strategically using relevant keywords in your description. Just like with the title, these keywords should reflect the terms buyers are most likely to use when searching for products. In eBay's case, this can help ensure that your listing shows up in the search results when buyers are looking for something specific. It's important to integrate these keywords naturally into your product description so that the text remains readable and engaging, while still ensuring that your listing is discoverable.

You should also consider the use of formatting in your description. While eBay doesn't allow rich text formatting, using paragraphs and bullet points can still help break up the text and make it easier for buyers to read. Long blocks of text can be overwhelming and difficult to skim. Organizing the description into short, digestible sections with clear headings helps buyers quickly find the information they need.

Another tip is to include social proof within your description. Social proof refers to the idea that people are more likely to trust a product or seller if they see that others have had a positive experience. This could be in the form of customer reviews, testimonials, or any awards or certifications your product may have. If your product has received glowing feedback from previous customers, including a snippet of that feedback can help persuade new buyers to make a purchase.

Always remember to review your product description before publishing it. A well-written description that is free of errors not only looks more professional but also reflects well on your credibility as a seller. Mistakes in spelling, grammar, or punctuation can detract from the overall presentation of your listing and make you seem less trustworthy.

Crafting detailed and persuasive product descriptions is both an art and a science. By focusing on clarity, accuracy, and persuasion, and by using language that emphasizes the benefits and value of the product, you can make your listings more appealing to buyers and increase your chances of success on eBay. Whether you're selling clothing, electronics, collectibles, or home goods, an effective description can help you stand out in a crowded marketplace, build trust with buyers, and ultimately drive more sales.

UTILIZING EBAY'S ITEM SPECIFICS FOR MAXIMUM VISIBILITY

When selling on eBay, visibility is one of the most important factors that can make or break a sale. With millions of listings available to buyers at any given moment, standing out in such a crowded marketplace requires strategic use of eBay's tools and features. One such feature that can significantly improve your product's visibility is the use of "Item Specifics." This feature, often overlooked by new sellers, is a powerful tool that allows you to provide detailed and standardized information about your products. When used correctly, Item Specifics can help your listings appear in relevant search results, increase your chances of being discovered by buyers, and ultimately boost your sales.

Item Specifics are attributes that are used to describe and categorize a product in a consistent manner. These details include key characteristics such as brand, model, size, color, material, and more, depending on the type of item you're selling. When buyers search for products on eBay, the platform uses these specifics to match their search queries with the most relevant listings. The more comprehensive and accurate your Item Specifics, the better chance your listing has of being surfaced in relevant search results.

The first step in effectively utilizing Item Specifics is to understand how they work. eBay automatically suggests relevant Item Specifics based on the category of the item you're listing. For example, if you're selling a pair of shoes, eBay may suggest specifics such as shoe size, brand, color, and material. If you're listing a phone, the specifics might include the brand, model, storage capacity, and operating system. These fields help ensure that your item is classified correctly and can be easily found by potential buyers. However, it's important to note that you should not rely solely on eBay's suggestions. Instead, take the time to review all the available specifics for your category and fill out every relevant field.

Filling out your Item Specifics as completely as possible is one of the best ways to ensure that your products will be discoverable by the right audience. When a buyer conducts a search, eBay filters listings based on specific criteria. This means that if you leave Item Specifics incomplete or ignore them entirely, you may miss out on valuable search visibility. Buyers often use filters to narrow down their search results, and the more specific and complete your listing is, the more likely it is to appear when those filters are applied. For example, if a buyer is looking for "blue leather jackets in size medium," they'll likely apply the size and color filters. If your listing accurately includes both the size and color in the Item Specifics, your jacket will have a higher chance of being shown.

Not only does using Item Specifics help buyers filter results, but it also improves the search engine optimization (SEO) of your listings. eBay's search algorithm takes Item Specifics into account when ranking listings, meaning that more complete and accurate specifics can help your products rank higher in search results. This increased ranking will give your listings greater visibility, leading to more traffic and, ultimately, more sales. Furthermore, eBay's search algorithm rewards sellers who are proactive in adding relevant details about their products. By thoroughly filling out the Item Specifics fields, you demonstrate to eBay that your listings are high-quality and well-maintained, which can result in better placement within search results.

When it comes to maximizing the effectiveness of Item Specifics, it's also crucial to be as detailed and accurate as possible. If you're selling a used item, for instance, be sure to indicate whether it is pre-owned, refurbished, or in brand-new condition. This not only helps to manage buyer expectations but also ensures that your product shows up when buyers filter for specific conditions. If there is any damage or wear to the item, be upfront about it. Accurate Item Specifics prevent negative feedback and returns, as buyers will know exactly what they are getting.

Another key aspect of maximizing visibility with Item Specifics is ensuring that you are using relevant keywords. These keywords should be naturally incorporated into the Item Specifics fields, as well as in your title and description. Think about the terms potential buyers might use when searching for your product. What words are they most likely to use when narrowing down their search? For example, if you are selling a "vintage 1970s leather jacket," make sure to include terms such as "vintage," "1970s," "leather," and "jacket" in the corresponding fields. These keywords will increase the chances of your listing being seen by buyers who are specifically looking for items with these characteristics.

It's also important to consider which Item Specifics are most relevant to your product and category. eBay provides a variety of specifics for different categories, but not every field will be relevant for every item. For instance, if you're selling a book, specifying the author and the genre is crucial, but size or material may not be. On the other hand, for a piece of furniture, specifying the material, color, and dimensions is essential. Always ensure that you're providing the most relevant and useful specifics to potential buyers. This helps not only with search optimization but also with creating a smooth and intuitive shopping experience for the buyer.

Using Item Specifics doesn't just help with searchability and SEO—it also gives your listing a more polished and professional appearance. Buyers are more likely to trust sellers who take the time to fill out all relevant details. A listing that includes a well-organized set of Item Specifics conveys that you are a thorough and reliable seller, which builds trust and credibility. On the flip side, a listing with sparse or inaccurate Item Specifics may cause buyers to hesitate or question the authenticity of your product.

eBay's system also rewards detailed listings with higher visibility in the form of the "Top Rated Seller" badge. This badge, which is awarded to sellers who meet certain performance metrics, can further increase your exposure and boost buyer confidence. Sellers with the Top Rated Seller status often see better placement in search results, as well as more visibility on eBay's homepage. By consistently filling out your Item Specifics and maintaining high-quality listings, you increase your chances of receiving this badge, which, in turn, can lead to more sales.

One aspect of Item Specifics that is often overlooked by sellers is the ability to update them after the listing has gone live. If you notice that certain specifics are missing or could be better optimized, don't hesitate to edit the fields and make the necessary changes. Updating your Item Specifics helps ensure that your product is consistently visible to the right buyers, especially if market trends or buyer preferences change. As you refine your listings over time, your understanding of which specifics matter most will improve, leading to even more effective listings in the future.

Utilizing eBay's Item Specifics for maximum visibility is an essential strategy for any seller looking to succeed in the competitive eBay marketplace. By ensuring that every field is filled out accurately, including relevant keywords, and staying up to date with eBay's suggestions, you increase the likelihood that your listings will be seen by the right buyers. Not only does this enhance your listing's searchability, but it also boosts the credibility of your listings, improves the buyer experience, and helps you stand out from the crowd. Ultimately, by leveraging Item Specifics to their fullest potential, you can ensure that your products receive the attention they deserve and achieve the sales success you're aiming for.

UNDERSTANDING CONDITION GUIDELINES AND BEING HONEST

When selling products online, one of the most crucial aspects of ensuring both a positive buyer experience and a solid reputation as a seller is providing clear, accurate, and honest information about the condition of your items. On eBay, condition guidelines are a key part of the process, and understanding how to navigate these guidelines can make a significant difference in your success as a seller. Whether you're selling new, used, refurbished, or collectible items, being transparent about the condition of your products will help you establish trust with your buyers and minimize disputes or returns.

eBay provides a comprehensive set of condition guidelines to help sellers describe their items accurately. These guidelines are not only a tool for setting expectations for your buyers, but they also help in improving the searchability of your listings. The more accurate your description of the product condition, the easier it is for buyers to find what they're looking for. Using the proper condition category helps buyers filter their searches and ensures that your items are displayed in relevant search results. However, beyond just categorizing your products correctly, being honest and thorough in your descriptions is essential to building long-term success on the platform.

One of the first things you'll need to familiarize yourself with is eBay's defined condition categories. These categories are designed to make it easy for buyers to understand what they are purchasing and allow sellers to present their items in a consistent and standardized way. The most common condition categories you'll encounter on eBay include "New," "Used," "Refurbished," and "For Parts or Not Working." Each of these categories comes with specific guidelines, and it's important to follow them carefully.

For example, when listing an item as "New," it's expected that the product has never been used or opened, and it should be in its original packaging. Any signs of wear, damage, or alterations to the product should disqualify it from being labeled as new. While this may seem straightforward, many sellers mistakenly list items as new when they may have been opened or used briefly. If you mistakenly list a product as new and it turns out to be used or damaged, the buyer could be dissatisfied and return the item, potentially leaving you with negative feedback and a damaged reputation. It's important to be scrupulously honest when categorizing an item as new to avoid misunderstandings.

On the other hand, when listing a "Used" item, you should clearly state whether the item has been worn, used, or otherwise altered. Used items often come with signs of wear, such as scratches, dents, or discoloration, and it is crucial to note these details in your description. Be specific about the item's condition to manage buyer expectations. If a used item is in excellent condition, you can describe it as "like new" or "excellent condition." If there are more visible signs of wear, such as scuff marks, fading, or minor damage, you should describe those clearly as well. Transparency is key here; the more detailed you are about any imperfections, the less likely buyers will feel misled.

"Refurbished" items typically refer to products that have been returned to the manufacturer or a third party for repairs or updates before being resold. These items are often in great working condition but may not be new. Be clear about the extent of refurbishing done to the item and any warranty it may carry. Some buyers may assume that a refurbished product is essentially like new, so it's important to communicate any nuances to avoid confusion. Including the fact that the product was refurbished by the manufacturer or a certified technician can provide buyers with the reassurance they need to proceed with the purchase.

Finally, "For Parts or Not Working" is a condition used for items that are either broken or cannot be used as intended without repairs. This condition often applies to electronics, appliances, or other products that have significant defects. When listing items in this condition, be detailed about the problem. Does the item fail to turn on? Is there missing or broken hardware? Providing as much information as possible will help potential buyers understand the extent of the issue and prevent misunderstandings. These types of items may be sought after by hobbyists, repair enthusiasts, or those looking to salvage parts, so an accurate description of the issues will attract the right audience.

Beyond choosing the correct condition category, the way you phrase your descriptions can also have a profound impact on how your listing is received. Being honest about the condition of your items doesn't just mean accurately labeling them—it's also about providing a full picture of the product. For example, if you're selling a pair of used shoes with scuff marks on the sole, take clear, close-up photos that show the condition. In your description, mention the scuff marks and any other wear and tear. If the shoes are missing their original box or if they have been cleaned or refurbished, note that as well. By offering this level of transparency, you help set accurate expectations for buyers, which can increase buyer confidence and reduce the likelihood of disputes.

Photos are another vital aspect of the condition description. Visuals are often the first thing that a potential buyer will look at when browsing listings. High-quality images that clearly show the condition of the item can reinforce the accuracy of your description and further establish your credibility as a seller. Make sure your photos are well-lit, high-resolution, and capture any imperfections or flaws. If you're listing a used item, taking pictures from different angles and zooming in on areas of wear will be especially helpful. Buyers appreciate clear, honest visuals that provide a true representation of the product, so never hide imperfections or fail to include them in your photos.

Maintaining honesty in your product descriptions goes beyond just avoiding negative feedback; it also helps to protect your seller account from penalties or suspensions. eBay has policies in place that hold sellers accountable for misrepresenting items. If a buyer feels that an item was inaccurately described, they can open a case against you, which could result in a return, a refund, and potentially even a suspension from eBay. By carefully adhering to the condition guidelines and being truthful about your items, you reduce the likelihood of these situations arising.

Additionally, honesty fosters long-term success. Buyers are more likely to return to a seller who is clear about product conditions and who delivers on their promises. Building trust is essential in creating a loyal customer base. Satisfied customers are more likely to leave positive feedback, which will, in turn, help your seller reputation and increase the visibility of your listings. This reputation for reliability and transparency can ultimately lead to repeat customers, which is key to sustaining a successful business on eBay.

In some cases, it's not just the condition of the product itself that you need to consider; the packaging and shipping method can also impact how buyers perceive the item. Even if an item is in perfect condition, poor packaging that results in damage during shipping can cause dissatisfaction and lead to negative feedback. Be sure to package your items securely and choose an appropriate shipping method to ensure they arrive in the condition you've described. This attention to detail adds to your reputation for being an honest and responsible seller.

Understanding and following eBay's condition guidelines is crucial for any seller. By accurately categorizing your items and providing thorough, honest descriptions, you create an environment of trust that encourages buyers to make confident purchases. The clearer and more transparent you are, the more likely buyers will be satisfied with their purchase and leave positive feedback. Building a reputation as an honest seller with high-quality listings is the foundation for long-term success on eBay. Always remember that the best way to maintain a thriving business is through honesty, transparency, and a commitment to providing excellent products and service.

SETTING COMPETITIVE PRICING STRATEGIES

Setting competitive pricing strategies is one of the most important aspects of running a successful eBay business. Pricing can determine whether your items attract buyers or sit unsold in your store. To effectively navigate this aspect of eBay selling, it is crucial to understand both the factors that influence pricing and the strategies you can use to remain competitive while maintaining profitability. By learning how to price your products strategically, you can ensure that your listings stand out in a crowded marketplace.

When setting prices for your products, the first step is to research the market. This means looking at similar items being sold by other sellers to get a sense of the going rate. eBay has millions of active listings, and buyers often shop around to find the best deals. If your product is priced too high compared to similar items, it may be overlooked. Conversely, pricing your item too low can raise suspicions about its quality or lead to missed profits. Finding the sweet spot—where the price reflects both the quality of the item and the market demand—is essential.

One of the key strategies in competitive pricing is understanding how to position your products relative to others in the market. Look at the listings of other sellers who are offering similar items. Pay attention not only to the price but also to the quality of their listings. Are their photos clear and well-lit? Is their product description thorough and accurate? If their items are priced similarly to yours, but their listings are more appealing, you may need to adjust your own listings to be more competitive. Enhancing your photos, improving your descriptions, and offering more value through extra services or benefits can justify a higher price, even if the base price is similar.

In addition to looking at competitors' prices, you also need to consider your costs and profit margins. When you list an item, the price you set needs to cover your costs, such as the cost of goods sold, shipping, eBay fees, packaging, and any other expenses associated with fulfilling the order. After covering these costs, you should aim to make a profit that is sufficient for you to sustain and grow your business. This is where understanding your expenses is vital. Calculate the total cost of each product and the fees you will incur on eBay. Then, ensure your pricing leaves room for a reasonable profit margin. Many new sellers make the mistake of setting prices too low without factoring in all of these variables, which can lead to financial strain and unsustainable business practices.

Another important element of competitive pricing is the use of pricing tiers. Many sellers offer different pricing for new, used, and refurbished items. For example, if you're selling electronics, a brand-new item might be priced at a premium, while a used or refurbished version might be priced lower to attract more price-sensitive buyers. Additionally, if you have variations of a product—such as different colors or sizes—consider offering a range of prices based on the options available. This allows you to cater to a broader audience with different budget levels, increasing the likelihood of making a sale.

In some cases, using a strategy like cost-plus pricing can help determine a baseline price for your products. This strategy involves calculating the total cost of the item (including shipping and eBay fees) and then adding a set profit margin on top. For example, if the total cost of the item is $30, and you want to make a $15 profit, your listing price should be $45. This approach is simple and effective, particularly for products that are relatively consistent in terms of cost and demand.

For sellers looking to differentiate themselves in competitive markets, dynamic pricing strategies can be highly effective. Dynamic pricing involves adjusting prices based on demand, competition, and other factors. For example, if you notice that a particular product is selling well at a certain price point, you might increase the price slightly to maximize profits. On the other hand, if demand decreases or competitors lower their prices, you can adjust your price to stay competitive. Dynamic pricing requires careful monitoring of market trends and competitor behavior, but when executed properly, it can lead to higher sales and improved profitability.

One tool that can help sellers manage dynamic pricing is eBay's own pricing tool, which provides insights into market trends, pricing history, and competitor prices. By using this tool, you can get a better sense of where your products fit in the broader market and adjust your pricing accordingly. This tool also helps sellers understand whether their prices are too high or too low relative to the market and can suggest adjustments to improve competitiveness.

When pricing your items, you should also take into account the psychological aspect of pricing. Certain price points tend to attract more buyers. For instance, prices that end in .99—such as $9.99 or $19.99—are often perceived as better deals, even if they're only a penny less than the next whole dollar. This tactic, known as "charm pricing," has been widely used in retail for decades and is just as effective online. Additionally, offering discounts or promotions can create a sense of urgency and encourage buyers to make a purchase. You could run a limited-time sale or offer free shipping on certain items to make them appear more attractive to potential customers.

However, it's essential to remember that not all pricing strategies work for every type of product. For example, luxury items or high-end collectibles may not benefit from the same pricing strategies as everyday products. High-end buyers may expect a certain price range and may view lower prices as a sign of lower quality. In these cases, it's important to focus on the value proposition of the product rather than the price alone. Offering detailed descriptions, highlighting the rarity or special features of the item, and emphasizing its quality can help justify the higher price point.

Additionally, offering free shipping can be a powerful pricing strategy, particularly when competing with sellers who charge separate shipping fees. Many buyers are attracted to the simplicity of "free shipping" offers, which can make the overall price more attractive even if the item itself is priced a little higher. When factoring in shipping, consider whether you can absorb the cost into the item's price without pricing yourself out of profitability. In some cases, you may find that offering free shipping can increase your sales volume, making up for the higher upfront costs.

One of the most common pricing mistakes sellers make is underpricing their products in an attempt to make quick sales. While it's tempting to offer the lowest price to attract buyers, this strategy can backfire in the long run. Underpricing your items can damage your perceived value, and buyers may associate low prices with low quality. It's also important to note that underpricing can make it difficult to scale your business and cover your operating costs as your volume increases. Instead, focus on pricing that reflects the value of the item and your business, considering both your profit goals and what the market will bear.

At the end of the day, the key to setting competitive pricing strategies is a balance between market research, cost management, and understanding your customers. By analyzing your competitors, considering your costs, and making adjustments based on market trends, you can establish a pricing strategy that positions you for success. Pricing is not static—it requires ongoing analysis and adjustment as you grow your business. By staying flexible, continually evaluating your strategies, and adjusting based on what works, you can maximize your chances of long-term success as an eBay seller.

CHAPTER 5
THE POWER OF VISUALS: TAKING AND OPTIMIZING PRODUCT PHOTOS

ESSENTIAL EQUIPMENT FOR GREAT PRODUCT PHOTOGRAPHY (EVEN ON A BUDGET)

Great product photography is an essential aspect of selling successfully on eBay. In the world of online shopping, images are often the first—and sometimes only—thing that buyers interact with before making a purchase decision. A well-lit, clear, and professional photo can make a world of difference when it comes to showcasing the quality and appeal of your products. While professional photography can be costly, you can achieve impressive results even on a budget by understanding the essential equipment needed and applying smart techniques.

One of the most fundamental pieces of equipment for great product photography is a good camera. While high-end professional cameras do offer exceptional image quality, they are not strictly necessary for beginners, especially if you're on a budget. Many smartphones today are equipped with high-quality cameras that can capture sharp, clear images with proper lighting. Modern smartphones often have features such as portrait mode, automatic focus, and enhanced resolution, which make them suitable for eBay photography. The key here is to ensure that the camera you use has enough megapixels (usually 8MP or more) and can shoot in high resolution.

The camera itself is just one piece of the puzzle. To achieve clear, sharp, and well-lit images, you also need to focus on lighting. Lighting is arguably the most important factor in producing high-quality product photos. In fact, no matter how good your camera is, poor lighting can make even the best product look unattractive or distorted. Natural light is always a good option for beginners, as it's free and easily accessible. Setting up your product near a large window with plenty of indirect sunlight will allow you to capture soft, natural light that minimizes shadows and highlights details. However, natural light can be unpredictable, so if you're photographing products at night or in low-light conditions, investing in affordable artificial lighting can make a significant difference.

A simple and budget-friendly lighting setup can include inexpensive LED lights, softboxes, or ring lights. Softboxes are great for diffusing light and minimizing harsh shadows, creating a soft, even glow around your product. These can be purchased online at an affordable price or even DIYed using household materials such as white fabric or parchment paper to cover the light source. Similarly, a ring light can be used to evenly illuminate small products, creating a professional and flattering look. The key with lighting is consistency—always aim for soft, even lighting to avoid any distracting glares or overly dark shadows. Lighting kits can be purchased for under $50, and the improvement in your images will justify the investment.

In addition to a camera and proper lighting, a clean and simple background is essential for product photography. A cluttered or busy background will distract from your product and may make it difficult for potential buyers to focus on what you're selling. A white background is often the most popular choice for eBay listings because it highlights the product without drawing attention away from it. Fortunately, achieving a clean white backdrop doesn't require expensive studio equipment. You can create an effective background by using a large sheet of white poster board, a roll of inexpensive backdrop paper, or a simple white cloth. The goal is to create a neutral space that lets your product take center stage.

If you're working with larger products or want to avoid reflections from the background, you can set up a "lightbox." A lightbox is essentially a box with translucent sides and a backdrop, which allows for controlled lighting and minimizes outside distractions. You can easily make a DIY lightbox with a cardboard box, white fabric, and some tape. By cutting out windows on each side of the box and lining them with the fabric, you create a soft diffusion of light that results in a professional-looking photo. These lightboxes are perfect for small to medium-sized items and can help you achieve studio-quality photos without the high costs.

For those willing to invest a little more into their product photography setup, a tripod is an excellent piece of equipment that can greatly enhance the quality of your images. A tripod stabilizes your camera or phone, ensuring that your photos are sharp and free from any blurriness caused by hand movement. This is especially important for product shots where you want to capture fine details or when photographing items that require precision and clarity. Tripods come in various price ranges, but even a budget-friendly tripod for around $20 can make a noticeable difference in your photos. They're particularly useful when shooting in low light, as they allow for slower shutter speeds without compromising image clarity.

Another important element to consider in product photography is the angle and composition of your shots. Even with great equipment, poorly composed images can fail to showcase your product in the best light. It's important to experiment with different angles to find the one that best represents the item. For instance, for clothing, a flat lay or mannequin shot may work best to display the fit and style. For smaller products like jewelry or electronics, a close-up shot from multiple angles can help buyers appreciate the details. Taking shots from a variety of angles, including front, side, and top views, provides buyers with a comprehensive look at the product and allows them to make an informed purchasing decision.

While the equipment and setup are crucial, post-processing is another area where you can elevate your photos without breaking the bank. Many smartphones and budget-friendly photo editing tools allow you to adjust exposure, contrast, and sharpness to improve your product images. Editing apps such as Lightroom, Snapseed, or even the built-in editing functions on your phone can help you fine-tune your photos to make them look more professional. It's important to avoid over-editing, as this can lead to unrealistic images that misrepresent the product. Instead, focus on enhancing the natural colors, removing any dust or imperfections, and ensuring that the image accurately reflects what the buyer will receive.

Lastly, when photographing products for eBay, it's important to keep the buyer's perspective in mind. Customers want to know exactly what they're getting, so make sure your images highlight both the positive attributes and any imperfections. If the product is used or has signs of wear, be transparent and show those details clearly. A good practice is to take multiple photos that showcase the item from different angles and perspectives. The more information you provide visually, the more confident buyers will feel about making a purchase.

Creating great product photography on a budget is entirely possible with the right tools and techniques. While investing in professional-grade equipment can certainly improve the quality of your images, it's not a necessity when you're just starting out. With a smartphone camera, affordable lighting, a simple background, and a little creativity, you can produce high-quality photos that highlight your products and make them more appealing to buyers. By paying attention to lighting, background, composition, and post-processing, you can significantly improve your eBay listings and increase the likelihood of making sales, all while keeping costs low.

LIGHTING TECHNIQUES FOR CLEAR AND APPEALING IMAGES

Lighting plays a crucial role in product photography, particularly when it comes to online marketplaces like eBay. Clear, vibrant, and well-lit images not only enhance the appearance of your product but also make a lasting impression on potential buyers. Poor lighting can distort colors, create shadows, and make your item appear dull or unappealing. By understanding and applying effective lighting techniques, even beginners can take professional-quality product photos without expensive equipment. This chapter will guide you through the essential lighting techniques you can use to ensure your images are bright, clear, and compelling.

The first thing to understand about lighting is that it directly affects how your product is perceived. Light can enhance the texture, color, and details of an item, making it more appealing to a potential buyer. It's the key factor in determining how clear and crisp your photos will be. Poor lighting can lead to shadows, harsh contrasts, or a loss of important details, all of which can turn customers away. Therefore, the right lighting technique can significantly increase your chances of making a sale.

The most natural and often the best source of light for photography is sunlight. When shooting indoors, placing your product near a large window allows natural light to illuminate the item without any harsh shadows. The most flattering light is indirect sunlight, which is soft and diffused. To avoid the harsh shadows that direct sunlight creates, it's best to shoot on overcast days, during early mornings, or in the late afternoon when the light is softer and more diffused. This type of light reduces the chances of having areas that are overly bright or too dark.

If you want to shoot during midday or in situations where the light is too harsh, you can use a sheer curtain or diffuser to soften the light. A simple white bedsheet or a piece of translucent fabric can help to diffuse the sunlight, giving it a soft and even quality. This will reduce harsh contrasts, create even lighting, and make the details of your product stand out clearly. This type of lighting is especially beneficial for reflective items, such as jewelry or electronics, where bright glares from direct sunlight can ruin the shot.

While natural light is free and easily accessible, it may not always be available at the time you need it. This is where artificial lighting comes into play. The key to successful artificial lighting is to mimic the qualities of natural light as closely as possible. The most common types of artificial lighting for product photography are LED lights and softboxes. LED lights are affordable, long-lasting, and can be adjusted to fit various lighting needs. They are a good option for beginners looking for a cost-effective solution. LED lights provide a crisp, clean light that enhances colors and details without creating harsh shadows, making them ideal for shooting a wide range of products.

For a more professional touch, a softbox is an essential piece of equipment. A softbox is a type of light modifier that softens and diffuses light, ensuring even coverage across the product. It works by enclosing a bulb in a reflective box with a diffusing fabric on the front. This setup creates a soft, shadow-free light that is ideal for showing products in their best light. Softboxes come in various sizes and can be placed at different angles to achieve the desired effect. The light they emit is gentle and natural-looking, eliminating the harsh, unflattering shadows that are common with direct lighting. Softboxes are perfect for photographing products that need even lighting, such as clothing, small gadgets, or beauty products.

Another lighting technique to consider is the use of a ring light. Ring lights are circular lights that emit an even, uniform light, which is perfect for products that need to be photographed from the front, such as cosmetics, jewelry, or small accessories. The unique shape of the light creates a signature ring-shaped reflection in the eyes or on shiny surfaces, which can make the product appear more dynamic. Ring lights are also highly portable, affordable, and easy to use. By placing your product in the center of the ring, you can ensure even, soft light that reduces shadows and highlights all the important details of the item.

In addition to lighting sources, how you position the lights plays a critical role in how the product is captured. The most common setup for product photography is a three-point lighting system, which involves using three light sources: the key light, the fill light, and the backlight. The key light is the main light source that illuminates the subject. It is typically placed at a 45-degree angle to the product, providing the primary illumination. The fill light is used to soften the shadows created by the key light, and it is usually placed opposite the key light at a lower intensity. The backlight, placed behind the product, adds depth to the image and helps separate the subject from the background. This setup is commonly used in professional photography, but even beginners can replicate it with basic equipment such as LED lights or softboxes.

While the three-point lighting system is effective, it can be complex and may require a bit of experimentation, especially if you're working with a limited budget. For those just starting out, a simpler two-light setup may be sufficient. A two-light setup involves using the key light and a fill light, both of which help to illuminate the product without the complexity of adding a backlight. This setup works well for most products and can still create high-quality, well-lit images with minimal equipment.

Reflectors are another helpful tool to consider in your lighting kit. A reflector is a simple object that bounces light back onto the subject, filling in shadows and enhancing the overall lighting. Reflectors are often used in conjunction with other light sources to ensure that all areas of the product are well-lit. They can be made from various materials, such as white foam board, silver or gold reflective material, or even shiny car sunshields. Using a reflector is a quick and easy way to improve your lighting without spending much money.

When shooting products, always consider the effect of shadows. While shadows can be a natural part of lighting, they should not overwhelm the product or obscure its details. If you're working with softboxes or LED lights, you can minimize the appearance of shadows by positioning the lights at different angles. Placing the lights above, to the side, or slightly behind the product will ensure that the light falls evenly, preventing any strong shadows from forming. A light tent or lightbox is also an excellent way to control shadows, as it diffuses the light evenly from all sides, providing an almost shadow-free environment.

Color temperature is another important consideration when lighting your product. Different light sources emit different color temperatures, which can affect the way the product's colors appear in your photos. Natural daylight has a color temperature of about 5000-6500K, which is ideal for product photography as it renders colors accurately. Artificial lights, however, can emit warm (yellowish) or cool (bluish) tones, so it's important to match the color temperature of your lights to ensure the product's true colors are represented. If you use a mix of different light sources, try adjusting your camera settings or using filters to ensure the color temperature remains consistent.

Lighting is one of the most important factors in product photography. Whether you are using natural sunlight or artificial lighting, understanding how to manipulate and position your light sources will allow you to create clear, appealing, and professional-quality images. By utilizing techniques such as diffusing light, using softboxes or LED lights, and positioning your lights strategically, you can showcase your products in the best possible light. With a little practice, you will be able to create images that not only look great but also help your products stand out on eBay, attracting more potential buyers.

COMPOSITION AND ANGLES TO SHOWCASE YOUR ITEMS

In product photography, composition and angles play an essential role in creating compelling, high-quality images that capture the attention of potential buyers. The way you arrange and photograph your items influences not only how they are perceived but also how easily buyers can assess their value, features, and condition. A well-composed photograph from the right angle can highlight the best features of your product, helping it stand out in a crowded marketplace. Whether you're a beginner or an experienced seller, understanding the principles of composition and utilizing effective angles is crucial to showcasing your products in the best light.

Composition refers to how the elements of a photo are arranged within the frame. It encompasses factors like the positioning of the product, the background, the use of space, and the balance of light and shadow. A well-composed photograph draws the viewer's eye to the most important aspects of the product, ensuring that nothing distracting or unnecessary detracts from its appeal. When taking photos of your items, the goal is to create a clear, aesthetically pleasing image that makes the product easy to understand at a glance.

The first principle of good composition is to focus on the subject. The item you're selling should be the focal point of the image, and it should be clearly visible without distractions. Whether you're shooting a piece of jewelry, a piece of furniture, or a vintage collectible, make sure that the product is positioned front and center. This ensures that buyers know exactly what they are looking at and can evaluate the item from all relevant perspectives.

Another important consideration is the use of negative space. Negative space refers to the areas around the product that are left empty. While this may seem counterintuitive, using negative space can actually enhance the composition of your photo. It helps to keep the viewer's focus on the product itself, without overwhelming them with too many elements. For example, if you're photographing a single product, you may choose to leave a generous amount of empty space around it to create a sense of balance and elegance. Negative space also helps to prevent the photo from feeling cluttered or chaotic, which can turn potential buyers off.

Lighting is another critical element of composition. Proper lighting ensures that the product is clearly visible and that its features are highlighted in the best way possible. When photographing products, make sure the light falls evenly across the subject. If you're using natural light, position the item near a window or in a well-lit area, making sure that there are no harsh shadows. If you're using artificial lighting, consider diffusing the light with a softbox or light tent to create even, flattering illumination.

In addition to focusing on the subject and using negative space, composition also involves considering the background. The background should complement the product, not compete with it. A cluttered or busy background can distract from the product itself and make it difficult for buyers to focus on what's important. A clean, neutral background works well for most products, as it allows the item to stand out without distraction. Plain white or light-colored backgrounds are particularly effective in e-commerce photography because they provide a consistent, professional look that emphasizes the product's details. Alternatively, for certain types of products, such as clothing or handmade goods, a lifestyle background or setting may be appropriate to give the buyer context about how the product might be used.

Once you've considered the composition of your photograph, the next step is to think about the angle from which you'll shoot your product. The angle at which you photograph an item can have a significant impact on how it is perceived by potential buyers. A flat, head-on shot may not always be the best choice for all products, as it can make the item appear less dynamic or difficult to assess from certain angles. On the other hand, shooting from an interesting or unique perspective can help reveal the product's features and create a more compelling visual story.

For example, when photographing a piece of clothing, a front-facing shot may be ideal for showcasing the item's shape and design. However, to highlight additional features such as buttons, zippers, or texture, a side angle or close-up shot may be more effective. Similarly, when photographing a piece of furniture, a side angle can reveal the contours and depth of the piece, while a top-down shot might showcase the seating or table surface.

A common angle used in e-commerce photography is the 45-degree angle. This angle provides a balance between showing the front of the product and revealing its sides, offering buyers a more three-dimensional view of the item. For products like electronics, jewelry, or books, the 45-degree angle helps highlight details like buttons, logos, and design elements that might not be visible in a flat-on shot.

For smaller items, such as jewelry, beauty products, or accessories, close-up shots are essential to showcase the fine details. Close-ups allow potential buyers to see textures, materials, and any imperfections that might affect the item's condition. Close-up shots are particularly important for items that are highly detailed or intricately designed, as they help convey the quality and craftsmanship of the product.

Another important consideration when choosing your angles is the context in which the product will be used. If you're selling a piece of furniture or home décor, lifestyle shots can add value by showing the item in a setting that demonstrates its purpose. For instance, a photograph of a lamp on a bedside table can help buyers visualize how the item will look in their own space. Similarly, clothing can be styled on a model or laid flat with accessories to show how it fits or complements other pieces.

Beyond standard angles, another powerful technique in product photography is the use of the "hero shot." This is typically a close-up shot that showcases the item from its most flattering angle, often highlighting the item's most important or unique feature. For instance, if you're selling a vintage wristwatch, the hero shot may focus on the watch face, emphasizing its design, craftsmanship, and details like the watch hands and numerals. The hero shot serves as a focal point for the buyer, drawing their attention to what makes the item special.

When photographing products from multiple angles, be sure to capture a range of perspectives to give buyers a complete view of the item. In addition to the front view, consider shooting the product from the side, back, and top, if applicable. Providing a full view of the product helps customers assess its condition and better understand its size and proportions.

Always remember that your goal is to present the product in the best possible light. While composition and angles are important, clarity and accuracy are equally essential. Make sure your images represent the product accurately and honestly. Avoid using angles that might hide flaws or imperfections unless you are also providing a clear, close-up image of the areas in question. Transparency builds trust with buyers and helps ensure they are satisfied with their purchase.

Mastering the art of composition and choosing the right angles for product photography is a critical skill for online sellers. By carefully considering the arrangement of your product within the frame, experimenting with different perspectives, and using proper lighting, you can create engaging, professional-looking images that attract potential buyers. Whether you're photographing jewelry, electronics, or home goods, the right composition and angles will not only showcase your products in the best light but also help build credibility with your customers. Taking the time to perfect your product shots will ultimately enhance your eBay listings and improve your chances of making a successful sale.

EDITING AND OPTIMIZING PHOTOS FOR EBAY'S REQUIREMENTS

In the world of e-commerce, product images serve as the first point of contact between you and your potential customers. Whether they are browsing through hundreds of listings or searching for a specific item, high-quality, well-edited images are crucial to capturing their attention and encouraging them to make a purchase. When selling on eBay, where competition is fierce and buyers often have many options to choose from, it's essential that your photos stand out in the best way possible. Editing and optimizing your photos not only enhances their visual appeal but also ensures they meet eBay's strict requirements, which can influence how easily your listings are found by buyers.

The first step in editing and optimizing your photos for eBay's platform is to ensure that they are clear, high-resolution images. eBay requires that the main image of your listing be at least 500 pixels on the longest side. However, it's advisable to upload images that are 1,000 pixels or more, especially if you want to take advantage of the platform's zoom function, which allows potential buyers to examine details in greater detail. Images with higher resolution will help buyers assess the condition and features of your product more accurately. Moreover, higher-quality images generally look more professional, which can enhance your credibility as a seller.

Once you've captured high-quality images of your product, the next step is editing them for optimal clarity and brightness. One of the first adjustments you might need to make is to correct the exposure of the image. Overexposed or underexposed images can make it difficult for buyers to assess the true color and condition of the product. By adjusting the exposure, you can brighten the image to make the product look more vibrant and appealing or darken it if it's too light. Proper exposure ensures that the details are visible and that the product appears as realistic as possible.

After adjusting exposure, it's important to pay attention to the white balance of your photos. White balance refers to the accuracy of the color representation in your images. If the white balance is off, your photos may appear too warm (yellow/orange tones) or too cool (blue tones), which can distort the true colors of the product. To achieve accurate white balance, you can use tools within editing software to adjust the temperature of the image. This ensures that buyers see the product as it truly is, reducing the likelihood of returns due to color discrepancies.

Cropping and straightening your images is another essential part of the editing process. Cropping helps to remove unnecessary background clutter or distractions, ensuring that the focus remains on the product itself. eBay's guidelines recommend using a white or neutral background to make the product stand out, and cropping your images can help achieve this. By removing any unwanted elements, such as tables, shelves, or other items in the background, you can create a cleaner, more professional-looking image. In addition, ensure that the product is centered within the frame. This will make the image appear more balanced and visually appealing.

Straightening your images is equally important. If your photos are taken at an angle or the camera is tilted, it can make the product look skewed and unprofessional. Ensure that the horizon line in your image is straight and that the product is aligned properly. Many editing software programs offer automatic straightening tools to help you correct slight tilts with minimal effort.

After cropping and straightening, another key consideration is optimizing the sharpness of your images. While it's tempting to rely on a perfectly clear and sharp photo straight from the camera, some photos may benefit from a slight sharpening adjustment. Sharpening enhances the edges of the product and ensures that finer details, such as textures or stitching on clothing, are clearly visible. However, be cautious not to over-sharpen, as this can introduce noise or unnatural-looking artifacts into the image. The goal is to highlight the important details of the product while maintaining a realistic appearance.

Additionally, removing any imperfections or blemishes from your images is vital in creating a clean and professional look. If your product has minor imperfections, such as dust, fingerprints, or scratches on its surface, you can use the clone tool or healing brush in photo editing software to remove these blemishes. This process can help eliminate distractions and ensure that your item is presented in the best possible light. However, it's important to note that honesty is key when listing items online. While removing minor imperfections is acceptable, you should never misrepresent the condition of your product by heavily altering the image to hide significant flaws.

To optimize your photos further, you should consider resizing them for faster loading times without compromising their quality. Large image files can slow down the loading speed of your eBay listing, which can result in a poor user experience and potential loss of sales. eBay recommends keeping the file size under 7 MB, but the key is to find the balance between image quality and file size. You can use image compression tools to reduce the file size without losing too much visual detail. There are numerous online tools and software options that allow you to resize and compress your images efficiently.

One of the most important aspects of optimizing your photos for eBay is ensuring that they meet eBay's image requirements. eBay's guidelines are specific about the types of images that can be uploaded to the platform. For example, images containing watermarks, promotional text, or logos are not allowed. eBay also prohibits images that are excessively manipulated or altered, as this can lead to misleading representations of the product. Always review eBay's photo policies to ensure that your images comply with their standards.

eBay also allows you to upload multiple images for each listing, which is a great opportunity to showcase your product from different angles and perspectives. In addition to your main image, include photos that display the product from various sides, close-ups of important details (such as labels, tags, or serial numbers), and any additional images that show the item in use or context. This gives buyers a comprehensive view of the product, which is essential for making an informed purchasing decision. It's important to remember that eBay recommends at least three images for each listing to improve your chances of standing out in search results.

When uploading your images to eBay, make sure to name your files descriptively, as eBay's search algorithm takes image file names into account when determining search rankings. For example, instead of naming your file "image1.jpg," name it something more specific, like "vintage-leather-jacket-size-medium.jpg." This will not only help with SEO but also make it easier for buyers to find your product when they are searching for specific items.

Lastly, it's worth considering the benefits of editing your photos for mobile users. With a significant number of eBay shoppers browsing and purchasing via mobile devices, it's important that your photos are optimized for smaller screens. Ensure that your images are clear and easy to view on mobile devices by focusing on the most important features of your product and making sure that they are visible even on smaller screens.

Editing and optimizing photos for eBay's requirements is a vital aspect of creating listings that attract buyers and drive sales. By investing time in improving the quality and clarity of your images, you are not only ensuring that your products meet eBay's guidelines but also enhancing their appeal to potential customers. High-resolution, well-edited photos that accurately represent the product's condition and features will increase your credibility as a seller and ultimately contribute to your success on the platform. Whether you are a seasoned seller or just starting, mastering the art of editing and optimizing photos will help you create professional listings that stand out and make a lasting impression on buyers.

USING MULTIPLE IMAGES TO INCREASE BUYER CONFIDENCE

When it comes to selling on eBay, creating a positive first impression is essential. Buyers are far more likely to engage with your listing and make a purchase if they can see clear, detailed images of the product from various angles. Using multiple images to showcase your item is not just a best practice; it is a proven strategy to increase buyer confidence, reduce uncertainty, and ultimately boost sales. By providing buyers with a comprehensive view of the product, you are helping them feel more assured about their purchase, which is critical in the online shopping world where they cannot physically touch or inspect the item.

The power of multiple images lies in their ability to tell a story about your product. Each image can highlight different features, details, and angles, giving the buyer a complete understanding of what they are purchasing. When a buyer is able to view your product from multiple perspectives, they feel like they are making a well-informed decision, which builds trust in both the product and you as a seller. The more informed a buyer is, the more likely they are to complete a purchase.

The first image in any eBay listing is crucial because it's the one that will appear in search results and attract potential buyers. This image should be the highest quality and should display the product clearly against a clean background. However, the other images that accompany this main one can play an equally important role in increasing buyer confidence. Imagine you are looking at a pair of vintage shoes. While the first image may show the shoes from a flattering, straight-on view, other images can show more detailed aspects, such as close-ups of the soles, stitching, brand tags, and any potential wear or imperfections. These additional photos provide transparency, which is an essential element of building trust with your customers.

One of the most compelling reasons to use multiple images is that it allows you to showcase the condition of the product more accurately. In eBay's competitive marketplace, many sellers are offering similar products. However, your photos can set you apart by giving buyers the reassurance that they are purchasing from a reputable seller who takes the time to showcase every detail. For example, if you're selling a pre-owned electronic device, you can include images of the device's buttons, screen, and ports, ensuring that any wear and tear is clearly visible. By being upfront about the condition of your product, you not only reduce the chances of negative feedback but also increase the likelihood of receiving positive reviews for your honesty.

Moreover, multiple images can help to eliminate any confusion about the product's features or specifications. A buyer may be drawn to a particular item because of its features, but they may need more visual context to fully understand how it functions. For instance, when selling a piece of furniture, photos showing how it looks in a room with different lighting or perspectives can give the buyer a clearer idea of how it fits into their own space. If you're selling a kitchen appliance, showing different angles, buttons, and features ensures the buyer can assess whether the item suits their needs. The more you provide in terms of visual context, the easier it will be for the buyer to visualize using the product, which builds confidence in their decision.

Aside from showcasing the product's features, multiple images also allow you to demonstrate its scale and proportions, which is often a challenge in online shopping. When browsing through listings, buyers might struggle to gauge the actual size of an item based solely on a single image. For example, if you're selling a piece of art or a decorative object, showing it in relation to an everyday object, like a chair or a coffee cup, can help buyers understand its size and fit. If you're selling clothing, showing the item worn on a model or mannequin provides buyers with a better sense of how it looks when styled. This approach helps avoid confusion and ensures that buyers receive the product they expect.

Another critical benefit of using multiple images is that they allow you to highlight both the strengths and any imperfections of the product. While it may seem counterintuitive, showing a potential flaw or imperfection can actually increase buyer confidence. Why? Because it shows transparency and honesty. If you're selling a used item, buyers appreciate seeing all sides of the product, including any scratches, dents, or discoloration. If the buyer knows exactly what they're getting, they are less likely to be surprised or dissatisfied when the product arrives. Additionally, highlighting imperfections can mitigate the risk of returns and disputes, as buyers are more likely to accept the item if they already know about any issues beforehand.

By including multiple images, you also improve your product's searchability on eBay. eBay's search algorithm takes into account the quality and quantity of the images you upload. Listings with more images tend to rank higher in search results, which increases visibility and exposure. This means that by simply uploading multiple high-quality photos, you're giving your listing a better chance of being discovered by more potential buyers. Additionally, eBay allows you to upload up to twelve images for each listing, and making use of all available slots can significantly increase the chances of your product being seen. Keep in mind that buyers are more likely to click on listings that feature multiple, high-quality images, as they feel they are getting a more complete picture of the product.

One often-overlooked advantage of using multiple images is that they help convey professionalism and credibility. Buyers are far more likely to trust sellers who put effort into their listings. High-quality, well-composed images give the impression that you are a serious, professional seller who is committed to providing great service. When sellers only upload one blurry image or fail to show essential details, it can create doubt in the buyer's mind about the product's quality or the seller's trustworthiness. On the other hand, providing a range of images that display every angle and feature shows that you are thorough, reliable, and invested in making the buying experience as transparent and easy as possible.

In addition to showcasing the product itself, multiple images can also help convey the product's packaging and any accessories that come with it. If you're selling an item with its original packaging, such as a brand-new watch or collectible toy, taking a picture of the packaging can add extra value to the product. Similarly, if the item comes with accessories like chargers, manuals, or cases, showing these items in separate photos will ensure that the buyer understands what they will receive when they make a purchase. This is especially important for used or refurbished items, where buyers may want to know if they will receive all the original components that came with the product.

To make the most out of your photos, it's essential to keep the images consistent in quality and style. Use the same lighting, background, and framing for each photo to ensure the entire set looks cohesive. A consistent presentation across multiple images creates a sense of professionalism and trustworthiness. Avoid cluttered backgrounds and distractions that might draw attention away from the product itself. Clean, simple backgrounds – like a white backdrop – help focus the viewer's attention on the item and prevent any unnecessary details from interfering with the product's visual appeal.

The Complete Guide to Selling on eBay for Beginners 2025

Using multiple images to showcase your products on eBay is one of the most effective strategies for building buyer confidence and driving sales. By providing clear, detailed, and varied images, you give potential customers a comprehensive view of what they're purchasing, helping to build trust and transparency. Whether you're displaying different angles, highlighting product features, or showing the item in context, multiple images allow buyers to make well-informed decisions and feel confident in their purchase. The more you can communicate through your photos, the less room there is for doubt or uncertainty, leading to a higher likelihood of a successful sale.

CHAPTER 6
MASTERING EBAY'S LISTING FORMATS AND OPTIONS

AUCTION VS. FIXED-PRICE LISTINGS: CHOOSING THE RIGHT APPROACH

When you start selling on eBay, one of the most important decisions you'll need to make is whether to use auction-style listings or fixed-price listings. Both have their advantages and disadvantages, and understanding how each works can help you choose the best option for your business. Your choice will depend on several factors, including the type of products you're selling, your business goals, and the behavior of potential buyers. Whether you're a beginner or someone looking to refine your selling strategy, knowing the nuances of each approach will enable you to maximize your profits and minimize risks.

Auction-style listings are the traditional method of selling on eBay. With this format, you set a starting price for your item, and interested buyers can place bids during a set period, usually between one and ten days. At the end of the auction, the highest bidder wins the item. This dynamic, competitive environment can generate excitement and sometimes drive the price up, especially for rare or highly desirable items. However, this model also has its drawbacks. If your item is not popular or if bidding is slow, you might end up selling it for less than you'd hoped, or even for less than what you paid for it. Moreover, auctions typically require a bit more time and effort in terms of monitoring bids and potentially relisting unsold items.

The appeal of auctions lies in their potential to create bidding wars. If you're selling a unique or in-demand item, an auction could work to your advantage, allowing you to sell it for a price higher than its initial value. For example, limited-edition items, collectibles, antiques, and rare pieces are perfect candidates for auction listings. Buyers who are interested in these types of items are often willing to place bids in a competitive manner, pushing the final price well above the starting bid. Auction-style listings create a sense of urgency, which can encourage faster decision-making from potential buyers. This makes them an excellent option if you want to generate excitement or if you're selling something that has a strong following.

On the other hand, auction-style listings also come with some uncertainty. You don't know exactly what price your item will sell for until the auction ends, and there is always the possibility that you'll end up with a lower bid than expected. Even if you set a reserve price (the minimum price you're willing to accept), there's still a risk that your item might not sell at all if the reserve is not met. This can be frustrating, especially if you're in a hurry to offload the item. Auctions are also time-sensitive, and once the bidding ends, your window of opportunity is gone. This is something to consider when you're weighing whether an auction-style listing fits into your business model.

In contrast, fixed-price listings, also known as "Buy It Now" listings, offer a more straightforward approach. With this format, you set a price for your item, and buyers can immediately purchase it at that price without having to wait for an auction to end. Fixed-price listings can be appealing because they provide more predictability and control over the sales process. As a seller, you know exactly what you'll receive for each item, which can help you plan your business finances more effectively. Additionally, fixed-price listings allow you to set up listings with a wider variety of options, including bulk purchasing or offering multiple quantities of the same item.

One of the biggest advantages of fixed-price listings is that they appeal to buyers who want instant gratification. In a world where consumers expect fast, easy transactions, fixed-price listings cater to buyers who don't want to wait for an auction to end or risk losing the item to another bidder. Buyers can instantly purchase the item, and they are often drawn to listings where the price is clearly stated upfront. If you're selling common, everyday products or items that are readily available, fixed-price listings are often the better choice. It's also worth noting that eBay has introduced the option to offer "Best Offer" in fixed-price listings, where buyers can submit an offer lower than the listed price, and sellers can accept or reject the offer. This adds some flexibility to fixed-price listings and makes them even more appealing to buyers.

For many sellers, fixed-price listings offer a more reliable way to sell products, especially those in stable or predictable markets. If you're selling items like clothing, electronics, or home goods, setting a fixed price might be a more effective strategy. It reduces the unpredictability of the auction format and ensures that you don't end up with an unsold item. Additionally, fixed-price listings can be relisted without the need for re-bidding, and you can easily make adjustments to the price if necessary, without worrying about the time constraints of an auction.

However, while fixed-price listings may seem like the safer choice, they do have their own challenges. For one, they don't carry the same sense of urgency or excitement that auctions do. Since buyers can take their time to decide whether to purchase, you may find that some listings sit idle for longer periods. The market for certain items may also become saturated, which means you could face increased competition and potentially have to adjust your pricing to stay competitive. In highly competitive categories, fixed-price listings may require more marketing and optimization efforts to stand out from the crowd.

When deciding between auction and fixed-price listings, it's crucial to consider the type of product you're selling. For items that are unique, rare, or highly collectible, auctions might be the better option because of the potential for higher bids. Think of rare comic books, vintage toys, or limited-edition sneakers—products like these tend to do well in an auction setting because buyers are often passionate about the item and willing to compete for it. Auctions can help you maximize the final selling price for these kinds of products, especially when there's demand for them.

For more common or mass-produced items, fixed-price listings tend to be more effective. Items like household goods, popular electronics, or clothing may not generate the kind of bidding excitement that rare collectibles would. In these cases, fixed-price listings allow you to set a reasonable price that buyers can accept right away, making the process faster and easier for everyone involved. This approach also allows you to focus on scaling your inventory, as you don't have to worry about the time-sensitive nature of auctions or the unpredictability of bidding wars.

It's also worth noting that eBay offers the option of combining both auction and fixed-price formats. You can start by listing an item as an auction and then switch to a fixed-price listing if the auction doesn't receive bids or doesn't reach the desired price. This hybrid approach can give you the best of both worlds, offering the excitement of an auction while providing the security of a fixed price if necessary.

Choosing between auction and fixed-price listings on eBay depends on the type of items you sell, your business goals, and the preferences of your target market. Auctions can be exciting and profitable for unique or collectible items, but they come with the risk of unpredictability and unsold listings. Fixed-price listings offer more control and reliability, making them an ideal choice for everyday products and items that don't generate auction-style competition. By understanding the strengths and weaknesses of both options, you can select the right approach for your business, optimize your listings, and increase your chances of making successful sales.

UNDERSTANDING "BUY IT NOW" AND "BEST OFFER" OPTIONS

When you begin selling on eBay, one of the most important aspects of your business strategy will be choosing the right listing format. eBay offers two highly effective and popular features for sellers: "Buy It Now" and "Best Offer." These options allow you to sell your products in a way that accommodates both your pricing strategy and the expectations of your potential buyers. To successfully use these tools, it's important to understand how each one works, how they differ, and how they can be combined to enhance your sales process.

The "Buy It Now" feature on eBay allows you to set a fixed price for your product, and buyers can purchase it immediately at that price without needing to wait for an auction to end or enter into a bidding war. It is a straightforward, no-hassle option for both sellers and buyers. As a seller, you have complete control over the price of the item, and the buyer has the certainty of knowing exactly what the cost will be. Once the buyer clicks the "Buy It Now" button, the sale is complete, and they immediately pay the listed price (plus any applicable shipping fees). This provides you with an efficient, predictable sales process that doesn't rely on time-sensitive bidding or the unpredictability of auctions.

The primary benefit of "Buy It Now" listings is that they offer both you and the buyer convenience. As a seller, you can set the price that you believe reflects the value of the item and move on with minimal time spent on managing the listing. You don't have to wait for the item to be auctioned off, and the transaction is usually completed quickly. For buyers, the "Buy It Now" feature caters to those who want to avoid the uncertainty of bidding and simply wish to pay for an item at a known price. This can be especially appealing to buyers who are not interested in waiting days or weeks for an auction to conclude, and they may appreciate the simplicity and transparency that "Buy It Now" offers.

This feature works particularly well for items that are in high demand or have a steady price. For example, if you are selling a popular piece of electronics, a brand-name handbag, or a commonly searched-for collectible, buyers may be more likely to choose the "Buy It Now" option because it allows them to secure the item right away. It also works for products with a known market value, where buyers expect to pay a fixed price, as opposed to taking a risk in an auction setting.

One of the key advantages of using "Buy It Now" is the potential for quicker sales. You can list an item and wait for it to sell immediately, without needing to follow up on the auction process or deal with time constraints. This is particularly useful if you have multiple items to sell or if you want to maintain a streamlined business operation. For sellers new to eBay, this can be a great way to get started without the added complexity of auctions.

However, there are also some limitations to the "Buy It Now" approach. The biggest challenge comes from competition. If you're selling products that are common or widely available, your listing could easily get lost among thousands of other similar items. Buyers might be less willing to pay your asking price if there are cheaper or more abundant options available elsewhere. Additionally, because the price is fixed, there's no flexibility for negotiation unless you choose to offer discounts or sales events.

To combat this, eBay allows you to pair "Buy It Now" with another powerful option: the "Best Offer" feature. This option lets buyers propose a price they're willing to pay for the item, which can be higher or lower than the original listing price. As a seller, you have the option to accept, decline, or counter the offer with a new price. This provides more flexibility and allows both buyers and sellers to engage in a form of negotiation, making it more appealing for buyers who may not be comfortable with the fixed price and want to get a better deal.

The "Best Offer" option works particularly well for products where the price might be negotiable or when you are willing to accept slightly lower offers to move inventory quickly. This feature can be useful in a variety of situations, such as when you have a limited number of items in stock or if you want to appeal to a larger audience by allowing for some price flexibility. By allowing buyers to make offers, you increase the chances of completing a sale, especially when there are price-sensitive customers who are looking for a deal. In essence, this option can expand your buyer base and help you close sales more effectively.

The combination of "Buy It Now" and "Best Offer" can be a powerful tool in your eBay selling strategy. It gives you the ability to set a fixed price while also leaving room for negotiation, providing the best of both worlds. If you set a reasonable price but are open to negotiation, you can attract a larger pool of buyers, some of whom might offer less than your asking price but still result in a successful transaction. For example, if you list a popular item for $50 and offer a "Best Offer" option, a buyer might offer $40. You can either accept the offer or counter with a price that's closer to your initial listing price. This helps you maintain control over your pricing while still engaging with buyers who are looking for some flexibility.

One of the significant advantages of using the "Best Offer" option is that it allows you to reach buyers who may not have initially considered your item due to price concerns. Even if a buyer is hesitant to purchase at the listed price, the ability to make an offer can prompt them to take the first step in initiating a conversation. Moreover, you can choose to accept offers that are close to your desired price or decline offers that are too low, giving you control over your sales strategy.

For many sellers, the decision to use "Buy It Now" and "Best Offer" in combination comes down to finding the right balance between fixed pricing and negotiation. You may find that certain items sell best with a fixed price, while others benefit from negotiation through offers. The key is understanding the nature of your products, the demand in the market, and how much flexibility you're willing to offer.

One additional consideration when using "Best Offer" is how to set the right price to encourage offers without undervaluing your item. The price you list should reflect the item's value but still leave room for negotiation. If you set the price too high, buyers may be discouraged from making an offer altogether. On the other hand, if your price is too low, you might end up selling for less than the value of your product. As a seller, you'll need to be mindful of how much wiggle room you leave in your pricing, ensuring that the "Best Offer" feature works in your favor.

Understanding how to use both "Buy It Now" and "Best Offer" options effectively can have a significant impact on your eBay business. These features give you the flexibility to control pricing while appealing to a wider range of buyers who appreciate the convenience of fixed prices or the ability to negotiate. By leveraging both options, you can enhance your sales strategy, improve buyer satisfaction, and create a more dynamic eBay selling experience. Whether you're new to eBay or have been selling for a while, mastering these tools will help you reach your sales goals while staying competitive in a crowded marketplace.

SCHEDULING LISTINGS FOR OPTIMAL VISIBILITY

Scheduling your eBay listings for optimal visibility is a key strategy that can significantly enhance the success of your online selling business. Timing is everything when it comes to selling on eBay, and knowing when to schedule your listings can make a noticeable difference in how quickly your items sell and how many potential buyers see them. This practice involves more than just listing an item when you have the time; it's about being strategic in order to capture the attention of your target audience at the right moment.

One of the fundamental factors to consider when scheduling your listings is understanding eBay's peak traffic times. eBay has millions of users who browse the site at various times throughout the day, but certain periods experience more traffic than others. Knowing these peak times allows you to position your listings when they are more likely to be seen by active buyers, improving your chances of a sale. For example, eBay generally experiences higher traffic during evenings, particularly between 8 p.m. and 10 p.m. EST, when many buyers are winding down from their day and browsing for products. Weekends, especially Sundays, also tend to see increased activity as people have more leisure time to shop online. By scheduling your listings to go live during these high-traffic periods, you are ensuring that your items receive maximum exposure.

While timing is critical, it's also important to consider the length of time you want your listings to remain active. eBay allows you to schedule listings to start at specific times, and it's essential to choose a duration that aligns with your business goals. Typically, eBay allows listings to last from one day to ten days, but the most common durations are three, five, and seven days. If you're selling items that are in high demand or limited supply, a shorter listing duration might work well to create urgency and prompt quicker bids. On the other hand, for products with lower demand or those that require more time for buyers to discover, longer listing durations might be more appropriate. Keep in mind that your listing duration also affects your visibility, as eBay's algorithm tends to favor listings that have more time remaining, as they are seen as more active.

Understanding eBay's search algorithm and how it ranks listings is another critical aspect of scheduling your listings for optimal visibility. eBay uses a variety of factors to determine which listings are shown to buyers, with the most significant factor being the relevance of your listing to the buyer's search query. This means that your title, description, and item specifics all play a role in getting your product seen, but timing is also an important consideration. Items that are listed more recently tend to appear higher in search results, especially if they have a longer duration left. Therefore, strategically timing your listings to ensure they are launched when they are likely to receive more views can give you a competitive edge in search rankings.

Another strategy to consider is the use of eBay's automated listing scheduling tools. These tools are designed to allow sellers to pre-schedule their listings for specific times and dates, ensuring that their items are posted when they're most likely to generate interest. By using this feature, you don't have to be online at the exact moment you want your listing to go live. Instead, you can prepare your listings in advance and set them to launch at peak times. This allows you to focus on other aspects of your business while still ensuring your products are reaching potential buyers when they're most likely to make a purchase.

Scheduling listings can also be an effective way to take advantage of specific events and seasonal trends. For example, if you are selling holiday-themed products, scheduling your listings to go live well in advance of the holiday season can give you a head start on your competitors. Similarly, if you're selling products related to a particular event or trend, timing your listings to coincide with that event can maximize your visibility. For instance, if you sell fitness gear, scheduling listings to launch in early January, when many people make New Year's resolutions, can be a great way to attract buyers who are looking to start their fitness journeys.

In addition to seasonal events, scheduling your listings to coincide with sales events or promotions is another great way to increase visibility. eBay often holds site-wide sales events, such as Black Friday, Cyber Monday, or their semi-annual sales events. If you know when these sales are happening, you can time your listings to align with them, ensuring that your products are included in these high-visibility, high-traffic periods. Sellers can also run their own promotions, such as discounts or free shipping offers, which can be scheduled to coincide with their listings. These promotions can attract additional buyers, and scheduling your listings to align with these offers can give you an edge in attracting potential customers.

It's also important to consider time zones when scheduling your listings. eBay is a global marketplace, and your buyers may be located in different parts of the world. To ensure that you are reaching the right audience at the right time, consider the time zones of your target market. For example, if you are selling to U.S.-based customers, it might make sense to schedule your listings during the late afternoon or evening hours, when buyers are more likely to be browsing. If you're targeting international buyers, you may want to adjust your timing to align with peak browsing hours in other countries. Taking the time zone differences into account can help you create a more strategic listing schedule that maximizes the chances of your products being discovered by the right buyers at the right time.

Using eBay's promotion tools, such as promoted listings, is another excellent way to complement your scheduling strategy. Promoted listings allow you to pay for additional visibility in search results, increasing the chances that your listings will appear at the top of buyers' searches. When paired with a carefully timed listing schedule, promoted listings can further amplify your efforts by ensuring that your products are shown at prime times. This combination of optimized scheduling and paid promotion can be especially powerful when you are selling highly competitive products, where it may be harder to stand out organically.

Scheduling your listings with flexibility in mind is crucial. While timing is essential, unexpected changes in market conditions, buyer behavior, or product availability can sometimes require you to adjust your plans. For example, if a product unexpectedly becomes more popular, you may want to extend its listing duration or relist it to keep it visible for longer. On the other hand, if a product isn't moving as quickly as anticipated, you may want to adjust the price or try a different timing strategy. Flexibility in your listing schedule allows you to respond quickly to market shifts and adapt to new opportunities as they arise.

Scheduling your eBay listings for optimal visibility is a key component of a successful selling strategy. By understanding peak traffic times, choosing the right listing duration, taking advantage of eBay's automated tools, and aligning your listings with seasonal trends and promotions, you can maximize your product's visibility and increase the likelihood of a sale. With careful planning and the right timing, your eBay store can gain a competitive edge in the marketplace, attracting more buyers and driving more sales. Scheduling listings is an easy yet powerful way to take control of your selling process and ensure that your items are reaching the right audience at the right time.

UTILIZING EBAY'S PROMOTED LISTINGS FOR INCREASED EXPOSURE (INTRODUCTION)

In the competitive world of online selling, standing out in a crowded marketplace can be a challenge. On eBay, where millions of items are listed daily, visibility is key to making sales. While listing your items optimally with great titles, descriptions, and high-quality images is important, sometimes it's not enough to reach the right audience. This is where eBay's Promoted Listings can make a difference. By leveraging this tool, sellers can significantly boost the visibility of their products, driving more traffic to their listings and increasing the likelihood of sales. Understanding how to effectively utilize eBay's Promoted Listings is an essential strategy for anyone serious about growing their online business.

Promoted Listings on eBay work by allowing sellers to pay for extra visibility in search results, meaning their listings are more likely to be seen by potential buyers. This feature is designed to help sellers increase the exposure of their items by positioning them higher in eBay's search results and within relevant product categories. Whether you are new to selling or an experienced seller looking to expand your reach, understanding how to use Promoted Listings effectively can significantly impact your sales performance.

When you use Promoted Listings, your products are displayed more prominently within the search results, giving them an edge over other listings. This service is not a fixed cost, but rather, it's based on a percentage of the sale price that you, the seller, choose to set. This is known as the "ad rate" or "ad fee," and it's a way of paying eBay for the additional exposure that comes with promoted listings. This is typically a performance-based fee, meaning that you only pay for the promotion if the item sells through the promoted listing. This makes it a risk-free way to increase visibility, as you only pay when you see results.

The process of using Promoted Listings begins when you create a campaign for your listings. In the campaign, you select which items to promote and choose your ad rate—an amount of money you're willing to pay eBay for the additional visibility. The higher your ad rate, the more likely eBay is to show your listing to potential buyers. However, setting the ad rate is a balancing act. While a higher ad rate increases the likelihood that your listing will appear at the top of search results, it's important to consider your profit margins and overall pricing strategy. You want to ensure that the fee you're paying for the promotion doesn't eat into your potential profits too much.

Once you've selected the listings to promote and set your ad rate, the listings will be automatically eligible for placement in more visible spots. Promoted Listings can appear in several key areas of eBay's platform, including the search results pages, on the sidebar of listing pages, and even within the "Recommended for You" section. These areas are prime real estate, where buyers are more likely to notice your items. The goal of these promoted placements is to increase your exposure to potential buyers who might not have otherwise found your listings in the organic search results.

One of the significant benefits of using Promoted Listings is that it helps you reach customers who are actively searching for items like yours. eBay's algorithm ensures that your promoted listings are shown to buyers who are most likely to be interested in your products. When shoppers search for items similar to yours, eBay's system considers factors like the relevance of your listing, the bidding history, and buyer behavior, making it a highly targeted form of advertising. Unlike traditional paid ads that can reach a broad audience, Promoted Listings provide a more focused approach, ensuring your products are displayed to the right people at the right time.

Additionally, Promoted Listings offer a form of visibility that organic listings cannot match. Organic search results on eBay are influenced by several factors, including the relevance of your title and item specifics, the quality of your product images, and your seller feedback. While these are important, there are many listings that may be competing for the same keyword or search term. Even if you have a well-optimized listing, your product may not appear at the top of the search results, especially when there are many other sellers offering similar items. Promoted Listings give you an edge by placing your item in prime spots, boosting its chances of being seen and clicked.

When it comes to setting the ad rate for your Promoted Listings, understanding eBay's system is crucial. eBay uses a bidding system for Promoted Listings, which means you can control the amount you're willing to pay for better placement in search results. The more competitive your bidding, the higher the likelihood your item will appear at the top of search results. However, it's important to strike the right balance between ad rate and the cost of goods. You don't want to overbid on promotions and risk reducing your overall profit margin. To find the optimal ad rate, many sellers experiment with different rates, adjusting them based on their results and profit goals. eBay also provides a "recommended" ad rate, which is based on the bidding history of similar items in your category, but this is just a guideline, and you can adjust it based on your budget and sales strategy.

An essential aspect of using Promoted Listings effectively is measuring your results. eBay offers sellers insights into the performance of their promoted listings, including the number of clicks, the total sales made, and the overall return on investment (ROI). Monitoring these results will help you determine whether your ad rates are set correctly and whether the promoted listings are driving meaningful traffic to your items. If a listing isn't performing as expected, you can adjust the ad rate, change the items you're promoting, or even stop the promotion entirely. This flexibility ensures that you have full control over your advertising strategy and can fine-tune it to achieve the best possible outcomes.

Another advantage of using Promoted Listings is that they help increase brand visibility. As your products get more exposure, more buyers become familiar with your brand. Over time, this can lead to greater brand recognition, and repeat customers may return to your store to make future purchases. Promoted Listings also allow you to showcase your best items or high-margin products, allowing you to prioritize which products you want to push into the market more aggressively.

One thing to keep in mind is that Promoted Listings are most effective when combined with other eBay selling strategies. For example, having an attractive listing with a detailed product description, high-quality photos, and competitive pricing can increase the effectiveness of your promoted listings. If your listing is visually appealing and well-crafted, it's more likely to catch the buyer's eye, which can lead to higher conversion rates. In this way, Promoted Listings work best as part of a holistic selling strategy where the promotion of your products complements all other aspects of your online store.

eBay's Promoted Listings offer a powerful way to increase your product visibility, drive traffic, and ultimately boost sales. By allowing you to pay for placement in high-visibility areas of eBay's marketplace, this tool provides a strategic advantage in a competitive environment. With careful planning, testing, and monitoring, using Promoted Listings can help sellers reach more buyers, increase sales, and grow their business over time. Understanding how to utilize this tool effectively is key to standing out in a crowded marketplace, especially in a time when consumers are bombarded with countless options online. By embracing this paid promotion tool, sellers can ensure their products are getting the attention they deserve.

EXPLORING EBAY'S INTERNATIONAL SELLING OPTIONS (INTRODUCTION)

Expanding your eBay business beyond domestic borders can be a game-changer, offering access to a global market of buyers. Whether you're looking to take advantage of untapped opportunities or simply wish to diversify your customer base, selling internationally opens doors to potential sales growth. However, navigating the complexities of international selling requires a solid understanding of the different eBay tools and features available to sellers, as well as awareness of the logistical, legal, and financial factors involved. eBay has developed several features to support sellers who wish to explore international markets, making it easier than ever to tap into the global eCommerce space.

When considering international selling, one of the first things to know is that eBay offers a range of services designed to help sellers reach buyers from different countries without the usual barriers. eBay's Global Shipping Program (GSP) and the international selling tools within the platform enable sellers to list and ship items to buyers across the globe, with as little complexity as possible. These services can make a significant difference in how you manage international sales, allowing you to tap into a vast network of buyers with minimal extra effort.

The Global Shipping Program is one of the most useful tools for sellers looking to reach international buyers. This program simplifies the process of selling to buyers outside your country by handling the complexities of international shipping, customs, and import duties. Under the Global Shipping Program, sellers ship their items to a domestic shipping center in their home country, and eBay takes care of the international shipping from there. This service reduces the administrative burden of calculating and handling customs fees, taxes, and the logistics of overseas shipping. As a seller, you don't need to worry about navigating international shipping regulations or customs paperwork—eBay's Global Shipping Program takes care of all of that for you, making the process much easier and less intimidating.

One of the most significant advantages of using the Global Shipping Program is that it provides sellers with a clear understanding of shipping costs and timeframes. eBay will automatically calculate the international shipping costs based on the buyer's location, so there are no surprises. This feature allows you to set your price with confidence, knowing that the buyer will be aware of the full cost of their purchase, including any applicable taxes or duties. Additionally, because eBay manages the shipping and customs process, sellers don't have to worry about unexpected delays or complications, as the entire process is streamlined and transparent.

For sellers who want to be more involved in the logistics of their international sales, eBay also offers an alternative to the Global Shipping Program: selling internationally without using the program. This option allows you to ship directly to buyers in other countries, bypassing eBay's domestic shipping center. While this gives you greater control over the shipping process, it also comes with added responsibility. As a seller, you would be in charge of determining the international shipping costs, handling customs paperwork, and dealing with any issues that arise during transit. For this reason, selling internationally outside of the Global Shipping Program requires more knowledge of international shipping regulations and a deeper understanding of the import/export process.

When it comes to listing your items for international buyers, eBay provides an easy way to reach global customers. eBay's global reach allows you to list your items in a way that makes them visible to buyers from multiple countries. When you create a listing, eBay automatically determines which international markets your product is eligible to be sold in, based on your chosen shipping method. You can choose to list your items in all available markets or select specific countries where you want your products to be visible. This is especially useful for sellers who may want to focus on certain countries or regions where their products are in high demand. Moreover, eBay's international search algorithms help ensure that your items are shown to the right buyers, improving your chances of reaching interested customers worldwide.

The ability to reach international buyers also comes with the benefit of being able to sell in different currencies. eBay offers currency conversion tools that help you easily manage international transactions, allowing you to price your items in the local currency of the buyer's country. By offering multiple currency options, you can attract a wider range of buyers and make your listings more appealing to customers who prefer to shop in their own currency. This feature simplifies the selling process for international buyers, as they can see prices that are specific to their country, reducing any confusion over pricing or conversion rates.

A critical aspect of international selling is understanding the different regulations and restrictions in various countries. Each country has its own rules regarding what can and cannot be sold, as well as specific requirements for shipping and customs. To navigate this, eBay provides detailed information about restrictions for international sales and helps sellers ensure that they comply with the necessary legal guidelines. By familiarizing yourself with the import/export regulations of the countries you plan to sell to, you can avoid unnecessary issues and delays. For example, some products may be restricted or banned in certain countries, and knowing these regulations is crucial to preventing legal problems and ensuring smooth transactions.

Another consideration when selling internationally is language barriers. Although eBay's platform is available in several languages, communication with buyers from different countries can sometimes be challenging. To alleviate this, eBay provides translation tools to help sellers interact with buyers who may speak different languages. These tools enable buyers and sellers to communicate more effectively and prevent misunderstandings that could result in disputes or poor customer experiences. Being proactive in offering clear communication and customer support can go a long way in ensuring that international buyers feel comfortable purchasing from you.

When you begin selling internationally, it's also important to assess the demand for your products in various regions. Different countries and regions may have varying preferences, cultural influences, and market trends that affect the types of products they're most interested in buying. Conducting research on international markets can help you identify areas where your products may perform well. Some sellers may even choose to tailor their inventory or product offerings based on the specific needs of certain markets. For example, some products might be more popular in Europe than in North America, or certain styles might be more fashionable in Asia. By understanding these regional differences, you can make better-informed decisions about where to focus your international selling efforts.

Shipping costs are another consideration when selling internationally. Shipping fees can vary significantly based on the destination country, and these costs may deter buyers from certain regions. To help manage shipping costs, eBay allows sellers to offer calculated shipping, where buyers can see the exact shipping cost based on their location. Additionally, sellers can offer free international shipping, though this can increase the cost of the item. By setting appropriate shipping fees and considering international delivery times, you can help reduce cart abandonment and increase your chances of closing the sale.

Exploring eBay's international selling options is an excellent way to expand your business and reach customers around the world. Whether through the Global Shipping Program, direct international shipping, or listing in multiple currencies, eBay offers a variety of tools and features designed to help sellers succeed in the global marketplace. By understanding the logistics, regulations, and best practices associated with international selling, you can take advantage of eBay's vast network to grow your online business and increase your sales. The key to success in international selling lies in preparation—doing your research, optimizing your listings for global buyers, and offering excellent customer service will help you build a strong international presence and ensure that your eBay business thrives on a global scale.

PART 3

Managing Sales, Shipping, and Customer Service

CHAPTER 7
MANAGING YOUR SALES AND ORDERS EFFECTIVELY

UNDERSTANDING EBAY'S SELLER HUB: YOUR CENTRAL COMMAND CENTER

The eBay Seller Hub is one of the most powerful tools available to online sellers, acting as the central command center for managing, tracking, and optimizing your entire eBay business. As a seller, the Seller Hub provides an intuitive and organized interface that consolidates all of the essential tools and features you need to manage listings, track orders, analyze performance, and enhance your selling strategy. It's designed to simplify the complex tasks of managing an eCommerce business, allowing sellers to focus more on growing their business and less on navigating the logistics of the platform.

When you first log into eBay as a seller, the Seller Hub is your starting point. It serves as the dashboard that provides a bird's-eye view of your eBay business, giving you immediate access to essential data and insights. With its user-friendly layout, you can quickly find the information you need to manage your listings, monitor your sales, and track the progress of your business. It is an all-in-one hub that combines several important features, from listing management to customer service tools, into one cohesive interface.

One of the key benefits of the Seller Hub is its ability to give you a detailed overview of your active listings. You can view your items in real-time, see how they are performing, and easily make any necessary adjustments to improve visibility or increase sales. For example, if you notice that a particular listing isn't performing as expected, the Seller Hub makes it simple to edit the listing, adjust pricing, or add promotional offers to attract more buyers. The ease of making adjustments in real-time allows you to remain agile and responsive to market trends, a crucial aspect of successful selling on eBay.

In addition to managing your listings, the Seller Hub also allows you to monitor your orders. It provides a detailed breakdown of all open orders, showing which items have been sold, which are pending shipment, and which need follow-up action. You can track the status of shipments, manage returns, and handle any disputes or issues with customers—all from within the Seller Hub. The ability to efficiently manage orders in one place ensures that you can maintain a high level of customer service and keep your operations running smoothly.

Tracking your performance is another important aspect of the Seller Hub. eBay provides a wealth of data and analytics that can help you understand how well your business is performing and where you can make improvements. Key performance metrics like total sales, number of items sold, customer feedback, and shipping performance are readily available. Seller Hub's performance analytics are broken down into easy-to-understand charts and graphs, so you don't have to be a data expert to analyze your sales trends. For example, you can view the total number of items sold over a specific time period and compare it to previous months to see if you're on track to meet your sales goals.

One of the most valuable features in the Seller Hub is its access to detailed insights about your buyer behavior. The platform provides you with data on who is visiting your listings, how long they stay, and whether they're engaging with your content. By using these insights, you can tailor your selling approach to better meet the needs and preferences of your target customers. For example, if you notice that a particular product is attracting a lot of views but not many purchases, you might consider tweaking your listing title, description, or photos to make it more appealing.

Seller Hub also provides valuable tools for improving your visibility on eBay. By optimizing your listings with the right keywords and ensuring they are well-structured, you can improve their ranking in search results. The Seller Hub offers guidance on how to improve your listings' SEO, including the use of the right keywords in titles, descriptions, and item specifics. This helps ensure that your products are more easily found by potential buyers, increasing your chances of making a sale. The Seller Hub's analytics also allow you to measure the success of your SEO efforts and adjust accordingly. By regularly reviewing these metrics, you can continually refine your listings for optimal visibility and performance.

For sellers who are looking to increase their sales, the Seller Hub provides options for creating promotional campaigns. Whether you want to offer discounts, run limited-time promotions, or create bundle deals, the platform makes it easy to set up and manage these marketing initiatives. You can even target specific segments of buyers with customized promotions, such as those who have previously viewed certain items or have purchased from you before. These promotions can significantly boost sales, and the Seller Hub makes it simple to track their success, so you can see which types of campaigns work best for your business.

Another important feature of the Seller Hub is its customer service tools. Providing excellent customer service is key to building a successful eBay business, and the Seller Hub offers a variety of tools to help you manage communication with buyers. From handling feedback and managing returns to resolving disputes, all customer service functions can be accessed through the hub. The platform even allows you to respond to customer inquiries quickly and efficiently, helping you maintain a positive reputation on the platform. Timely responses to buyer messages and prompt resolution of any issues are crucial for maintaining high seller ratings, which in turn boosts your credibility and trustworthiness.

Seller Hub also simplifies the process of handling payments and managing your financials. Through the platform, you can view your sales and revenue, track your expenses, and access reports that help you manage your profits. The financial tools within the Seller Hub are designed to help you stay organized and on top of your cash flow, so you can make informed decisions about reinvesting in your business or scaling your operations.

Beyond these core features, the Seller Hub also offers access to eBay's vast educational resources. Whether you're new to selling or looking to refine your strategy, the platform provides access to learning materials that cover topics ranging from listing optimization to shipping best practices. The Hub also provides tips on how to improve your seller rating, which is crucial for gaining buyer trust and increasing sales. By regularly engaging with these resources, you can stay up to date with the latest selling strategies and eBay platform changes.

Another major benefit of using the Seller Hub is the streamlined approach it offers for managing your inventory. Sellers can easily track their stock levels, ensure that items are listed accurately, and keep their inventory up to date. This is especially helpful for those managing a larger volume of products, as it reduces the risk of overselling or running out of stock unexpectedly. Through the Seller Hub, you can make bulk changes to your listings, update pricing, or adjust inventory quantities quickly and efficiently, all from one central location.

The Seller Hub is not just about monitoring your business but also about staying compliant with eBay's rules and guidelines. It helps you keep track of your seller performance, ensures you meet eBay's shipping and return standards, and reminds you of deadlines or potential policy changes. By staying on top of these details, you can avoid penalties or disruptions to your selling account, ensuring that your eBay business remains in good standing.

eBay's Seller Hub is a vital tool for anyone serious about building and managing a successful online business on the platform. From managing listings and orders to tracking performance and engaging with customers, the Seller Hub consolidates everything you need into one central location. By making full use of its features, sellers can not only improve their efficiency but also gain valuable insights that will help them grow their business over time. It's the one-stop shop for managing every aspect of your eBay business and is essential for anyone looking to succeed on the platform. Whether you're a beginner or an experienced seller, mastering the Seller Hub is key to achieving long-term success on eBay.

TRACKING SALES AND MONITORING YOUR INVENTORY

Keeping track of your sales and monitoring inventory is the beating heart of any thriving eBay business. Without a solid grasp of what is selling, what's still on your shelves, and what needs restocking, it's easy to lose control, miss opportunities, or worse—disappoint your customers. Selling on eBay is not just about posting items and hoping for the best; it's a living, evolving process that requires continuous attention to detail. Every transaction, every return, every item that lingers too long in your store without a buyer is data speaking to you, offering insights that, when properly understood, can sharpen your strategy and fuel your growth.

Sales tracking is more than just checking how many items you sold in a week. It's about understanding the patterns—seasonal trends, popular categories, buyer preferences, and even which listings generate more interest than others but don't convert into sales. The ability to spot these patterns is what transforms a casual seller into a strategic one. On eBay, every sale leaves a trail of valuable information: what time the item sold, how long it took to sell, the final sale price, any accepted offers, and the type of listing used. When you begin paying close attention to these variables, you begin to learn what resonates with your audience and what doesn't.

The most effective way to track sales is by using eBay's built-in tools. The Seller Hub offers real-time data that gives you access to your order history, current sales, and performance trends. You can break down your sales over time—daily, weekly, or monthly—and measure them against previous periods to assess growth or identify any concerning dips. These insights are crucial in deciding whether your pricing is competitive, your keywords are strong, or if your product selection needs tweaking. If your average selling price starts to decline while your volume increases, that might indicate it's time to evaluate your margins and reassess your sourcing strategy.

But tracking sales alone isn't enough. You also have to keep your finger on the pulse of your inventory. Without organized inventory management, it's easy to oversell items, disappoint customers with delays, or waste time looking for stock you thought you had. As your eBay store grows, the stakes become higher. Buyers expect fast shipping, accurate listings, and no surprises when they open the package. These expectations require a seller to maintain control over their inventory at all times.

Inventory management begins with knowing what you have, where it is, and what condition it's in. If you're just starting out, this might be as simple as keeping a spreadsheet of your items, stored neatly in labeled bins or shelves. But as your operation grows, manual systems can quickly become a bottleneck. That's when inventory management software becomes essential. Whether you use third-party tools or eBay's own features, the goal is to have real-time insight into your stock levels, SKU tracking, and low-inventory alerts. The faster you know when something is running low, the faster you can restock and keep your sales pipeline flowing without interruption.

The link between sales tracking and inventory monitoring is tight. They feed into each other. If a product starts to sell rapidly, you need to be alerted quickly enough to reorder before it goes out of stock. A pause in availability can lead to missed opportunities, lost revenue, and lower placement in eBay search results. eBay's algorithm favors sellers who maintain consistent inventory levels and fulfill orders quickly, so being proactive is not just about customer satisfaction—it directly affects your visibility on the platform.

Understanding your top sellers is a critical part of this process. Not every item in your store carries the same weight. Some products are steady performers that sell regularly and generate reliable profits. Others might be seasonal or dependent on trends. Then there are those that never quite take off. By consistently reviewing your sales reports, you can separate the winners from the stragglers. With this knowledge, you can prioritize your inventory purchases to focus on high-converting items. You'll also become more strategic with your pricing, promotions, and listing optimization for your best-performing products.

Equally important is your ability to handle returns and relist items efficiently. Every time a product is returned, it needs to be accounted for in your inventory. Is it still in sellable condition? Does it need a new listing, or can it be added back to the original one? These small tasks can become overwhelming if not handled systematically. That's why sellers benefit from building a simple routine around returns—checking the item, updating inventory counts, adjusting the listing if needed, and restocking promptly.

There's also a psychological aspect to tracking your sales and inventory effectively. It gives you clarity. Running an online business can feel chaotic, especially in the early stages when you're wearing all the hats—seller, photographer, marketer, packer, and customer service rep. Having a reliable system to track what's coming in, what's going out, and what needs attention gives you a sense of control. You're not just reacting; you're planning. You're not guessing; you're analyzing.

One often overlooked benefit of consistent tracking is fraud prevention. Knowing exactly what you've sold, when you shipped it, and where it was delivered helps protect you against unfair claims or disputes. If a buyer says they never received an item, your records—complete with tracking numbers and timestamps—can make all the difference. Organized records are not only useful for your daily workflow but also offer protection in situations that require evidence or resolution.

Beyond the operational side, there's the financial reality to consider. Properly tracking your sales helps you stay on top of your revenue and expenses. You'll know how much profit you're making per item after fees, shipping, and sourcing costs. You'll see which items generate repeat business or higher customer satisfaction. You'll also be better prepared when it comes time to file taxes or apply for business financing. An accurate record of sales and inventory is the backbone of responsible financial management.

Staying ahead of your inventory also allows you to capitalize on trends quickly. When you notice a spike in demand for a particular item, being ready with stock on hand gives you the advantage. If you run out while others are still selling, you miss out on a window of opportunity. That's why many successful eBay sellers make it a habit to review inventory data daily or weekly. It becomes part of their rhythm—an essential business check-up that keeps things running smoothly and profitably.

No matter how big or small your operation is, staying organized with your sales and inventory management is non-negotiable. The tools are there. The data is available. The real question is whether you're using it to your advantage. Success on eBay doesn't happen by accident. It happens by understanding the numbers behind your business and acting on them with clarity and intention. The more precisely you track your sales and monitor your inventory, the more agile, efficient, and profitable your business becomes. What begins as a few listings in your spare time can evolve into a full-scale operation—one rooted in smart tracking, smart restocking, and the kind of attention to detail that separates good sellers from great ones.

COMMUNICATING WITH BUYERS PROFESSIONALLY AND PROMPTLY

Communicating with buyers on eBay is not just about exchanging information—it's a cornerstone of building trust, securing sales, and encouraging repeat business. In a marketplace where the seller and buyer often never meet face-to-face, your written words become your handshake, your tone becomes your smile, and your responsiveness becomes your integrity. The impression you leave through your messages can directly influence a buyer's decision to purchase from you, leave a positive review, or even recommend your store to others.

Professional and prompt communication starts the moment a buyer sends a question about an item. Whether they're asking for more details, requesting additional photos, or clarifying shipping options, how quickly and respectfully you respond often sets the tone for the entire transaction. Many buyers will message multiple sellers with the same inquiry and choose to buy from the one who responds first or with the most clarity. Delayed or vague replies risk making a buyer feel ignored, unimportant, or uncertain—none of which inspire confidence.

A key part of professionalism is understanding that every interaction with a buyer, no matter how small, should be approached with courtesy and patience. Even when faced with repetitive questions or messages that seem rushed or overly demanding, your tone should remain calm and constructive. Think of every buyer as someone evaluating not just your product but your overall reliability. Avoid slang, unnecessary abbreviations, or overly casual responses, especially with new buyers. A clear, friendly tone—paired with direct answers—reassures the buyer that you are knowledgeable, reliable, and focused on customer satisfaction.

Spelling and grammar might seem like small matters, but they have a significant psychological impact. Well-written messages convey a sense of professionalism and attention to detail. If you were buying from a store and the staff handed you a brochure filled with typos, it might make you second-guess the credibility of the business. The same applies here. Clean, polished writing subtly reinforces that the buyer is in good hands.

Timeliness is another critical component. In the world of e-commerce, where buyers can click and buy within seconds, expectations around speed are high. If a buyer sends a question or makes an offer and doesn't hear back within a reasonable timeframe—usually within 24 hours or less—they may move on. Many successful sellers make it a habit to check their eBay messages multiple times throughout the day, treating it with the same priority as checking sales. The faster you respond, the more likely you are to capture interest before it fades.

Once a sale is made, communication doesn't stop—it simply shifts in purpose. After purchase, buyers appreciate confirmation that their order has been received, processed, and shipped. While eBay's automated systems send out basic notifications, a personalized message from you goes a long way. A quick thank-you note sent after the sale, a short message confirming the item is on its way, or a heads-up if there's a delay in shipping helps reinforce the buyer's confidence and shows that you care about the full experience, not just the transaction.

In situations where problems arise—such as delays, inventory errors, or returns—your communication style can either defuse tension or make matters worse. If an item arrives damaged or the buyer is unhappy with it, a defensive or dismissive response can escalate the issue. On the other hand, an empathetic, solution-focused message often transforms a dissatisfied customer into a loyal one. Apologizing sincerely when things go wrong, offering options, and explaining how you plan to resolve the issue turns a potential negative into a chance to earn trust.

Handling returns and refunds, in particular, is a sensitive area that requires clear and kind communication. Whether or not the return is your fault, it helps to approach the situation with a mindset of resolution rather than resistance. Buyers want to feel heard, not blamed. A professional tone, coupled with a willingness to listen, often diffuses frustration before it has a chance to grow into a formal complaint or a negative review.

It's also important to manage buyer expectations early on. Detailed item descriptions, accurate shipping timeframes, and up-to-date tracking information help prevent misunderstandings. Still, when a buyer reaches out for clarification, your response can reinforce their expectations or realign them as needed. For example, if there's a shipping delay due to weather or courier issues, informing the buyer promptly and providing updates—even if you're not at fault—can prevent impatience from turning into anger.

Another often underestimated skill is knowing when to stop communicating. While staying engaged is important, over-communication or pushing for feedback or follow-up sales too aggressively can turn a positive experience into a pressured one. Let your tone be confident but not clingy. Once the transaction is complete and you've thanked the buyer or addressed their concerns, allow the relationship to breathe. Trust that the quality of your service will inspire them to return or leave positive feedback.

Dealing with difficult buyers can test your patience, but remaining professional under pressure is a mark of a seasoned seller. When faced with unreasonable demands, rude comments, or persistent complaints, the best approach is to remain factual, courteous, and calm. Never engage emotionally or retaliate in kind. Remember, your responses are visible to eBay in the case of disputes, and maintaining professionalism helps protect your standing.

Templates can be useful for maintaining consistency, especially for common scenarios like confirming orders or responding to frequently asked questions. However, avoid using canned responses that feel robotic or cold. Buyers can usually tell when they're getting a copy-paste message. Personalizing even a short line in your template—like mentioning the buyer's name or referencing the specific item—can make a big difference in how the message is received.

Lastly, communication is not just about resolving issues or answering questions. It's also about building relationships. A brief message that expresses appreciation or encourages the buyer to return in the future can plant the seed for repeat business. Some sellers even include handwritten thank-you notes in their packages or offer small gestures like coupons for future purchases. These thoughtful touches speak volumes and are often mentioned in glowing reviews.

Ultimately, every message you send is a reflection of your brand, your values, and your commitment to excellence. Whether you're explaining product features, resolving a return, or thanking a buyer for their purchase, your words carry weight. They influence whether a buyer trusts you, recommends you, and chooses to buy from you again. In a marketplace built on reputation and feedback, strong communication isn't just a skill—it's a competitive advantage. Mastering it gives you a powerful edge that technology alone can't replace.

HANDLING PAYMENTS AND UNDERSTANDING EBAY'S PAYMENT PROCESSES

Getting paid on eBay is one of the most crucial parts of the selling experience, and understanding how the platform handles payments is essential for managing your business smoothly. The process has evolved significantly in recent years. What was once a decentralized system involving third-party services is now a more integrated and streamlined operation managed entirely by eBay. This shift means sellers can operate with fewer moving parts, but it also requires a solid understanding of how the money moves, how fees are applied, and what you can expect during the payment lifecycle.

eBay now manages all payments directly through a unified system. This transition means buyers can pay using a wide range of methods—including credit and debit cards, Apple Pay, Google Pay, PayPal, and even bank transfers in some regions—while sellers receive their funds directly into their bank accounts. You no longer need to manage or link a PayPal account separately, which simplifies bookkeeping and customer service issues. However, the simplicity of the new system doesn't mean it's hands-off. On the contrary, you need to be aware of how payouts are scheduled, how long they take, and how to read your financial reports to keep your business on track.

Once a buyer completes a purchase and submits payment, eBay begins the process of verifying and securing those funds. This process generally takes a short time, and you're notified when the payment is confirmed and it's time to ship. It's critical that you wait for this confirmation before dispatching the item. Shipping before payment is cleared introduces unnecessary risk, as the funds may be held, delayed, or rejected due to fraud detection measures. Only once eBay verifies that the payment has been successfully processed should you move forward with fulfilling the order.

One key factor to understand is how eBay handles your funds. Rather than transferring the buyer's money to you immediately upon sale, eBay typically deposits your earnings into your linked bank account according to a set payout schedule. You can choose a daily, weekly, or biweekly schedule, depending on what suits your cash flow needs. Daily payouts mean funds are sent each business day, but this doesn't mean instant access. Banks often take an additional one to three business days to process deposits, so the full cycle from sale to usable cash can vary.

It's important to build a buffer in your financial planning to accommodate these timelines. If your business depends on reinvesting sales revenue into purchasing inventory or supplies, understanding these delays is essential for maintaining smooth operations. Planning ahead allows you to avoid situations where you're waiting for payments to land before you can fulfill another order or restock popular items.

eBay deducts selling fees and other associated charges before your payout is issued. These deductions include the final value fee, which is a percentage of the sale price including shipping and taxes, as well as any listing upgrades, promotional fees, or international transaction charges. Since these costs are removed before funds are deposited, your net payout may be lower than the actual sale amount. Regularly reviewing your transaction reports ensures that you're not surprised by these deductions and allows you to price your products accurately to maintain healthy profit margins.

Another element to be aware of is how eBay handles refunds and chargebacks. If a buyer opens a return request and you accept it, or if a chargeback is filed through the buyer's payment provider, eBay may place a temporary hold on those funds. If a refund is issued, eBay typically deducts it directly from your pending or next available payout. In the case of a chargeback, eBay may reach out to you for supporting documentation, and depending on the outcome, the amount may be reversed or refunded to the buyer.

Managing disputes effectively and maintaining transparency in your listings helps reduce the risk of chargebacks. Clear communication, accurate descriptions, and prompt handling of issues build a strong seller reputation and offer protection in case of financial disputes. eBay does offer a Seller Protection program, which can cover you in cases where a buyer falsely claims an item wasn't delivered or returns an item in worse condition than it was sent. However, this protection is contingent on meeting certain standards—such as providing tracking information, shipping promptly, and maintaining strong feedback ratings.

Understanding your financial dashboard within eBay's Seller Hub is another important part of handling payments effectively. This dashboard provides a detailed breakdown of your sales, fees, pending payouts, and expected deposits. Regularly reviewing these insights not only gives you a clear picture of your business's performance but also helps in making strategic decisions about pricing, inventory management, and investment in promotional tools.

It's also worth considering the tax implications of your eBay income. eBay is required to report your earnings to the IRS once they exceed certain thresholds, and you'll receive a 1099-K form for tax reporting purposes. It's your responsibility to maintain accurate records of your expenses, deductions, and net income so you can file your taxes properly. Many sellers choose to use accounting software or consult with a professional to ensure their records are thorough and compliant. Ignoring tax obligations can lead to serious issues down the line, especially as eBay continues to expand its regulatory oversight.

One potential pain point for new sellers is the possibility of initial payment holds. eBay may temporarily hold funds from your early sales as part of its seller performance monitoring. This practice is common for new accounts and usually lifts once you've established a history of successful transactions and satisfied buyers. These holds are not punitive but are designed to ensure that you're shipping items and buyers are receiving what they ordered. During this period, funds may be released a few days after the item is marked as delivered. The better your performance and the more reliable your service, the faster this restriction disappears.

Another factor that can affect your payouts is disputes regarding item not received or item not as described. If these cases arise and are decided in the buyer's favor, the transaction amount may be deducted from your upcoming payouts. Staying ahead of this by providing excellent customer service, offering accurate product details, and using tracked shipping methods goes a long way in avoiding these complications.

As your sales volume grows, you may consider integrating accounting and inventory management tools that synchronize with eBay's payment system. These tools can offer detailed insights into cash flow, profit margins, and tax obligations, allowing you to scale your business with greater control. While these services come with a cost, the investment often pays for itself in saved time, reduced errors, and better financial forecasting.

Navigating eBay's payment ecosystem is not just about getting paid—it's about understanding how the money flows, where it goes, and how to manage it wisely. The more knowledgeable you are about fees, timelines, and policies, the better equipped you'll be to build a resilient and profitable operation. Payment is the final step in a successful sale, but it's also the starting point for the next one. With the right systems in place, each transaction can fuel your momentum, supporting steady growth and a business that is built to last.

The Complete Guide to Selling on eBay for Beginners 2025

DEALING WITH CANCELLATIONS AND RETURNS

Cancellations and returns are a natural part of the e-commerce ecosystem, and while they can be inconvenient, how you manage them often determines whether your business thrives or stalls. Navigating these situations with professionalism, empathy, and a clear understanding of platform policies is crucial. Selling online isn't just about closing sales; it's about sustaining relationships and trust—two things that are often tested during returns and cancellations.

When a buyer requests to cancel an order, the first step is not to take it personally. Buyer behavior varies widely, and sometimes customers change their minds. They may have ordered the wrong item, found a better deal, or misunderstood the product listing. In most cases, if the order hasn't been shipped yet, it's best to approve the cancellation request quickly. Prompt action avoids unnecessary complications, like shipping something the customer no longer wants, which could result in a more expensive return later.

That said, it's important to ensure your listings are clear and accurate to reduce the frequency of cancellations due to confusion or mistaken expectations. Carefully written descriptions, quality photos, and correct specifications help buyers make informed decisions. Inaccurate or vague listings often lead to regretful purchases, and regret is a prime driver of cancellations. Prevention starts before the order is even placed, through transparency and detail.

Once an order has been shipped, cancellations become more complex. If a buyer contacts you after the package is in transit, the only real option is for them to return the item once it arrives. In such cases, it's important to communicate clearly and politely. Let the buyer know the package has been shipped and explain how the return process works, including whether they will be responsible for return shipping costs. Most customers will appreciate honesty and a straightforward approach.

Returns, on the other hand, require a more structured system. Every seller should have a return policy that's fair, easy to follow, and clearly stated in each listing. eBay allows sellers to set their own return terms—whether you accept returns at all, within how many days, and under what conditions. While offering returns might seem like an invitation for hassle, it often has the opposite effect. Buyers feel safer purchasing from sellers who offer returns, and your listings may even rank higher in search results. A strong return policy can increase conversion rates, attract more serious buyers, and improve your seller rating.

There are different types of return scenarios you may face, and each needs to be handled appropriately. A "buyer's remorse" return—where the buyer simply changes their mind—should be treated with understanding. Even if it's frustrating, allowing the return graciously and quickly issuing a refund helps protect your reputation. On the other hand, a "not as described" return can be a bit more involved. These typically occur when a buyer believes the item they received doesn't match the listing. This can be due to a variety of factors, such as an incorrect size, a missing feature, or damage not disclosed in the photos or description.

If the item was accurately described and the buyer made a mistake, you may be able to dispute the claim, especially if you have clear evidence. But in many cases, especially early on, it may be better to accept the return, refund the money, and learn from the experience. Each return, even the tough ones, is an opportunity to evaluate your listings and improve the accuracy and quality of your communication.

In cases where the item arrives damaged, the first question to ask yourself is whether the damage happened during shipping or if the item was defective before it left your hands. If it was a packaging issue, consider upgrading your materials—bubble wrap, stronger boxes, or additional padding. A small investment in better shipping materials often pays for itself many times over by reducing return rates due to damage.

Another return scenario involves counterfeit or fraudulent claims. Though rare, some buyers attempt to exploit return policies by sending back the wrong item or something entirely different from what they received. To protect yourself, always take clear, time-stamped photos of the item before shipping it—especially for high-value goods. This documentation can be crucial in proving your case if a dispute arises. Additionally, use tracked shipping with delivery confirmation whenever possible, and retain receipts or invoices in case eBay requests proof of shipment.

Once a return is initiated, the process typically involves the buyer printing a return shipping label—often provided through eBay—and sending the item back. When you receive the returned item, inspect it carefully to confirm it's in the same condition as when it was sold. If it is, promptly issue a refund to close the transaction on good terms. Delaying refunds after receiving returned items can lead to negative feedback, reduced seller ratings, and even account restrictions.

From a business management perspective, keeping track of returns helps identify patterns that may indicate systemic issues. Are certain items being returned more frequently than others? Are there common complaints across different buyers? Use returns as data points. They provide real-time feedback on what may need fixing in your listings, product sourcing, or fulfillment process.

You also need to factor returns and cancellations into your financial planning. They represent not just lost revenue but also sunk costs in shipping, packaging, and potentially restocking. Maintaining a reserve fund to account for these losses is a smart move. It helps you weather unexpected return spikes without straining your cash flow. Some sellers also implement a restocking fee, though this should be used sparingly and transparently to avoid alienating customers.

Customer service is key in how returns and cancellations affect your long-term success. Buyers who feel heard and respected—even when things don't go perfectly—are more likely to leave positive feedback, come back for future purchases, and recommend your shop to others. A courteous tone, prompt replies, and a willingness to resolve issues can turn a disappointing transaction into a memorable one.

There's also a psychological component to consider. Dealing with returns and cancellations can be disheartening, especially when you're just starting out and every sale feels significant. But keeping a level head, staying solution-focused, and treating each case as part of the business process helps preserve your motivation. These bumps are not failures; they're proof that you're operating in a real marketplace, with real people and real variability. Over time, you'll develop a rhythm and confidence that makes handling returns just another part of your daily routine.

Ultimately, how you handle cancellations and returns defines your reputation as a seller. Buyers talk. They leave reviews, they rate experiences, and their voices contribute to the long-term health of your store. Excellence in handling difficult interactions is often what separates casual sellers from successful business operators. Be generous when you can, firm when you must, and always grounded in the knowledge that great customer service isn't just about pleasing the customer—it's about building a foundation of trust, reliability, and long-term growth.

CHAPTER 8
STREAMLINING YOUR SHIPPING PROCESS FOR SUCCESS

UNDERSTANDING EBAY'S SHIPPING OPTIONS AND POLICIES

Shipping is one of the most crucial elements of running an eBay business. It connects the dots between a successful sale and a satisfied customer. Getting it right means delivering not just a package, but a positive experience. Understanding the range of shipping options available, the expectations eBay has for sellers, and how to set your shipping policies strategically can significantly impact your efficiency, profitability, and buyer satisfaction.

At the most fundamental level, shipping on eBay involves choosing how your items will get from you to your buyer. eBay offers a wide array of carrier integrations and shipping services, and it's up to you to determine which ones work best based on what you're selling, where you're located, and who your buyers are. The platform supports a mix of domestic and international shipping providers, with the most common options in the United States including USPS, UPS, FedEx, and DHL. Each carrier offers different rates, delivery speeds, and service tiers—from economy to express—and you can tailor your shipping approach for each listing.

One of the first decisions you'll need to make is whether to offer free shipping or charge the buyer. Offering free shipping can be a strategic move. It simplifies the buying decision for customers, especially those who compare prices across listings. Many buyers gravitate toward listings that include shipping in the item price, even if the total cost is similar to one where shipping is listed separately. Free shipping can also improve your visibility in eBay's search results, as the algorithm often favors listings with this feature. However, the cost isn't really "free"—you'll need to factor it into your pricing strategy carefully to ensure you're not cutting into your profit margins.

On the other hand, charging for shipping gives you more flexibility. You can itemize the cost and adjust it depending on the buyer's location or the shipping method they choose. This approach can be useful when dealing with large, heavy, or fragile items that require extra packaging or incur higher shipping fees. Many sellers use calculated shipping for this purpose, which determines the exact cost based on the buyer's ZIP code, the weight and dimensions of the package, and the selected shipping service. eBay's built-in shipping calculator automates this process, ensuring buyers see accurate costs at checkout.

Another key concept to grasp is handling time—the amount of time between when a buyer pays for an item and when you ship it. eBay allows sellers to set their own handling times, typically within one business day to several days, depending on your capacity. Fast handling times can improve your seller rating and customer satisfaction, and they often contribute to better visibility in search rankings. Buyers appreciate quick shipping, and eBay's standards are increasingly aligned with the expectations set by other major e-commerce platforms. Consistently meeting your handling time commitments shows reliability and helps build buyer trust.

When you're preparing your shipping options, you'll also encounter the decision between flat-rate and calculated-rate shipping. Flat-rate shipping charges the same amount to every buyer, regardless of where they're located. It's a simple and predictable method, ideal for sellers who ship similar items regularly and want to streamline their listings. Calculated-rate shipping, by contrast, varies based on the distance between you and the buyer, which can help prevent overcharging or undercharging on postage. For sellers with variable inventory or buyers in diverse locations, calculated shipping often provides a more accurate reflection of true shipping costs.

Insurance is another consideration that can protect your business, especially when shipping valuable or fragile items. Most major carriers offer optional insurance coverage, and eBay also offers its own shipping insurance through partnerships. If an item gets lost or damaged during transit, insurance can help you recover the cost and avoid absorbing the loss. Buyers expect to receive their orders intact and on time, so preparing for rare but inevitable issues like postal mishaps is part of a responsible shipping policy.

Tracking is another pillar of modern e-commerce logistics. Providing tracking information on all shipments, whether required or not, is one of the best ways to reassure buyers that their order is on the way. eBay allows you to upload tracking numbers, and in many cases, this is done automatically when you purchase labels through eBay's shipping interface. Tracking helps prevent disputes, reduces the number of "where is my item" messages, and gives both parties visibility over the delivery timeline. It also plays a role in eBay's performance metrics and seller standards, contributing to your eligibility for benefits like Top Rated Seller status.

eBay also allows you to offer expedited shipping options for buyers who are in a hurry. While many buyers are happy to wait for standard delivery, others are willing to pay extra to receive their items sooner. By offering choices like priority or overnight shipping, you can cater to a wider audience and potentially increase your conversion rates. Just be sure to clearly communicate your options, prices, and expected delivery windows in each listing.

Shipping internationally opens your store to a global customer base. eBay supports international shipping through several programs, including the eBay International Shipping (EIS) service. This program simplifies the international selling process by allowing you to ship your package to a domestic shipping center, where eBay then handles the customs paperwork and final delivery abroad. This relieves sellers of the most complicated parts of international logistics, including calculating duties or navigating country-specific shipping regulations. You can also choose to handle international shipping directly, allowing you more control over the carriers and methods used, though this requires a solid understanding of customs procedures and regional policies.

Return shipping is another layer of your overall shipping policy. Whether you offer free returns or ask the buyer to pay for return shipping, it's essential to have a clear return shipping process outlined. Free returns may increase the likelihood of a sale, particularly in competitive categories, but they also increase your risk of absorbing two-way shipping costs. Consider this when deciding whether to include a prepaid return label in your shipments or issue one only upon request.

Label printing is another operational task you can streamline by using eBay's integrated tools. Through eBay's shipping center, you can purchase postage, print labels, and automatically upload tracking numbers all from your seller dashboard. This integration saves time, ensures accuracy, and often gives you access to discounted commercial rates that are more competitive than retail pricing at the post office. Investing in a thermal label printer can further speed up your shipping workflow, reducing manual effort and helping you process orders faster, especially during busy sales periods.

Packaging is part of your shipping ecosystem, and it deserves careful attention. Beyond protecting the product, your packaging influences how your brand is perceived. A well-packaged item tells the buyer you care about their purchase. Use appropriately sized boxes, adequate padding, and durable materials to ensure safe transit. Reused materials are acceptable, but make sure they're clean and sturdy. Tamper-evident tape, thank-you notes, or branded stickers can all enhance the customer experience and make your store more memorable.

Your shipping performance directly affects your seller rating and eligibility for eBay's various perks. Late shipments, lost packages, or delivery disputes can all lead to negative feedback and lower seller metrics. By mastering the logistics side of your business, you protect your reputation, improve buyer satisfaction, and position your store for long-term growth.

Shipping is more than just moving goods from point A to point B. It's a service experience that buyers remember and a logistical challenge that sellers must manage with precision. By fully understanding eBay's shipping options, policies, and best practices, you transform shipping from a backend task into a competitive advantage that sets your store apart.

CALCULATING SHIPPING COSTS ACCURATELY

Accurately calculating shipping costs is one of the most critical elements of managing a successful online business. It not only protects your profits but also ensures that buyers receive fair, transparent pricing, which in turn builds trust and encourages repeat purchases. Misjudging shipping charges can easily turn a profitable sale into a financial loss. Either you overcharge and deter customers, or you undercharge and end up absorbing unexpected fees. Finding the right balance requires a thorough understanding of the variables involved in shipping, as well as the tools and strategies that make the process more predictable and efficient.

Shipping costs are not a one-size-fits-all equation. They are determined by a complex interplay of factors including the package's weight, dimensions, destination, carrier selection, delivery speed, packaging material, and even optional services like tracking and insurance. Understanding how each of these elements affects the final cost is the key to building a sustainable pricing and logistics model.

The starting point in calculating shipping costs is the actual weight of your item, including its packaging. Most shipping carriers price packages based on either the actual weight or the dimensional weight—whichever is greater. Actual weight is straightforward: it's what the package physically weighs on a scale. Dimensional weight, on the other hand, considers the size of the package and the amount of space it occupies in a delivery vehicle. To calculate dimensional weight, you typically multiply the length, width, and height of the package, then divide the result by a factor set by the carrier, often 139 for domestic shipments using inches. This method prevents shippers from using large, lightweight boxes that take up space without adding much weight.

Once the weight and dimensions are known, the next variable is destination. Shipping rates are highly dependent on the distance between your shipping location and the buyer's address. Carriers often divide the country into zones, with rates increasing as the package moves farther from its origin. For example, shipping a package from New York to Boston is less expensive than shipping the same package to Los Angeles. When selling to international buyers, costs increase even more due to customs, duties, and longer transit times. You'll also need to consider whether you'll be responsible for those additional fees or if the buyer will pay them upon delivery.

Carrier selection is another major cost factor. Different shipping providers offer a range of service levels, from economy ground services that take several days, to premium options like overnight or two-day delivery. USPS is often the most affordable for small packages, while FedEx and UPS are preferred for larger or heavier items. Each carrier has its own pricing structure, surcharges, and service guarantees, so it's important to compare them regularly. Many sellers create accounts with multiple carriers to access discounted rates and choose the most cost-effective option on a per-order basis.

Packaging materials should never be overlooked in your cost calculations. The type and quantity of packaging you use adds to the total expense of shipping. Boxes, bubble wrap, tape, void fill, labels, and even ink for your printer are part of the total shipping cost. While it might seem small, it adds up quickly, especially when you're fulfilling a large number of orders. Using free packaging materials from carriers like USPS can help reduce expenses, but you must ensure they match the services you're using. Misusing a branded Priority Mail box for a First-Class shipment can lead to penalties or returned packages.

The choice between offering flat-rate or calculated shipping plays a strategic role in how you present shipping costs to buyers. Flat-rate shipping allows you to charge a consistent amount regardless of where the buyer is located. This simplifies the listing and removes any guesswork for buyers, but it only works well if you have a clear understanding of your average shipping costs across regions. Calculated shipping, by contrast, uses real-time data to determine the shipping fee based on the buyer's location. This method ensures accuracy and fairness but can introduce variability that might surprise buyers if the price jumps at checkout. Using calculated shipping is often a safer option for new sellers who are still learning the cost dynamics of different destinations.

To make calculated shipping effective, you must enter accurate package weights and dimensions when creating your listing. Guessing or rounding too generously can lead to errors and underestimations. A digital postal scale and a measuring tape are essential tools in your seller toolkit. Consistently weighing and measuring items before they are listed—not after they sell—prevents last-minute surprises and ensures your listings reflect real costs.

eBay offers a shipping calculator that helps sellers determine the most accurate shipping prices for their listings. This tool allows you to input package details and see the cost of shipping using various carriers and services. It also integrates directly with the listing process, ensuring that buyers receive real-time estimates based on their location. Using this calculator regularly, especially when listing new items or adjusting prices, keeps your shipping strategies aligned with your actual costs.

Another tactic to keep shipping costs in check is to pre-package items. If you routinely sell the same type of product—such as phone accessories or collectibles—you can pre-weigh and measure your packages in advance, allowing you to confidently input the correct shipping data when creating your listings. This also speeds up order fulfillment, which is a bonus for your workflow and helps meet eBay's handling time expectations.

Offering multiple shipping options on each listing can also work in your favor. Some buyers will prioritize cost, selecting the cheapest option available, while others may be willing to pay extra for expedited delivery. By giving your customers the freedom to choose, you increase the chances of meeting their individual expectations and reducing cart abandonment. It's also a way to upsell faster delivery without forcing it on everyone.

Free shipping is a tempting promotional tool, and many sellers use it to gain a competitive edge. However, the shipping cost still needs to be covered somewhere, usually within the item price. This means you must have a strong handle on your average shipping expenses and bake that into your pricing without losing profitability. It also requires a clear understanding of your margins—how much profit you make on each sale after all costs, including shipping, are factored in.

Shipping discounts are another powerful tool available to sellers who purchase labels through eBay. eBay's negotiated rates with USPS, FedEx, and UPS often come with discounts that are better than retail prices. Buying and printing your labels through eBay not only saves money but also ensures that tracking information is automatically uploaded to your order, reducing the chance of disputes or late shipment claims. Taking full advantage of these savings requires regular use of the platform's shipping tools and an awareness of the best service for each package.

Beyond these practical concerns, accurate shipping cost calculation also supports long-term business growth. As your order volume increases, small miscalculations can scale into substantial losses. By tracking your actual shipping spend against what you charge customers, you can continually refine your pricing strategies and identify areas where you can improve efficiency. Keeping records of your shipping activity—such as postage spend, packaging costs, and delivery time performance—gives you the insight to make better decisions over time.

Shipping is often the last touchpoint between you and your customer, but it has the power to shape their entire buying experience. A well-calculated, transparent shipping cost shows professionalism and care. It reassures buyers that there will be no surprises, no hidden fees, and no excuses. It also enables you to operate your business with confidence, knowing that every package you send is contributing positively to your bottom line, not eroding it.

Shipping costs may seem like a minor technical detail in the broader world of online selling, but in reality, they are a financial and logistical cornerstone. Mastering this area allows you to sell with clarity, speed, and precision—and gives your customers every reason to buy from you again.

CHOOSING THE RIGHT PACKAGING MATERIALS

Packaging is far more than a routine task in the selling process—it's a pivotal aspect of your customer's experience and a crucial element that protects your reputation as a seller. Choosing the right packaging materials is not merely about aesthetics or keeping costs down; it's about delivering your product safely, securely, and professionally while maximizing efficiency and minimizing risk. Whether you're shipping vintage collectibles, clothing, electronics, or delicate ceramics, the materials you use reflect the seriousness of your business and can either solidify customer trust or invite costly returns and negative feedback.

At the core of smart packaging lies the goal of protection. Once an item leaves your hands, it's vulnerable to an unpredictable journey—bumps, drops, stacking, moisture, and temperature fluctuations are all real threats. Choosing the correct packaging material is your first and most effective defense. The type of product you're shipping determines what you'll need. Fragile items like glassware or electronics demand cushioned layers, strong outer boxes, and careful internal support to prevent jostling. In contrast, apparel or soft goods might only require poly mailers or padded envelopes to arrive in perfect condition. The right material selection reduces the likelihood of returns due to damage and increases customer satisfaction upon unboxing.

Cardboard boxes remain the most universally used shipping container, and for good reason. They are sturdy, stackable, widely available, and recyclable. However, not all cardboard boxes are created equal. Single-wall boxes are suitable for lightweight, less fragile items, while double-wall or even triple-wall corrugated boxes are recommended for heavier or more delicate shipments. Sizing also matters—a box that's too large can allow the item to shift inside, while one that's too tight may burst under pressure. Ideally, the box should be slightly larger than the item, allowing room for cushioning materials but not excessive empty space that invites movement.

Padded envelopes and poly mailers are excellent choices for lightweight, non-fragile items. Padded envelopes, with their built-in bubble lining, offer light protection while keeping shipping weight and costs down. These are especially useful for books, DVDs, small accessories, or clothing items. Poly mailers, especially the high-strength tear-resistant types, offer water-resistant protection and are ideal for apparel, fabrics, or any product that won't suffer from slight compression. Many of these mailers are now available in eco-friendly or recyclable versions, which appeal to environmentally conscious consumers.

Protective inner packaging is just as important as the exterior. Bubble wrap is a go-to choice for cushioning delicate items. It creates a barrier against shocks and vibrations, making it perfect for fragile goods. When wrapping, it's important to ensure full coverage, including corners and edges, which are most susceptible to impact. Wrapping in multiple layers and securing with tape prevents the bubble wrap from slipping during transit. Foam inserts, air pillows, or molded pulp trays are other options that offer high levels of protection for specific products, especially electronics or items with intricate shapes.

Packing paper and kraft paper are ideal for filling voids inside a box. These prevent items from shifting and add a layer of shock absorption. Compared to materials like packing peanuts, paper is easier for customers to dispose of and often more eco-friendly. However, if you do choose to use packing peanuts, opt for biodegradable versions, which are better received by buyers and help reduce your environmental footprint. Regardless of the filler you use, the key is to ensure that the item doesn't move inside the package when you gently shake it—movement equals risk.

Tape might seem like a minor detail, but it plays a vital role in package integrity. High-quality shipping tape is designed to stick securely to cardboard and withstand the rigors of transportation. Standard office tape or masking tape is insufficient and often peels away under stress, especially when exposed to temperature or humidity changes. Reinforced water-activated tape offers even more security for heavier packages, creating a tamper-evident seal that signals professionalism. Always use enough tape to seal all edges and seams, especially the bottom of the box, which bears the full weight of the contents.

Labels are another packaging component that deserves careful attention. A clear, legible shipping label not only ensures the package reaches its destination but also reflects well on your operation. Thermal labels are preferred by many professional sellers because they don't smudge, don't require ink, and produce a crisp, professional appearance. Make sure the label is firmly adhered to a flat surface and not placed over box seams or curves. Covering the label with clear packing tape can help protect it from rain or abrasion, although it should not obscure any barcode, which must remain scannable throughout its journey.

Branding through packaging is an advanced strategy that adds polish to your business. While it's not essential for beginners, using custom-branded packaging—such as boxes with your logo, thank-you cards, or tissue paper—can enhance the unboxing experience and encourage repeat business. Just as important as aesthetics, however, is maintaining cost control. Custom packaging should be introduced gradually, once you have a clear understanding of your profit margins and customer base.

Sustainability is becoming an increasing concern among online shoppers, and your packaging choices can make a statement about your brand's values. Opting for recyclable, compostable, or biodegradable materials shows that you're conscious of environmental impact. Some sellers even encourage customers to reuse or recycle packaging, and this gesture can enhance goodwill and customer loyalty. Sourcing packaging materials from suppliers that prioritize sustainability not only benefits the planet but can also attract a niche of eco-conscious buyers.

When sourcing packaging materials, it's important to compare prices across multiple suppliers. Buying in bulk often yields discounts that reduce your per-package cost. Online marketplaces, office supply stores, and even local wholesalers offer deals on boxes, mailers, and tape. Many sellers also take advantage of free packaging provided by shipping carriers, such as USPS Priority Mail boxes. These materials can only be used with specific services, but they are a cost-effective and convenient solution for certain types of shipments.

Staying organized with your packaging supplies is another aspect of operating efficiently. Designating a dedicated packing station stocked with all necessary materials—boxes, mailers, wrap, tape, scissors, labels, and a scale—saves time and ensures consistency. It also allows for faster order fulfillment and fewer errors. Running out of a key supply mid-shipment can cause delays and affect your seller performance metrics, so maintaining inventory of your materials should be part of your routine.

Testing your packaging is a smart habit, especially when introducing new materials or shipping new product types. You can do this by packing a sample, shaking the box to check for movement, and even doing a light drop test from a few feet to simulate the shipping process. If the item survives intact and the packaging remains secure, you've likely made solid choices. If not, adjust your materials and methods accordingly.

Packaging is more than a functional step—it's a strategic component of your entire operation. It determines the first physical impression a customer receives and plays a direct role in whether the transaction ends in satisfaction or frustration. Selecting the right materials doesn't require guesswork when you understand your product, your shipping methods, and your customers' expectations. With careful planning, appropriate investment, and ongoing adjustments, your packaging can support growth, increase positive reviews, and set the stage for a scalable, professional online business.

PRINTING SHIPPING LABELS THROUGH EBAY AND OTHER SERVICES

Printing shipping labels efficiently and correctly is one of the most essential behind-the-scenes processes in running a successful eBay store. It might not seem like the most glamorous part of online selling, but it is deeply tied to how smoothly your orders are fulfilled, how quickly buyers receive their items, and ultimately how satisfied they are with the overall shopping experience. A delayed or incorrect label can lead to shipping errors, returns, added expenses, and frustrated customers. On the other hand, a professional label, generated promptly and accurately, keeps your operation running like a well-oiled machine.

One of the most convenient features eBay offers sellers is its integrated shipping label system. As soon as a buyer completes a transaction, you have the option to print a shipping label directly from the platform. This process not only saves time but also helps you access discounted postage rates, track shipments seamlessly, and manage everything in one centralized dashboard. eBay's shipping label tool integrates with several major carriers, including USPS, UPS, and FedEx, allowing you to compare prices and delivery speeds in real-time. That means you don't have to jump from one website to another to figure out which carrier gives you the best deal for that particular package.

Using eBay's built-in label printing tool begins by accessing the "Sold" section under your Seller Hub or My eBay page. There, you'll see all completed orders that are awaiting shipment. By clicking "Print shipping label" next to the order, you're directed to a page where you enter package dimensions, weight, and service preferences. The accuracy of the information you input at this stage is crucial. An incorrectly weighed or measured package can lead to underpaid postage, which may result in the carrier returning the package or even charging you a fee after delivery.

The best way to ensure accuracy is by using a digital postage scale. These scales are relatively inexpensive and provide precise weight readings, which are essential when dealing with rate-based shipping charges. Likewise, a simple measuring tape helps you capture the exact dimensions of the package. Round up measurements slightly to avoid disputes with carriers that rely on dimensional weight pricing. Once you've input the details, eBay's system automatically calculates the cost based on your chosen carrier and shipping speed. You can preview different service levels—such as Priority Mail, First Class, or Ground Advantage—to determine what works best for your budget and timeframe.

Another advantage of printing shipping labels through eBay is the inclusion of tracking. As soon as you purchase and print the label, tracking is automatically uploaded to the order, and your buyer is notified. This immediate communication builds trust and assures the customer that their item is on its way. In the case of disputes or claims, the tracking information also provides a layer of protection, showing exactly when the item was shipped and scanned along its route. Additionally, eBay integrates tracking data into its seller performance metrics, so timely updates can help you maintain a strong seller rating.

The label itself can be printed using a standard inkjet or laser printer on regular paper, which is then affixed to the package with clear packing tape. However, many sellers opt for thermal label printers like the Zebra or Rollo, which are specifically designed for shipping. These printers use heat-sensitive labels that don't require ink or toner, making them faster and more cost-effective in the long run. Thermal labels also produce clear, smudge-proof barcodes that are easier for carriers to scan. Investing in a thermal printer becomes especially worthwhile as your volume increases, allowing you to prepare packages quickly and professionally.

While eBay's native label printing solution works well for most sellers, some choose to explore third-party shipping services to gain additional features or consolidate orders across multiple platforms. Services like Pirate Ship, ShipStation, or Stamps.com offer powerful shipping solutions with competitive rates, more flexible automation tools, and broader integrations. These platforms allow you to import your eBay orders and generate labels from a single interface, especially helpful if you also sell on other platforms like Etsy, Amazon, or your own website.

Third-party services can also offer more advanced customization, such as branded packing slips, bulk label printing, or international documentation. Pirate Ship, for example, offers USPS Commercial Pricing and a user-friendly interface that appeals to both new and seasoned sellers. ShipStation provides automation rules that can assign shipping methods based on order weight or destination, streamlining repetitive tasks. Stamps.com is a long-standing option that integrates with eBay and allows offline postage printing, which can be useful during internet outages or system maintenance.

When using third-party platforms, it's essential to ensure your eBay store settings reflect the changes. While most reputable services automatically update tracking numbers back into your eBay dashboard, double-checking that the correct tracking is displayed helps prevent confusion or delays. Buyers rely on this information, and eBay uses it to assess your shipping performance, so consistency is key.

Another detail to consider is label layout and printer settings. Depending on your chosen printer, you might print a 4x6 thermal label or an 8.5x11 sheet with two labels per page. Each shipping software allows you to choose the label format, and it's important to test a few options to ensure the barcode is sharp and positioned correctly. Some sellers even create templates to add a small "Thank You" message or store branding to the shipping label page, creating a more polished look without extra expense.

Scheduling pickups or dropping off your packages at the right location is the final step that ties into the label printing process. Many sellers coordinate USPS pickups directly from their home or office, a free service that adds convenience and efficiency. Other carriers, like UPS or FedEx, offer scheduled pickups for a fee or allow drop-offs at nearby locations. The important part is to scan the package in as soon as possible. A tracking number that sits unscanned for days may raise questions with customers or affect your seller metrics.

Shipping labels are more than just postage—they are the vehicle that carries your product to your buyer's doorstep, and the accuracy, appearance, and timeliness of that label play a defining role in your store's reputation. Learning how to print them correctly, choose the best platform, and optimize your process is a skill that pays dividends over time. As your business grows, mastering label printing can shave hours off your workflow, eliminate errors, and elevate the overall professionalism of your brand. The sooner you build a streamlined label routine, the smoother your shipping operation becomes, helping you deliver not only packages but also trust, reliability, and lasting customer satisfaction.

TRACKING SHIPMENTS AND KEEPING BUYERS INFORMED

Once an item is packaged and sent out the door, a significant part of the transaction may feel finished for the seller, but for the buyer, the journey is just beginning. From that moment on, they become acutely interested in one thing: when the item will arrive. In this waiting period, communication becomes critical, and effective shipment tracking is one of the most powerful tools a seller can use to maintain trust and reinforce professionalism. In the world of online commerce, transparency and timing are everything, and keeping buyers informed during the shipping process is no longer optional—it's expected.

When a buyer places an order, they are entrusting you not only with their money but also with their time and expectations. One of the first steps in upholding that trust is making sure the item is shipped within the stated handling time. If a listing promises shipping within one business day, then that window becomes the buyer's baseline for expectation. Fulfilling this promise by generating a label promptly and getting the package into the carrier's system without delay reflects your reliability as a seller. However, it doesn't stop there. Once shipped, buyers want updates. That's where tracking plays a pivotal role.

Modern buyers are used to watching packages move in real-time, down to the minute a box lands on their doorstep. This habit has been shaped by large e-commerce platforms, and eBay sellers are held to the same standard. Fortunately, eBay makes it relatively easy for sellers to provide tracking updates. When a shipping label is printed directly through eBay or an integrated third-party service, tracking numbers are automatically uploaded to the order details and emailed to the buyer. This immediate communication sends a strong signal of professionalism and accountability.

Tracking numbers are more than just digital receipts—they are a living log of a package's journey. From acceptance at a post office to arrival at a distribution hub, and eventually delivery, each scan provides reassurance to the buyer that the item is progressing toward its destination. These updates become even more crucial when delivery times are longer, or when weather, holidays, or logistical delays disrupt normal shipping routes. During these periods, buyers are often on edge, and proactive tracking can be the difference between a satisfied customer and an impatient complaint.

Sellers should also be aware that eBay uses tracking information as a performance metric. If you consistently upload valid tracking numbers and ensure that items are scanned within your stated handling time, eBay recognizes you as a dependable seller. This contributes positively to your seller rating, search visibility, and even eligibility for certain selling benefits like Top Rated Seller status. Conversely, failing to upload tracking, providing incorrect numbers, or shipping late can hurt your seller metrics and lead to account restrictions or lower placement in search results.

Beyond automated updates, there's tremendous value in personalized communication. Buyers appreciate a short, professional message confirming that their item has been shipped and including the tracking number again, even if it's already in the system. This small gesture creates a personal touch that large corporate sellers often lack. A message that says, "Hi [buyer name], your item has been shipped and is on its way! Here's your tracking number again: [tracking number]. Let me know if you have any questions. Thank you again for your purchase!" reinforces that a real person is behind the transaction and actively ensuring a smooth process.

Sometimes, despite best efforts, shipments can get delayed or stuck in transit. When this happens, the worst thing a seller can do is go silent. Buyers who feel abandoned during a delay are far more likely to escalate to eBay for a refund or leave negative feedback. Instead, monitoring your shipments regularly—even after they leave your hands—

allows you to spot problems early. If a package hasn't moved for several days, consider reaching out to the carrier for more information or submitting a help request. Simultaneously, send a polite and honest message to the buyer acknowledging the delay, assuring them that you're monitoring the situation, and letting them know you're available to help resolve any concerns. Proactive transparency often diffuses frustration before it escalates.

Another aspect of effective tracking involves being strategic about the carriers you choose. Some carriers offer more detailed tracking and faster updates than others. For example, USPS offers robust tracking services on Priority Mail, but its lower-cost First Class or Ground Advantage options may provide more limited scan visibility. UPS and FedEx generally offer more frequent tracking updates and estimated delivery dates, which some buyers find more reassuring. Choosing the right service based on the item's value and the buyer's expectations can enhance the overall delivery experience.

For sellers handling international orders, tracking becomes even more critical. Many international buyers are understandably more anxious about receiving their items due to longer transit times and the involvement of multiple postal systems. Ensuring that your chosen shipping service offers end-to-end international tracking is vital. eBay's Global Shipping Program simplifies this process by providing full tracking through a central US hub before forwarding the item internationally, reducing the burden on sellers. If using your own international shipping method, always select one with tracking and make sure buyers understand the estimated delivery windows upfront.

A best practice in maintaining long-term buyer satisfaction is to build a routine around shipping and tracking updates. Set aside time each day to verify that all shipments from the previous day were scanned into the carrier's system. Occasionally, packages can miss initial scans, which may lead buyers to believe their item hasn't been shipped. In these cases, contacting the carrier or resending the tracking information with an explanation can prevent misunderstandings.

Technology can also assist in tracking. Some sellers use shipment tracking tools or apps that compile all their outgoing packages into one dashboard, allowing them to monitor statuses without visiting each carrier's site individually. These tools often send alerts when packages are delivered or delayed, giving sellers a real-time overview of their operations and helping them take swift action when needed.

Ultimately, tracking shipments and keeping buyers informed is a cornerstone of trust-building in e-commerce. Buyers don't just purchase products—they purchase experiences. Every clear update, every timely delivery, and every helpful message contributes to that experience. In a competitive marketplace where buyers have countless options, these small acts of communication and transparency become the glue that holds a business together and transforms one-time buyers into repeat customers. They signal not just logistical competence, but care and consistency—the trademarks of a seller committed to delivering excellence with every order.

EXPLORING DIFFERENT SHIPPING CARRIERS AND THEIR ADVANTAGES

Shipping is one of the most crucial aspects of any e-commerce business. It directly impacts the customer experience, the seller's reputation, and ultimately, the success of your business. When you sell on platforms like eBay, choosing the right shipping carrier is just as important as choosing the right product to sell. With several shipping carriers available, each offering different services, delivery speeds, pricing structures, and tracking options, it's essential to understand the advantages and limitations of each. By carefully selecting the best carrier for each situation, sellers can not only ensure timely deliveries but also enhance their customers' shopping experiences and maintain competitive pricing.

The most commonly used shipping carriers are USPS (United States Postal Service), UPS (United Parcel Service), FedEx, and DHL, with each offering distinct services tailored to different needs. While it's tempting to rely on a single carrier for all shipments, savvy sellers take the time to evaluate each option based on the type of item being sold, delivery speed, pricing, and geographic location of both the seller and the buyer. By leveraging the strengths of each carrier, you can offer more flexibility to your customers, which can ultimately boost satisfaction and sales.

USPS is one of the most widely used carriers for eBay sellers, particularly because it offers a broad range of affordable services for both domestic and international shipments. One of the primary advantages of USPS is its pricing, especially for lighter items. The Postal Service offers flat-rate shipping boxes through its Priority Mail and Priority Mail Express services, which allow sellers to ship items at a fixed cost regardless of weight (up to certain limits). This can be particularly advantageous when shipping items like clothing, electronics, or books that may weigh less but require sturdy packaging. Furthermore, USPS provides free packaging materials for its flat-rate boxes, which can help sellers save money on packing supplies.

USPS is also known for its accessibility, offering drop-off points at numerous locations, including post offices, retail stores, and even mailboxes. This can make it incredibly convenient for sellers who need to quickly ship products. Additionally, USPS offers First-Class Mail, which is a budget-friendly option for shipping small items weighing up to 13 ounces, and it also provides free delivery tracking with all services, including First-Class and Priority Mail. For eBay sellers, USPS integrates seamlessly with eBay's system, allowing for easy printing of shipping labels directly through eBay, streamlining the process and saving valuable time.

Despite these advantages, there are some drawbacks to using USPS. One of the most significant concerns is its delivery speed, which, while reliable, can sometimes be slower than UPS or FedEx, particularly with First-Class or standard Priority Mail services. While tracking is available, there may be times when it is not as detailed or frequent as that provided by other carriers, particularly for international shipments. Additionally, USPS is not always the best option for shipping large or heavy items, as its pricing structure can become prohibitively expensive for packages over a certain weight.

UPS, on the other hand, is a powerhouse when it comes to reliable, fast shipping, especially for larger or heavier packages. Known for its efficiency and global reach, UPS is a go-to option for eBay sellers looking to ship items with expedited delivery. One of the key advantages of UPS is its wide range of services that cater to different needs. For example, UPS Ground offers affordable rates for domestic shipments, and UPS 2nd Day Air or UPS Next Day Air are great options for expedited delivery when time is of the essence. UPS also excels in international shipping, providing a reliable and efficient service to a variety of destinations worldwide.

Another benefit of UPS is its tracking capabilities. UPS provides in-depth tracking details, including estimated delivery windows and updates at every stage of the package's journey, making it easier for both the seller and the buyer to stay informed about the status of the shipment. This level of transparency helps build trust with customers, especially when shipping expensive or valuable items.

However, while UPS provides superior services for larger or more time-sensitive shipments, it can also be more expensive than USPS, especially for smaller, lighter packages. This is particularly true for international shipments, where UPS's rates can be significantly higher. As a result, while UPS is an excellent option for premium services, sellers must consider the cost-effectiveness of this carrier based on the type of products they sell and their profit margins.

FedEx is another carrier that provides robust shipping solutions, particularly for time-sensitive shipments and international deliveries. Like UPS, FedEx is well-regarded for its fast and reliable service, with options such as FedEx Ground, FedEx Express Saver, and FedEx 2Day, providing a wide range of choices for domestic shipping. FedEx also excels in international shipping, offering global reach with services that can get packages delivered within days. With its global network and high level of service, FedEx is a top choice for eBay sellers shipping items like electronics, fragile goods, or high-value merchandise.

One of FedEx's standout features is its reputation for timely deliveries and its guarantee for express services like FedEx Overnight or FedEx Express. These services are backed by a money-back guarantee, which is a unique advantage for sellers who want to ensure a certain level of reliability for urgent shipments. In addition, FedEx offers excellent customer service and real-time tracking, which makes it easier for sellers to manage shipments and address any potential issues quickly.

That said, similar to UPS, FedEx's pricing can be steep, especially for smaller items or packages that do not require expedited delivery. For eBay sellers, the higher costs associated with FedEx's premium services may not always justify the added speed, particularly for lighter, less expensive items. Additionally, while FedEx provides detailed tracking information, its delivery options may not always be as convenient or widely available as those of USPS, especially in rural areas.

DHL, though less commonly used in the United States, is a dominant player in international shipping, particularly to Europe and Asia. DHL is often chosen by sellers who need to reach global customers quickly and reliably. One of the advantages of DHL is its ability to navigate customs efficiently, ensuring that packages reach international destinations without significant delays. DHL offers a variety of services tailored to international markets, including Express Worldwide and Express 12:00, which guarantees delivery by noon the following business day to major international cities.

For eBay sellers focusing on global sales, DHL can be an excellent option, as it offers door-to-door service and allows for full tracking throughout the package's journey. However, like FedEx and UPS, DHL's services can be pricey, and its availability may not be as widespread as USPS or UPS in certain regions.

Choosing the right shipping carrier is an essential decision that affects your eBay business's profitability, reputation, and customer satisfaction. USPS is a great choice for small, lightweight items and budget-conscious sellers, while UPS and FedEx provide fast, reliable, and detailed tracking options, especially for larger or time-sensitive shipments. DHL stands out as an international shipping option for sellers looking to expand globally. Ultimately, it's important to evaluate your product type, customer needs, and shipping goals when selecting the right carrier, and consider using a combination of services to meet the diverse demands of your eBay store. By understanding the advantages of each shipping carrier, you can make informed decisions that enhance your business's efficiency and help build a strong reputation as a reliable seller.

CHAPTER 9
PROVIDING EXCELLENT CUSTOMER SERVICE: BUILDING LOYALTY

THE IMPORTANCE OF POSITIVE CUSTOMER INTERACTIONS

In the world of e-commerce, where competition is fierce and thousands of sellers are vying for buyers' attention, positive customer interactions are not just a nicety—they are a necessity. The way you communicate with your customers, address their concerns, and resolve any issues that arise can make or break your business. In fact, it can be the difference between securing a loyal, repeat customer and losing a potential sale for good. For eBay sellers, who are essentially running small businesses within a global marketplace, the importance of cultivating positive relationships with customers cannot be overstated.

The foundation of any successful business lies in its ability to foster trust and loyalty among its customers, and one of the best ways to do that is through positive, professional, and effective communication. In the eBay marketplace, where buyers and sellers interact remotely, it is especially critical to go above and beyond to ensure that customers feel heard, respected, and valued. Positive interactions not only help resolve issues but also contribute to creating a favorable reputation, which is key in a platform where ratings and feedback play a significant role in a seller's success.

One of the most significant ways in which positive customer interactions influence your eBay business is through customer feedback and ratings. The eBay feedback system is a powerful tool that allows buyers to leave reviews based on their experience with a seller. These reviews—whether positive, neutral, or negative—are visible to all potential buyers and have a direct impact on a seller's reputation. A single negative review, if not handled appropriately, can have lasting consequences on your reputation, while a consistent stream of positive feedback can increase buyer confidence and set you apart from the competition. Therefore, how you manage your interactions with customers will directly affect your feedback score and, in turn, your overall sales.

Timely communication is one of the most fundamental aspects of positive customer interactions. eBay buyers, much like shoppers in any other retail environment, expect quick responses to their inquiries. Whether they are asking about product details, shipping times, or return policies, responding promptly demonstrates professionalism and a commitment to customer satisfaction. In many cases, buyers are more likely to make a purchase from a seller who responds quickly, even if they are still deciding between multiple options. A timely response shows that you are attentive and reliable, which reassures the buyer and fosters a sense of trust.

Effective communication goes beyond simply responding to messages quickly; it also involves being clear, courteous, and helpful. Whether you are addressing a simple question or a more complex issue, being clear and straightforward in your responses can prevent misunderstandings and avoid unnecessary frustration. Providing detailed, accurate information not only helps buyers make informed purchasing decisions but also builds your credibility as a seller. When customers feel they can trust the information provided, they are more likely to purchase from you and return for future transactions.

In addition to answering inquiries, addressing any concerns or complaints swiftly and professionally is essential for maintaining a positive customer experience. While you may not always be able to avoid problems such as delayed shipping, damaged goods, or incorrect orders, how you handle these situations will leave a lasting impression on your customers. The key to turning a potentially negative situation into a positive one lies in your ability to empathize with the buyer, apologize for the inconvenience, and offer a satisfactory resolution. Whether that means offering a replacement item, issuing a refund, or covering the cost of return shipping, taking responsibility for the issue and offering a solution shows your commitment to customer satisfaction. This kind of proactive approach helps to prevent negative feedback and ensures that customers leave the interaction feeling heard and respected.

One of the best ways to create a lasting positive impact is by going above and beyond in your customer interactions. While it's important to resolve issues efficiently, small gestures of goodwill can also make a big difference. For example, including a handwritten thank-you note in a package or offering a small discount on a future purchase can leave customers with a favorable impression of your business. These thoughtful actions not only strengthen the buyer-seller relationship but also demonstrate that you value your customers as more than just sources of revenue. Going the extra mile to exceed customer expectations can lead to repeat business and positive word-of-mouth referrals, which are invaluable for growing your eBay store.

Consistency is another critical factor when it comes to customer interactions. Providing excellent customer service consistently builds trust over time and helps you establish a reputation for reliability. When buyers know they can count on you to deliver quality products, timely shipments, and clear communication, they are more likely to return to your store for future purchases. Furthermore, a consistent record of positive customer interactions can help mitigate the occasional slip-up. If you occasionally make a mistake, whether it's shipping a wrong item or experiencing a delay, your history of positive communication can make it easier for buyers to overlook the error, as they know you are a trustworthy and reliable seller.

Customer interactions also play a significant role in managing returns and cancellations. While it's always best to try to avoid returns by providing accurate descriptions and images, there will inevitably be occasions when a customer needs to return an item. Handling these situations effectively is crucial for maintaining a positive relationship with the buyer. Make sure your return policy is clearly stated and easy for customers to understand, and always be prompt and courteous when processing returns. A smooth, hassle-free return experience can turn a potentially dissatisfied customer into a loyal one, as it shows that you prioritize their satisfaction.

While the feedback system is one of the most public ways to gauge the success of your customer interactions, don't underestimate the importance of building personal connections with your customers. Personalized communication, such as addressing buyers by name and responding to their concerns in a thoughtful manner, can create a more positive and memorable experience. Customers who feel valued are more likely to leave positive feedback, return to your store, and recommend your products to others. These personal touches can help humanize your business and differentiate you from other sellers who may rely on impersonal, transactional interactions.

In an increasingly digital world, maintaining positive customer interactions also involves being mindful of your online presence. Many buyers will research a seller before making a purchase, so it's important to ensure that your profile, store, and product listings reflect professionalism and trustworthiness. Regularly checking and responding to customer inquiries, keeping your listings updated, and maintaining a positive tone in all of your communications can help reinforce the impression that you are a reliable and approachable seller.

Positive customer interactions are the cornerstone of any successful eBay business. Through timely, clear, and courteous communication, you can build trust with your buyers, enhance their shopping experience, and increase the likelihood of repeat business. By handling issues with empathy and offering thoughtful gestures of goodwill, you not only resolve conflicts but also turn potentially negative situations into opportunities for growth. Consistency, personalization, and a commitment to customer satisfaction will help you cultivate a loyal customer base, strengthen your reputation, and ultimately set you on the path to long-term success in the competitive e-commerce marketplace.

RESPONDING TO INQUIRIES AND RESOLVING ISSUES EFFECTIVELY

In the fast-paced world of eBay selling, the ability to respond to inquiries and resolve issues effectively can make a significant difference in the success of your business. In a marketplace where trust and customer satisfaction are paramount, how you handle buyer inquiries, questions, or complaints can determine whether or not they choose to complete a purchase and whether they will return for future transactions. Developing strong communication skills and a systematic approach to resolving issues can lead to improved feedback, repeat business, and an overall positive reputation that will set you apart from the competition.

Buyers often reach out to sellers with questions or concerns regarding items before making a purchase. It could be about the product's condition, specific features, shipping times, or return policies. How you handle these initial inquiries can directly influence the buyer's decision to move forward with the transaction. Prompt, clear, and professional responses are essential in creating a positive impression. Buyers tend to appreciate sellers who take the time to respond to their questions quickly, as it reflects on the seller's commitment to customer service and reliability. If buyers feel they are being treated with respect and their concerns are addressed thoroughly, they are far more likely to make a purchase and become repeat customers.

Clear communication is key to ensuring that your response is effective and leads to a favorable outcome. It's crucial to ensure that you provide accurate, detailed information, as well as to be transparent about any limitations, such as shipping delays, availability of certain products, or restrictions in your return policy. Being upfront about these potential issues can prevent misunderstandings and avoid negative feedback down the line. Additionally, maintaining a polite and professional tone in your responses is paramount. It's easy to become defensive if a buyer's inquiry comes across as demanding or critical, but responding in a calm and understanding manner will always serve you better. A polite response helps to de-escalate any tension and shows the buyer that you are willing to work with them to find a satisfactory solution.

On the other hand, how you handle issues that arise post-sale can be just as important as responding to inquiries before a purchase. Once a sale is made, it's important to remain available to address any concerns or complications that arise. Whether the issue is related to an item being damaged during shipping, a buyer receiving an incorrect product, or dissatisfaction with the quality of the item, how you handle these problems can impact your reputation as a seller. When dealing with post-sale issues, it is essential to approach the situation with empathy. Even if the issue seems like it may not be your fault, it's important to acknowledge the buyer's frustration and express understanding. Empathy goes a long way in smoothing over potentially negative situations. Simply acknowledging a buyer's disappointment and showing that you are willing to assist them can diffuse a lot of tension.

When resolving issues, offering clear, practical solutions is crucial. This might mean issuing a refund, sending a replacement item, or guiding the buyer through the process of returning the item. When you provide a straightforward and efficient solution, it demonstrates that you are committed to making things right, which helps to retain the buyer's trust and confidence. In some cases, offering something extra, such as covering return shipping costs or offering a small discount on a future purchase, can go a long way in keeping the customer satisfied. Even though these steps might require additional resources or effort on your part, the benefits of fostering positive customer relationships outweigh the costs. A customer who feels valued and taken care of is more likely to leave positive feedback, recommend your store to others, and return to make additional purchases in the future.

Communication plays a critical role in the resolution of issues, but it is also important to act quickly. Time is of the essence when resolving problems with buyers. The longer an issue goes unresolved, the more likely the buyer is to become frustrated, and this could result in a negative review or, worse, a dispute. Many sellers make the mistake of delaying their responses, thinking that the issue will simply resolve itself, but in reality, an unresolved issue can escalate quickly and cause damage to your reputation. By addressing problems promptly, you signal to your customers that you value their business and are dedicated to providing excellent service.

When you're addressing inquiries or resolving issues, it's also important to be flexible and adaptable. Not every situation is going to have a straightforward solution, and each customer is unique. There may be instances where a buyer requests something outside of your standard policies, such as an extended return window or a custom request. In these situations, it's important to assess the request on a case-by-case basis and make a reasonable judgment. While it's essential to set clear policies for your business, being too rigid can sometimes alienate customers who might have genuine concerns. On the other hand, being overly lenient with exceptions can lead to misuse of your policies. Striking the right balance between upholding your policies and being open to reasonable adjustments can help you maintain both customer satisfaction and your business integrity.

Effective communication also extends to following up after an issue is resolved. Once a problem is addressed, it's a good idea to follow up with the buyer to ensure they are satisfied with the solution. This small step demonstrates that you are committed to their satisfaction beyond just the immediate resolution of the issue. A follow-up message also gives the buyer an opportunity to voice any further concerns, which you can address before they leave feedback. This proactive approach can help you avoid negative reviews by giving you a chance to ensure that the buyer is truly happy with the outcome.

Furthermore, if a customer reaches out with an inquiry, take advantage of the opportunity to build a relationship. Engaging with customers and demonstrating that you care about their experience can go a long way in making them feel valued. For example, thanking a buyer for their inquiry or offering additional information about related products may not only resolve the current issue but also increase the likelihood of a future sale. By creating a dialogue, you create an atmosphere of trust, which is vital in building long-term customer relationships.

Another important aspect of responding to inquiries and resolving issues is handling disputes and claims professionally. eBay has a well-established resolution process in place for situations where a buyer and seller cannot come to an agreement. If a buyer opens a case against you, it's essential to stay calm and follow the guidelines set by eBay. Responding in a professional manner, keeping all communication through eBay's platform, and adhering to eBay's policies will help protect your reputation and ensure that any disputes are resolved fairly.

While it's important to address issues promptly, it's also vital to recognize when to escalate matters. In some cases, an issue may be too complex or contentious to resolve directly with the buyer. In these instances, turning to eBay's customer support services can help facilitate a solution. By involving eBay in the process, you ensure that the situation is handled fairly, and you have a third party to help mediate any unresolved issues.

Responding to inquiries and resolving issues effectively is an essential skill for any eBay seller. The way you handle communication with buyers can directly influence your reputation, sales, and overall success in the marketplace. By responding promptly, maintaining professionalism, offering clear solutions, and following up, you can turn potential problems into opportunities for customer satisfaction and loyalty. These positive interactions not only protect your seller reputation but also enhance your overall standing in the eBay community, fostering a successful and sustainable business.

HANDLING NEGATIVE FEEDBACK PROFESSIONALLY

Handling negative feedback is an inevitable part of selling online, especially on platforms as expansive as eBay. While receiving positive feedback can feel rewarding, negative feedback can feel disheartening and, at times, even threatening to your reputation. However, the way you handle negative feedback can make a significant difference in maintaining a strong customer relationship and in the overall success of your business. By responding to negative feedback professionally, you not only demonstrate resilience but also show potential customers that you are a seller who values transparency, improvement, and customer satisfaction.

It's essential to understand that negative feedback is not always a reflection of your overall business performance or your capabilities as a seller. In some cases, buyers may leave negative feedback due to misunderstandings, unrealistic expectations, or issues that are outside of your control. For example, a buyer may leave negative feedback due to shipping delays caused by the postal service, or they may not fully understand your product's specifications. Therefore, the first step in handling negative feedback is to take a deep breath and assess the situation without jumping to conclusions or reacting impulsively.

Once you have a clear understanding of the feedback, the next step is to respond calmly and professionally. Buyers who leave negative feedback are often frustrated or upset, and it is important to approach the situation with empathy. Acknowledge the buyer's concerns and express your willingness to work with them to resolve the issue. This type of empathetic response can go a long way in diffusing tension and showing that you care about the customer's experience. When crafting your response, it's essential to stay polite and avoid using defensive language. For example, instead of saying "I didn't cause the problem," say "I'm sorry for the inconvenience this has caused you, and I'm happy to help resolve this."

Professionalism in your response is crucial not only for addressing the immediate issue but also for the public nature of eBay feedback. When you respond to negative feedback, it is visible to other potential buyers. A well-crafted, respectful response can turn a negative situation into an opportunity to demonstrate your commitment to excellent customer service. It shows prospective buyers that you are a seller who cares about resolving issues and is willing to go the extra mile to make things right. This can inspire confidence and trust in your future customers.

Another key aspect of handling negative feedback is to evaluate whether the feedback is justified or if it stems from an issue that could have been avoided. If the feedback is warranted, such as a mistake you made with an order or an item description, take full responsibility and apologize. A sincere acknowledgment of your mistake shows buyers that you are accountable for your actions and willing to learn from your errors. On the other hand, if the feedback is based on an issue that wasn't your fault, such as a delayed shipment due to a postal service error, calmly explain the situation without sounding defensive. You might say, "I understand your frustration, and I apologize for the delay. Unfortunately, the postal service has been experiencing delays, but I assure you that I shipped the item promptly. If there's anything else I can do to assist, please let me know."

In some cases, the buyer may have made an error or misunderstanding that led to the negative feedback. If this is the case, you should reach out to the buyer privately through eBay's messaging system to clarify the situation. Politeness and respect are paramount in these situations. Instead of accusing the buyer of making a mistake, gently explain the misunderstanding and offer to work together to resolve it. If a buyer mistakenly purchased an incorrect item, for instance, offer to provide additional clarification or to assist in a return if appropriate. You may also want to politely ask if they would consider revising the feedback if the issue is resolved to their satisfaction.

While addressing the situation directly with the buyer is important, you should also be aware of eBay's feedback revision policy. If the issue is resolved and the buyer is satisfied with the solution, you can politely ask if they would be willing to amend or remove the negative feedback. However, it's important to note that eBay's policy prohibits sellers from offering incentives in exchange for feedback changes, so your request should remain respectful and based purely on your resolution of the issue. If the buyer agrees to revise their feedback, this can be a positive outcome for both parties.

Sometimes, despite your best efforts, a buyer may be uncooperative or unreasonable. In such cases, eBay provides mechanisms for sellers to report abusive or unfair feedback. If you believe the feedback violates eBay's feedback policies, such as being irrelevant to the transaction or containing personal attacks, you can request that eBay investigate the matter. eBay typically has a process for determining whether the feedback should be removed or altered, but it's important to use this option sparingly and only in cases where the feedback is truly unjustified.

While negative feedback can feel discouraging, it can also be an opportunity to grow as a seller. Every negative review provides insight into your business operations, and it can highlight areas where you might need to improve. If you frequently receive negative feedback about your shipping times, for instance, you might want to review your shipping processes or explore faster shipping options. If the negative feedback concerns the condition of your items, it might be time to reassess your packaging or quality control processes. By analyzing the feedback, you can identify trends and take proactive steps to avoid similar issues in the future.

It's also important to remember that negative feedback does not have to define your business. On platforms like eBay, your reputation is built over time, and a single negative comment won't necessarily harm your success if you continue to provide excellent customer service and improve where necessary. What matters most is how you handle these situations and the consistency of your efforts to meet and exceed customer expectations.

Building a strong reputation on eBay involves more than just receiving positive feedback; it also involves learning how to handle criticism with grace and professionalism. Negative feedback, when managed correctly, can even help to enhance your reputation. Buyers appreciate sellers who are not only responsive but also open to feedback and willing to make things right. As long as you remain committed to customer satisfaction and keep a calm, respectful approach in all interactions, you will build a loyal customer base and improve your standing as a reliable and professional seller.

Handling negative feedback professionally is an essential skill for any eBay seller. Whether the feedback is justified or stems from a misunderstanding, your response is an opportunity to demonstrate professionalism, empathy, and a commitment to customer satisfaction. By responding calmly, addressing issues promptly, and using negative feedback as a learning tool, you can turn potential setbacks into valuable experiences that help you grow and succeed as a seller. The way you handle negative feedback will not only impact your relationship with the buyer but will also shape your reputation on the platform and determine your long-term success in the online marketplace.

ENCOURAGING POSITIVE FEEDBACK AND REVIEWS

Building a strong and reputable presence on eBay is not only about delivering great products and offering competitive prices but also about receiving positive feedback and reviews from satisfied customers. Positive feedback plays a significant role in attracting future buyers, as many people rely heavily on reviews and ratings when making purchase decisions. Therefore, it's essential to understand how to encourage positive feedback and reviews and leverage them to grow your business.

Positive feedback is one of the most critical factors that potential buyers consider when evaluating whether to purchase from a seller. On platforms like eBay, a high rating can build trust and credibility, making you stand out in a crowded marketplace. It is no longer enough to just offer quality products at a fair price. You need to actively engage with your customers to ensure that their shopping experience is as seamless and enjoyable as possible. The more positive experiences you provide, the more likely you are to receive favorable feedback. This feedback, in turn, will generate more business and contribute to the long-term success of your eBay store.

The process of encouraging positive feedback begins with the basics of providing excellent customer service. Start by clearly communicating with buyers about the products you sell, including detailed descriptions and accurate images. Ensuring that the buyer understands exactly what they are purchasing can prevent misunderstandings and disappointments. When buyers know what to expect, they are more likely to leave positive reviews. Misleading product descriptions or inaccurate images can lead to dissatisfaction, which often results in negative feedback. To avoid this, always take extra care when creating your listings, double-check product details, and provide honest representations of your items.

Another critical factor in earning positive feedback is ensuring prompt and reliable shipping. Buyers appreciate timely deliveries, and delays or shipping issues can quickly lead to frustration. One of the best ways to encourage positive feedback is to provide quick shipping and a seamless tracking process. Use eBay's integrated shipping options, which offer discounted rates and streamlined services for sellers. Offering fast and reliable shipping builds buyer confidence and increases the chances of receiving praise for your efficiency. However, delays may still occur due to unforeseen circumstances, such as postal service issues or weather conditions, so it's essential to communicate with buyers if there are any unexpected delays. By providing tracking numbers and keeping buyers updated on the status of their shipments, you can demonstrate your commitment to customer service.

While the logistics of selling are important, equally crucial is the way you communicate with buyers throughout the process. Always be courteous, professional, and timely in your responses. If a buyer has questions or concerns, respond as quickly as possible with helpful and informative answers. A friendly, personalized message thanking the buyer for their purchase and offering assistance if needed can go a long way in making a buyer feel valued. Buyers are more likely to leave positive feedback if they feel that they have had a pleasant and personalized shopping experience. The simple act of showing genuine interest in your customer's satisfaction can encourage them to leave a positive review.

It's also essential to address any issues or complaints before they escalate. Negative feedback can often be prevented if sellers are proactive in resolving problems. If a buyer expresses dissatisfaction, take the time to understand their concern and work with them toward a solution. Offer solutions that are fair, reasonable, and in line with eBay's policies, such as providing a refund, offering an exchange, or working out a partial refund. By resolving issues amicably, you demonstrate a willingness to go the extra mile to ensure that the buyer has a positive experience. This not only prevents negative feedback but also increases the likelihood that the buyer will leave a favorable review after the situation is resolved.

A more direct way to encourage positive feedback is by simply asking for it. After a successful transaction, consider sending a polite, short message to your buyer thanking them for their purchase and kindly asking if they would be willing to leave feedback. This message should be brief, sincere, and respectful of the buyer's time. A simple message such as "I hope you are enjoying your item! If you have a moment, I would greatly appreciate it if you could leave feedback about your experience." This type of request is often appreciated, especially after a smooth transaction. However, it's essential not to be overly insistent. Some buyers may not be inclined to leave feedback, and that's perfectly fine. Respect their decision and don't press the matter further.

In addition to asking for feedback, it's important to ensure that you're making the feedback process as easy as possible for your customers. Most eBay users are familiar with leaving reviews, but for those who are less experienced or who are new to the platform, a little guidance can help. Consider including a note or instructions in your shipment thanking the buyer and encouraging them to leave feedback if they're satisfied with the purchase. A small gesture like this can show that you value their input and that it's important to you. It doesn't hurt to remind them that feedback helps sellers improve and maintain a high standard of service, which benefits the entire eBay community.

Another effective strategy for encouraging feedback is building relationships with buyers. Buyers who feel personally connected to a seller are more likely to leave positive reviews. Consider offering small tokens of appreciation, such as a handwritten thank-you note or a small discount on their next purchase. These personalized touches make customers feel valued, which in turn increases the likelihood of them leaving positive feedback. Building a positive reputation through personalized customer care will set you apart from other sellers and cultivate customer loyalty, which is key to long-term success.

While encouraging positive feedback is crucial, it's also important to stay professional when dealing with negative feedback. Sometimes, despite your best efforts, a buyer may leave a less-than-ideal review. However, rather than being discouraged, view negative feedback as an opportunity to learn and improve. Responding to negative feedback in a calm and professional manner shows other potential buyers that you are committed to resolving any issues. This professionalism can mitigate the impact of negative reviews and may even encourage other buyers to trust your service more.

Remember that consistency is key. Building a reputation as a reliable, trustworthy, and customer-focused seller takes time. It's the culmination of hundreds or even thousands of positive transactions. By consistently providing great products, excellent customer service, and fast shipping, you will create a base of satisfied customers who are more likely to leave positive reviews and recommend your store to others. Over time, this will result in a higher overall rating, a more significant number of positive feedback, and a stronger reputation on eBay.

Encouraging positive feedback and reviews is an ongoing process that requires dedication, attention to detail, and a genuine commitment to customer satisfaction. By providing excellent service, communicating effectively with buyers, and addressing any issues promptly, you can significantly increase your chances of receiving positive feedback. While you can't control everything, your efforts to build strong relationships with customers, ask for feedback politely, and handle complaints professionally will go a long way in ensuring your success on eBay. Ultimately, positive feedback is a reflection of your hard work and dedication to delivering exceptional value to your buyers, and it will help propel your business to new heights.

BUILDING LONG-TERM RELATIONSHIPS WITH YOUR CUSTOMERS

Building long-term relationships with your customers is one of the most powerful ways to sustain and grow your eBay business. While attracting new customers is essential for expansion, the true value lies in nurturing existing relationships and turning one-time buyers into repeat customers. Establishing trust and maintaining positive communication is the foundation of any successful business, and when it comes to eBay, the significance of fostering long-term relationships cannot be overstated.

When customers return to buy from you again, it's an indication that they trust your products and services. These customers are not only more likely to make future purchases but can also become advocates for your brand, spreading positive word-of-mouth to their friends and family. The trust you build with them will help protect your business from fluctuations in sales or market trends, making it more resilient in the long run.

One of the most important aspects of building lasting relationships with customers is delivering exceptional service that exceeds expectations. This goes beyond offering a quality product at a competitive price. To establish a reputation that encourages customers to return, you must provide an outstanding overall experience from the moment they discover your listing to the final delivery of their purchase. When customers feel valued and respected, they are more likely to come back for future purchases.

Communication plays a pivotal role in this process. Clear and prompt communication helps avoid misunderstandings and builds trust. Right from the start, it's essential to establish your brand as reliable and approachable. Respond to customer inquiries quickly, whether it's about a product detail, shipping time, or a question about returns. By demonstrating responsiveness, you show customers that you care about their experience and are committed to assisting them. People appreciate being heard, and even if you cannot meet a buyer's every demand, being honest and open about what you can provide builds goodwill.

After the sale, keeping the lines of communication open remains essential. Sending a brief thank-you message or email after each transaction shows your customers that you are genuinely grateful for their business. It's a simple gesture, but it can make a huge difference in creating a positive experience. You can also ask them for feedback once their order has been processed. This shows that you value their opinion and are always striving to improve your service. Some sellers even include small personal touches, such as a handwritten note or a small freebie with the product. Such gestures can go a long way in building rapport and ensuring that your buyers feel special.

To further develop long-term relationships, personalized interactions with customers are crucial. Rather than treating each transaction as a one-time event, approach it as part of a bigger picture. For instance, if you notice that a customer has purchased from you multiple times, take the opportunity to send them a personalized message, thanking them for their continued support. You can even recommend products they might like based on their previous purchases. Showing customers that you recognize their buying habits and are willing to offer tailored solutions will make them feel more connected to your brand.

Offering loyalty incentives is another effective way to encourage customers to return to your eBay store. Whether it's through occasional discounts, special offers, or loyalty points, rewarding repeat customers helps solidify their commitment to your store. You can also create exclusive sales events where only repeat customers can access certain discounts. These loyalty programs not only reward customers for their continued support but also create a sense of belonging and appreciation.

In addition to providing personalized service and loyalty rewards, ensuring consistent product quality is vital for maintaining long-term customer relationships. If customers are continually pleased with the products they purchase from you, they will naturally return. On the flip side, even one negative experience due to subpar product quality can tarnish your reputation and push customers away. Therefore, always double-check your products, provide accurate descriptions, and ensure that they match the photos you've displayed. Customers will appreciate knowing exactly what they are getting when they buy from you, which will build trust over time.

Transparency is another key aspect of long-term customer relationships. When selling on eBay, it is important to provide clear and honest information about your products, including any potential defects, flaws, or limitations. If a product is pre-owned or has any issues, be upfront about it rather than trying to hide it. Buyers appreciate honesty, and when they feel they can trust your descriptions, they are more likely to purchase from you again. Likewise, providing transparent shipping policies and estimated delivery dates prevents confusion and frustration, ensuring customers feel confident in their purchase decisions.

Effective handling of issues or disputes also plays a significant role in maintaining strong relationships. It's inevitable that, from time to time, problems may arise with a transaction. Whether it's a delayed shipment, a product that arrives damaged, or a customer who is unhappy with their purchase, how you respond to such issues will determine whether the customer remains loyal. A swift, professional, and empathetic response to any issues can turn a potentially negative situation into a positive one. Offering fair resolutions, such as refunds or exchanges, and taking responsibility for any mistakes builds trust and encourages customers to return despite the occasional hiccup.

In addition to offering great service and handling issues efficiently, maintaining consistency is crucial in fostering long-term relationships. This means ensuring that every transaction, communication, and product meets the same high standards. When buyers know they can consistently rely on you for fast shipping, excellent customer service, and quality products, they are more likely to return for future purchases. Consistency gives customers a reason to choose your store over others.

Furthermore, encourage customers to stay engaged with your store through ongoing communication. Sending regular updates about new products, sales events, or special promotions can keep your store top-of-mind for customers. Many eBay sellers use newsletters, store promotions, or special offers to remind buyers of the value they offer. While it's important not to bombard customers with too many messages, occasional updates can help keep the relationship alive and encourage repeat business.

As your business grows, consider expanding your relationship-building efforts through a loyalty program or a VIP club for your most dedicated customers. This can include offering early access to sales, birthday discounts, or free shipping for frequent buyers. By creating exclusive perks for loyal customers, you not only show your appreciation for their business but also incentivize them to continue shopping with you.

Lastly, it's important to remember that building long-term relationships is not a quick process. It requires time, consistency, and effort to establish trust and credibility. However, the rewards of a loyal customer base are well worth the investment. As these customers continue to return to your store and refer others, your business will grow, and your reputation will be solidified in the marketplace. Positive feedback and customer referrals will further increase your visibility and boost your chances of long-term success.

Building long-term relationships with your customers requires more than just offering good products. It involves providing exceptional customer service, being responsive to inquiries, maintaining transparency, and always ensuring the quality of your offerings. By creating personalized experiences, offering loyalty incentives, and addressing any concerns swiftly and professionally, you can foster a base of loyal, repeat customers who are integral to your success. By focusing on these key principles, you'll not only retain your current customers but also build a foundation for sustainable growth in your eBay business.

The Complete Guide to Selling on eBay for Beginners 2025

PART 4

Growing and Scaling Your eBay Business

CHAPTER 10
OPTIMIZING YOUR LISTINGS FOR MAXIMUM VISIBILITY

DEEP DIVE INTO EBAY SEO: UNDERSTANDING SEARCH ALGORITHMS

eBay's search engine optimization (SEO) is a powerful tool that can significantly impact the success of your listings and, ultimately, your eBay business. Understanding how eBay's search algorithms work is crucial for any seller looking to increase visibility, attract more buyers, and generate more sales. While eBay's search process may seem complex at first, once you grasp the basics of how its algorithms function, you can optimize your listings to ensure they rank higher in search results.

At the core of eBay's search algorithm is its goal to deliver the most relevant and best quality products to buyers. When a buyer enters a search query, eBay's system works tirelessly behind the scenes to match the user's intent with the best possible listings. This is accomplished using a ranking system that takes multiple factors into account, such as the title, description, price, shipping options, and seller performance. By understanding how these factors interact, you can make small adjustments that result in large improvements in visibility.

One of the most critical elements of eBay SEO is the title of your listing. The search algorithm places significant weight on keywords within the title, which is why it is essential to create a title that accurately describes your item while incorporating relevant search terms. While it's important to avoid keyword stuffing (repeating keywords unnecessarily), using descriptive keywords that potential buyers would likely type into the search bar is crucial for visibility. For instance, if you're selling a vintage leather jacket, include specific details such as the material, brand, and size in the title to attract the right audience. Using all 80 characters allowed in your title can maximize your chances of appearing in relevant search results.

The description is another key factor that eBay's algorithm uses to evaluate the relevance of your listing. A detailed and clear product description provides not only potential buyers with all the necessary information but also the search engine with data to index your listing. Be sure to highlight the key features of your product, including its condition, size, color, material, and any unique selling points. Additionally, the use of keywords in your description is also essential, though they should be naturally incorporated into the content rather than forced. The more thorough your product description, the better chance you have of your listing being ranked higher in search results.

Images play a crucial role in eBay SEO as well. Listings with high-quality, clear images not only provide a better shopping experience for potential buyers but are also more likely to rank well in search results. High-quality photos, showing the item from multiple angles and highlighting any specific features or defects, give buyers a better understanding of the product they're purchasing. It's important to follow eBay's image guidelines, such as using a clean background and ensuring that your photos are sharp and properly lit. The clearer the images, the more likely your listing will attract clicks and, ultimately, sales.

Shipping options are also a vital consideration in eBay's ranking algorithm. The platform prioritizes sellers who offer fast, affordable, and reliable shipping options. eBay's algorithm rewards listings that provide free shipping, as it is a highly valued feature by buyers. If you are able to offer free shipping, it's important to factor that cost into your product's price so that it remains competitive. In addition to offering free shipping, offering expedited or same-day shipping can increase the likelihood of your listing appearing higher in search results. Additionally, offering multiple shipping options allows buyers to choose what works best for them, enhancing the overall customer experience.

Seller performance metrics play a significant role in determining how your listings rank in eBay search results. eBay's system takes into account factors such as feedback ratings, return rates, and shipping times when evaluating a seller's overall reliability. To improve your performance metrics, ensure that you provide excellent customer service, respond promptly to inquiries, and maintain a fast shipping turnaround. Positive feedback from buyers will help enhance your reputation as a reliable seller, further boosting your SEO ranking.

Another key element in eBay's search algorithm is the use of "Best Match," which is the default sorting option used by eBay's search engine. The Best Match algorithm ranks listings based on factors such as relevance, buyer activity, seller reputation, and price competitiveness. While Best Match is not a static set of rules, the general principle is to prioritize listings that have a higher likelihood of satisfying the buyer's needs. For example, if a buyer is searching for a "brand new iPhone 13 case," the algorithm will favor listings that accurately match that search term and come from a highly rated seller with a strong shipping record.

A key aspect of understanding the search algorithm is knowing that eBay continually updates and refines its algorithms to improve user experience. As a result, eBay sellers must stay on top of these changes to maintain their SEO performance. Periodically reviewing and adjusting your listings according to eBay's guidelines is necessary to remain competitive in search rankings. This might involve tweaking product titles, revising descriptions, or updating your shipping policies to meet new standards.

To further optimize your eBay listings for search, it's important to stay active within the platform. Regularly adding new items, updating existing listings, and participating in promotional offers or sales events can help increase visibility. The more activity you have on your account, the more eBay's algorithm will recognize your presence and reward you with higher rankings. A consistent flow of new listings and positive interactions with buyers signals to eBay that your business is legitimate and committed to providing a high-quality shopping experience.

One powerful tool that can help sellers improve their SEO performance is eBay's Promoted Listings feature. Promoted Listings allow you to pay for additional exposure of your items, increasing the likelihood of them appearing at the top of search results. While using this feature doesn't guarantee that your items will automatically rank first, it can give your listings a boost, especially in competitive categories. The Promoted Listings algorithm works by considering factors like keyword relevance, item quality, and ad performance. By utilizing this tool strategically, you can increase your visibility and reach more potential buyers.

The use of eBay's advertising tools, including Promoted Listings, is just one aspect of a broader SEO strategy. To achieve the best possible results, sellers should regularly analyze their performance and optimize their listings based on data. eBay provides analytics tools that show how well your listings are performing in search, allowing you to identify opportunities for improvement. By analyzing which keywords drive the most traffic, you can make adjustments to your titles, descriptions, and tags to align with buyer behavior and maximize visibility.

eBay SEO is a dynamic and evolving field that requires sellers to be proactive and adaptable. By understanding the key factors that influence search rankings and staying ahead of changes to eBay's algorithms, you can improve the visibility of your listings, increase your sales, and establish a successful eBay business. As you refine your listings, focus on providing a seamless customer experience and maintaining a strong seller reputation. When combined with SEO best practices, these elements will help ensure your success on the platform for years to come.

UTILIZING KEYWORDS EFFECTIVELY IN TITLES AND DESCRIPTIONS

When selling on eBay, one of the most critical factors influencing the visibility of your listings is the use of keywords in your titles and descriptions. These keywords play a significant role in how your products are discovered by potential buyers, and understanding how to use them effectively can dramatically increase your sales. Whether you're selling a rare collectible, a piece of fashion, or electronics, choosing the right keywords and strategically incorporating them into your product titles and descriptions is essential for boosting your listing's ranking in search results.

To begin, it's important to understand how eBay's search algorithm works. The platform relies on a system called Best Match, which ranks listings based on several factors, with keywords being one of the most crucial. When a buyer types a search term into the search bar, eBay's algorithm will scan the listings for relevance to the keywords entered. If your listing matches the search query, it's more likely to appear at the top of the search results. Therefore, ensuring that your titles and descriptions contain the right keywords is key to increasing visibility.

The title of your listing is the first and most obvious place to focus on when it comes to keyword usage. eBay allows sellers up to 80 characters for the title, and using this space wisely is vital. The title should be both descriptive and concise, including essential details about the item that a potential buyer would search for. Think of keywords that buyers would likely use when searching for the type of product you're selling. For example, if you're selling a vintage 1990s Nike T-shirt, including key details like "vintage," "Nike," and "1990s" can help buyers looking for that exact product find your listing.

The key to success with keywords in titles is finding the right balance between specificity and broad appeal. While it's tempting to use as many keywords as possible, you don't want to overstuff your title with irrelevant terms. Instead, focus on the most important and relevant keywords that are likely to drive traffic to your listing. Also, avoid repeating words unnecessarily. For instance, if your product is a "Sony PlayStation 5 Console," there is no need to say "Sony PlayStation 5 Console Console." Instead, make use of those 80 characters to add more specific details like the model, condition, or any included accessories. Remember that titles should flow naturally and be readable to human eyes, not just the algorithm.

When writing product descriptions, you need to extend the keyword strategy beyond the title. While titles are crucial for initial visibility, descriptions help to provide more context and additional keywords that can attract a broader audience. Descriptions should be comprehensive and give potential buyers all the information they need to make an informed purchase. However, they should also be optimized for eBay's search algorithm by using relevant keywords throughout. For example, if you're selling a vintage leather handbag, your description might include terms like "genuine leather," "vintage," "designer," "luxury," and "authentic." These keywords will help the search engine connect your product to buyer queries searching for these specific characteristics.

It's important to avoid keyword stuffing, a practice where too many keywords are crammed into a description to manipulate search rankings. This can result in a poor customer experience and could even hurt your rankings. Instead, focus on crafting a natural, detailed description that incorporates keywords in a way that feels authentic. Using keywords within the context of complete sentences helps make the description sound natural while still benefiting from SEO optimization. For example, instead of listing keywords like "authentic leather, vintage handbag, designer purse" in a jumbled manner, write something like, "This authentic vintage leather handbag from a renowned designer is the perfect accessory for those who appreciate high-quality craftsmanship."

Incorporating long-tail keywords can be another powerful strategy. Long-tail keywords are longer, more specific phrases that target niche searches. These can help you stand out in competitive markets. For instance, instead of just "camera," a long-tail keyword could be "Canon DSLR camera with 18-55mm lens." Long-tail keywords are often less competitive, meaning they can help attract a more targeted audience who is specifically searching for what you're offering. While these phrases might have lower search volume than shorter keywords, they often lead to higher conversion rates because they're tailored to what the buyer is actually looking for.

One of the best ways to discover relevant keywords is through eBay's own search tools and the platform's autocomplete function. By typing in the first few letters of a search term, eBay will suggest popular phrases that buyers frequently search for. Additionally, eBay's Seller Hub provides valuable insights into the search terms that are driving traffic to your listings. These analytics can help you refine your keywords and identify new opportunities. Tools like Google Keyword Planner and third-party eBay keyword research tools can also be useful in identifying keywords with high search volumes.

Another effective strategy for utilizing keywords is to incorporate them into your item specifics. Item specifics are attributes like brand, size, color, material, and condition that help eBay's search algorithm understand your listing better. Including the right item specifics can increase the likelihood of your listing being found by buyers who are looking for specific product characteristics. While item specifics may not directly impact your search ranking, they improve the accuracy of search results and can help you reach the right audience.

While keywords are essential for visibility, it's equally important to focus on creating a positive buyer experience. If your listing has a high-quality description, accurate keywords, and well-chosen titles, it will be more likely to gain traction in search results. However, great content alone isn't enough. Buyers are looking for sellers who provide value, transparency, and trustworthiness. A well-written description that helps buyers understand exactly what they're purchasing, coupled with professional and friendly communication, can help you build a reputation that encourages repeat business.

In addition to optimizing your listings for keywords, it's important to stay current with eBay's ever-evolving SEO practices. As eBay continues to refine its search algorithm to improve buyer experience, keeping an eye on the platform's updates and trends will ensure that your listings remain relevant. Regularly refreshing your listings, revisiting your keywords, and keeping your product descriptions updated will keep you ahead of the competition.

Utilizing keywords effectively in both your titles and descriptions is vital for improving the visibility of your eBay listings and driving traffic to your store. By thoughtfully selecting keywords that match what buyers are searching for, creating clear and comprehensive descriptions, and keeping up with eBay's search practices, you can greatly increase your chances of standing out in a crowded marketplace. At the same time, always focus on providing value to your customers by crafting engaging, accurate, and honest content that enhances their buying experience. This balanced approach to keyword optimization will not only help improve your eBay SEO but also help establish you as a trusted and successful seller.

LEVERAGING ITEM SPECIFICS AND CATEGORIES

One of the most important aspects of creating a successful eBay listing is leveraging item specifics and categories effectively. These tools play a critical role in ensuring that your products are accurately represented and easily discoverable by potential buyers. On a crowded marketplace like eBay, standing out is crucial, and utilizing item specifics and categories can make a significant difference in how well your listings perform in search results.

When it comes to item specifics, think of them as the building blocks that give eBay's search engine the detailed information it needs to match your listing with relevant buyer queries. Item specifics are attributes like size, color, brand, model, material, condition, and more, which help describe the product in greater detail. These details help eBay's algorithm categorize your product correctly, making it easier for buyers to find it when searching for similar items. The more accurate and detailed your item specifics, the better your chances of ranking higher in search results and reaching the right audience.

One of the biggest advantages of using item specifics is that they directly impact how your listings are filtered in search results. eBay's search engine relies on these specifics to match buyers' search queries with relevant listings. For instance, if a buyer is looking for a "blue leather handbag," the search engine will use item specifics to filter through thousands of listings and show only those that match the color and material. If your listing includes the correct specifics for "color" and "material," it will be more likely to appear in this buyer's search results.

To take full advantage of item specifics, sellers should complete every applicable field when creating or editing their listings. eBay provides a list of standard item specifics for each category, which sellers should take care to fill out. While it might be tempting to skip over some fields or leave them blank, doing so can harm your listing's visibility. Buyers may not be able to filter your product through search filters if it lacks essential item specifics like size or brand, which could result in missed sales opportunities. Always make sure that the information you provide is accurate, as misleading or incorrect specifics can lead to poor customer experiences and negative feedback.

The categories you choose for your products are just as important as the item specifics. Categories help eBay's search engine classify your products into specific sections of the marketplace, ensuring that potential buyers are shown products that fit their search criteria. Choosing the correct category is critical, as it determines where your product will appear within eBay's vast catalog. If you place an item in the wrong category, buyers who are searching within that category may never even see your listing.

When selecting a category, it's essential to carefully consider the nature of your product and the search behavior of your target audience. Think about how buyers would typically search for your product. For example, if you're selling a vintage bicycle, don't just place it in a broad category like "Sports & Outdoors." Instead, you should refine your search to more specific categories such as "Cycling" or "Vintage Bicycles" to increase the likelihood of reaching the right buyers. By selecting a more precise category, you improve your chances of ranking higher in search results for relevant queries, as your listing will be associated with a more specific group of potential buyers.

In addition to choosing the correct category, you should also pay close attention to eBay's subcategories. eBay often breaks larger categories into more refined subcategories, which can help your product get even more specific visibility. For instance, if you're selling a used video game, you might select the category "Video Games & Consoles" and then choose a subcategory such as "Video Games" and further narrow it down to "PlayStation 4" or "Action & Adventure Games." This helps your product show up in more targeted searches, ensuring that only buyers who are interested in exactly what you're selling will see your listing.

Taking the time to optimize your item specifics and categories is particularly important for sellers who are competing in high-demand or competitive markets. In these cases, the extra effort can help you stand out from the crowd. Even small differences in how your product is categorized or described can lead to a significant increase in visibility. Additionally, many buyers use eBay's search filters to narrow down results based on specific item criteria, such as size, condition, and brand. By accurately selecting item specifics and categories, you ensure that your listing is more likely to meet the criteria that buyers use to filter search results.

Another benefit of using item specifics and categories properly is that they allow you to leverage eBay's search filters. These filters let buyers search for products based on specific criteria, such as price range, location, condition, and more. When your product is correctly categorized and includes the appropriate item specifics, your listing becomes eligible to appear in these filtered searches, which increases the chances that it will be seen by relevant buyers. For example, if a buyer is looking for a new iPhone 12 in "mint condition," they can filter their search to show only listings that match that description. If your listing has the correct item specifics filled out, your product will be displayed within that filter, putting it in front of an even more targeted audience.

In addition to improving your listing's search ranking, item specifics and categories also help to establish trust with buyers. When a listing includes accurate and detailed information about the product, buyers are more likely to feel confident in their purchase. Transparency is key when selling online, and providing clear, specific details about your product's features and condition helps to minimize any confusion or misunderstandings. Buyers are more likely to leave positive feedback and return for future purchases when they know exactly what they're getting.

One often-overlooked benefit of properly using item specifics and categories is that they can improve your chances of appearing in eBay's "Best Match" search results. The Best Match algorithm takes into account factors such as relevance, price, and shipping options, but it also considers how well your listing is categorized and whether it includes the right item specifics. Properly optimized listings are more likely to appear at the top of search results, giving you an edge over competitors.

It's important to stay up-to-date with eBay's evolving guidelines for item specifics and categories. eBay frequently updates its item specifics requirements to reflect changes in product trends and buyer behavior. New categories and item specifics fields are often introduced, while others may be removed or altered. Regularly reviewing eBay's updates ensures that your listings are always optimized for the latest search trends, which can help you maintain a competitive edge.

Leveraging item specifics and categories effectively is crucial to the success of your eBay business. These tools help eBay's search engine accurately categorize your listings, increase their visibility in search results, and ensure that buyers can find exactly what they're looking for.

By taking the time to select the right categories, fill out all relevant item specifics, and regularly update your listings, you can improve your chances of standing out in a competitive marketplace, build trust with potential buyers, and ultimately increase your sales.

UNDERSTANDING EBAY'S BEST MATCH ALGORITHM

eBay's Best Match algorithm is the backbone of the marketplace's search functionality. When potential buyers enter a search term, eBay's algorithm decides which listings will appear first, based on various factors that determine relevance and appeal. Understanding how Best Match works is critical for any seller looking to increase visibility and drive sales. The goal for sellers should always be to ensure their listings are optimized for Best Match so they can consistently appear at the top of search results.

At its core, the Best Match algorithm is designed to provide buyers with the most relevant and appealing results for their search queries. When a buyer types in a keyword or phrase, the algorithm sifts through millions of listings and ranks them according to several factors. The more relevant and high-quality a listing is, the higher it will appear in search results. Best Match is constantly evolving, and it is important for sellers to stay current on the changes that eBay introduces.

One of the key components of the Best Match algorithm is the relevance of the keywords in your listing. When you choose your keywords, you need to think like a buyer. What words would a buyer use to search for your product? Make sure that your title and description contain those words, as this is the primary way the algorithm identifies what your listing is about. The more specific and accurate your keywords, the more likely your listing is to appear for relevant searches.

But relevance alone doesn't guarantee a high ranking. eBay also takes into account the listing's overall quality. This includes factors like item condition, price, and shipping options. For example, a well-priced item in excellent condition will perform better than an identical item priced too high or in poor condition. Sellers who offer competitive prices and present their items in top condition are rewarded by the Best Match algorithm.

Shipping is another crucial factor in Best Match rankings. eBay has long emphasized the importance of providing fast and affordable shipping. The algorithm takes into account the seller's shipping performance, including how quickly items are shipped after payment is received and whether the seller offers free shipping. Listings that include free shipping tend to rank higher, as buyers are drawn to the convenience of not having to factor shipping costs into their purchase decision. If you are a seller who offers expedited shipping or faster delivery times, this can also give your listing a boost in the search rankings.

Another important element that influences Best Match is the seller's overall performance. eBay wants to promote listings from sellers who consistently meet or exceed buyer expectations. The algorithm takes into account metrics such as the seller's feedback score, customer service ratings, and shipping time. A seller who has a high positive feedback score and consistently ships items quickly is more likely to rank higher in search results. Sellers with a history of negative feedback or poor customer service can see their listings suppressed in search results.

The number of sales you make also impacts how your listing ranks in Best Match. eBay rewards listings with a high number of sales because they are perceived as more trusted and more popular with buyers. This is why having a steady flow of sales and positive feedback is crucial. The more successful sales you have, the more likely eBay is to push your listings higher in search results. However, this is a cumulative factor; you will need a solid track record of successful transactions to consistently rank well.

The listing's format and listing structure can also play a role in Best Match rankings. For instance, eBay's algorithm takes note of the quality of your listing description. A detailed and clear description can enhance your search ranking because it helps buyers find exactly what they're looking for. Furthermore, listings with clear, high-quality images of the product have a better chance of ranking well because they are more likely to convert views into purchases. If your listing has multiple high-quality images showing the product from different angles, the chances of appearing in the top results are increased.

Additionally, Best Match rewards sellers who consistently update their listings. Regularly reviewing and refreshing your listings shows eBay that your items are up-to-date and still available for sale. If you don't regularly refresh your listings, especially if they are older or outdated, eBay may lower your ranking in search results.

One factor that many sellers overlook is the item's return policy. eBay places significant weight on whether a seller offers a returns policy. Buyers tend to trust sellers who offer a reasonable return policy, which is why listings that offer free returns or a long return window generally perform better in Best Match rankings. A generous return policy can reduce a buyer's hesitation, knowing they can return the item if it doesn't meet their expectations.

eBay also pays attention to whether your listing is part of the eBay Top Rated Seller program. Sellers who have earned Top Rated Seller status through their consistent performance in shipping, customer service, and other metrics often receive priority in Best Match rankings. To qualify for this program, sellers must meet a set of specific criteria, including a minimum percentage of positive feedback and a certain level of shipping performance. Sellers with Top Rated Seller status have the added benefit of receiving a discount on their final value fees, which can improve profitability.

Another increasingly important factor in Best Match is the use of eBay's Promoted Listings feature. While Promoted Listings are a paid option, they give sellers the ability to increase the visibility of their listings by promoting them in sponsored spaces. Promoted Listings can help drive more traffic to your products, but they don't guarantee that your listing will be ranked higher in organic search results. However, by using Promoted Listings, you can effectively increase the visibility of your products and attract more potential buyers. This can indirectly help increase the number of sales and, ultimately, improve your standing in Best Match.

The final element to consider is mobile optimization. More and more buyers are shopping via mobile devices, and eBay has designed its search algorithm with this shift in mind. Listings that are optimized for mobile users tend to rank higher in Best Match results. This means using concise and clear descriptions, high-quality images, and easy-to-navigate listings. If your listing is not mobile-friendly, it will likely perform poorly in search results, especially when buyers are accessing the platform via smartphones or tablets.

To sum up, understanding and optimizing for Best Match is a multi-faceted process. The Best Match algorithm considers a variety of factors, including the relevance of keywords, the quality of the listing, shipping options, and the seller's overall performance. To succeed in eBay's competitive marketplace, sellers must focus on improving each of these factors. By creating high-quality, well-optimized listings, offering competitive prices, providing excellent customer service, and regularly refreshing your listings, you can increase your chances of ranking higher in Best Match results. Regularly reviewing eBay's guidelines and adjusting your strategies as the platform evolves will ensure that you stay competitive and visible to potential buyers.

KEEPING UP WITH EBAY'S SEARCH UPDATES (2025 CONSIDERATIONS)

In the ever-evolving landscape of eBay, staying ahead of changes in the platform's search algorithms and updates is a crucial part of building a successful selling business. As eBay continues to refine its search features and algorithms, sellers must be vigilant in adapting their strategies to maintain visibility and competitiveness. The importance of keeping up with eBay's search updates cannot be overstated—especially in 2025, where there are new trends, tools, and shifts in user behavior to consider.

The core of eBay's search engine is its ability to match buyers with the most relevant products based on their search queries. This process is largely governed by the Best Match algorithm, which takes into account various factors, including keywords, listing quality, shipping, and seller performance. eBay regularly updates this algorithm to improve user experience, refine search results, and adapt to emerging e-commerce trends. For sellers, staying informed about these updates is vital for ensuring that their listings remain competitive and visible.

One of the most noticeable shifts in eBay's search updates in recent years is the growing importance of artificial intelligence (AI) and machine learning in the platform's search algorithms. In 2025, eBay continues to enhance its AI-driven systems to deliver more personalized and relevant search results for buyers. As a seller, this means that simply relying on traditional methods like optimizing keywords or listing titles may not be enough to stay ahead. AI algorithms are designed to learn from user behavior, refining their ability to rank listings based on subtle nuances and patterns. Sellers who actively monitor and adapt to these changes will be in a better position to benefit from the evolving system.

Another major consideration is the increased focus on mobile-first experiences. As mobile commerce continues to rise, eBay has made significant strides in optimizing its platform for mobile users. For sellers, this means that listings need to be fully optimized for mobile devices in order to perform well in search rankings. In 2025, eBay's search updates are expected to place even greater emphasis on mobile-friendliness, considering how buyers interact with listings through their smartphones and tablets. This includes ensuring that product images are clear and high-quality, descriptions are concise and scannable, and the overall user experience is seamless on smaller screens. Sellers who fail to optimize their listings for mobile risk being buried in search results, as eBay increasingly prioritizes mobile-friendly content.

Additionally, eBay's continued push for sustainability and eco-friendly practices is another update that sellers should take note of in 2025. eBay is actively encouraging sellers to adopt green business practices, and this shift is reflected in its search updates. Listings that showcase eco-friendly or sustainable attributes may receive preferential treatment in search results, particularly if they align with buyer preferences for environmentally responsible products. Sellers who highlight their commitment to sustainability, whether through using recyclable packaging or promoting products made from sustainable materials, may benefit from this new focus in eBay's search algorithm. In this sense, staying updated on eBay's search updates goes beyond technical optimizations and extends to aligning with evolving consumer values.

Equally important is the increase in the role of eBay's Promoted Listings in 2025. While Promoted Listings have always been a paid option for sellers looking to increase visibility, recent updates to the search algorithm suggest that the influence of this feature will continue to grow. In 2025, sellers who want to stand out in search results may need to invest more heavily in Promoted Listings. This feature enables sellers to pay for better placement of their listings in search results, and eBay uses its AI to determine the most relevant listings for these promoted spaces. As more sellers turn to Promoted Listings, competition for these premium spots will intensify, making it more important than ever to monitor the performance of promoted listings and adjust bids accordingly.

eBay is also placing a greater emphasis on the overall quality of the buyer's experience, including how quickly items are shipped and whether they are accurately described. In 2025, sellers are likely to see more updates that reward excellent customer service and penalize sellers who fail to meet buyer expectations. A timely response to customer inquiries, offering free or expedited shipping, and having a clear, easy-to-understand return policy are all factors that contribute to a positive buyer experience and, therefore, to a better search ranking. To keep up with eBay's updates, sellers will need to continuously monitor their performance metrics, including shipping times, customer feedback, and return rates, and take action to maintain a high level of service.

One of the most important aspects of keeping up with eBay's search updates in 2025 is understanding how changes to search algorithms may impact your listing optimization strategy. As eBay refines its search criteria, sellers must be agile in adapting their listings to stay relevant. For example, while keyword optimization used to be the primary way to rank in search results, eBay's focus on listing quality and customer satisfaction has grown in importance. In 2025, simply using the right keywords in your title and description may not be enough to rank highly in search results. Instead, eBay's algorithms are more likely to prioritize listings that have clear, concise descriptions, high-quality images, competitive pricing, and strong customer service metrics.

To stay ahead of these changes, sellers should regularly audit their listings to ensure they meet eBay's current standards. This includes reviewing their titles, descriptions, item specifics, and images to ensure they are optimized for the latest search trends. Sellers should also keep an eye on their sales performance and customer feedback, as eBay's algorithm takes both of these into account when ranking listings. High-performing sellers with excellent feedback and customer service ratings are more likely to appear higher in search results than those with lower performance metrics.

In addition to optimizing individual listings, sellers should also stay informed about broader eBay policy updates and trends that could affect their business. For instance, eBay has made efforts in recent years to standardize pricing and shipping policies across the platform. Sellers who do not comply with these policies may find their listings penalized in search results. In 2025, eBay may introduce new policies or updates aimed at improving the platform's overall user experience, and sellers who are quick to adapt to these changes will have a competitive edge.

Another crucial consideration is the impact of eBay's integration with external platforms and channels. As eBay continues to expand its presence across social media and other online marketplaces, sellers must be mindful of how their listings perform across these platforms. In 2025, search updates may favor listings that are cross-promoted or integrated with social media platforms like Instagram, Facebook, or Pinterest. Sellers who leverage these external platforms and link them to their eBay listings may see an increase in visibility and traffic, as eBay's algorithm rewards listings that engage with a wider audience.

To stay on top of these updates, it is important to follow eBay's official seller channels, including blogs, forums, and newsletters. eBay often announces search updates and algorithm changes through these outlets, and staying informed will allow sellers to adjust their strategies quickly. Sellers should also consider participating in eBay's community forums, where they can share experiences with other sellers and learn about best practices for optimizing listings based on the latest search trends.

Keeping up with eBay's search updates in 2025 is essential for any seller who wants to remain competitive on the platform. With the growing influence of AI, mobile optimization, sustainability, and changes to search algorithms, sellers need to be proactive in adapting their strategies. By staying informed about eBay's search updates and aligning their listings with current trends, sellers can maintain strong visibility and continue to drive sales in an increasingly dynamic online marketplace. Regularly auditing your listings, optimizing for mobile, and focusing on customer satisfaction will ensure that your products are always in front of the right buyers, no matter how the search algorithms evolve.

CHAPTER 11

LEVERAGING EBAY'S MARKETING AND PROMOTIONAL TOOLS

MASTERING PROMOTED LISTINGS: ADVANCED STRATEGIES

Mastering Promoted Listings on eBay is an essential component of a successful selling strategy, particularly as competition grows and more sellers vie for visibility on the platform. While understanding the basics of Promoted Listings is critical, leveraging advanced strategies will allow sellers to not only enhance their visibility but also maximize their sales and profitability. In 2025, as eBay's marketplace becomes increasingly sophisticated, using Promoted Listings effectively has become more than just a tool to increase exposure. It is now an essential tactic for competing in a crowded marketplace, and sellers who master this feature stand to significantly boost their sales.

At its core, Promoted Listings is a paid advertising option on eBay that allows sellers to have their products appear more prominently in search results and on other parts of the platform. eBay uses an auction-style bidding system for Promoted Listings, meaning sellers bid a percentage of their sale price in exchange for better placement in search results. However, the real challenge lies in understanding the nuances of the Promoted Listings system and how to use it strategically to maximize return on investment (ROI).

One of the advanced strategies for mastering Promoted Listings lies in the ability to choose the right products to promote. While it might seem tempting to promote every item in your store, focusing your efforts on the products with the highest potential for success is a more effective approach. Analyze your sales data and identify the items that have the highest demand but aren't getting enough organic visibility. These are the products that will benefit most from additional promotion. Additionally, consider promoting high-margin products where the cost of the promoted listing will be outweighed by the profit you stand to make from a sale.

Another key strategy is understanding the different types of Promoted Listings and when to use them. eBay offers two primary types of Promoted Listings: Promoted Listings Standard and Promoted Listings Advanced. The Standard option allows you to pay for increased visibility in eBay's search results, while the Advanced option gives you more control over the bidding process, allowing for advanced targeting options and the ability to place your promoted listings in specific locations throughout eBay's site, including on the homepage, category pages, and in recommendations. Sellers who are looking to fine-tune their advertising approach should consider utilizing Promoted Listings Advanced, especially if they have a well-defined customer base or are looking to target specific demographics.

To fully master the power of Promoted Listings, it is essential to understand how eBay's algorithm works and how it interacts with bidding strategies. eBay's search engine, called Best Match, determines the ranking of promoted listings based on a variety of factors. These include how competitive your bid is, the relevance of your listing's title, and the quality of your listing itself. To improve the chances of your listing appearing in the top search results, make sure that your listing is optimized with relevant keywords, high-quality images, and accurate descriptions. Additionally, consider using eBay's Dynamic Pricing feature, which adjusts your bids based on factors like the item's competitiveness and the time of day. This feature allows you to automate some of the decision-making in your promotions, ensuring that you remain competitive without having to manually adjust bids every day.

One of the most advanced techniques in using Promoted Listings effectively is leveraging eBay's reporting and analytics tools. After running a promotion for a period of time, eBay provides sellers with detailed insights into the performance of their promoted listings. These reports include important metrics such as impressions, clicks, and conversions, which can help sellers understand which promotions are working and which ones need adjustment. By studying this data, you can identify trends and patterns that will allow you to make more informed decisions about where to allocate your promotional budget in the future. For example, you might discover that a certain product is performing exceptionally well with a high bid, while another product requires a lower bid to be competitive. The key is to continuously monitor your campaigns and optimize them based on real-time performance data.

Further sophistication comes in the form of using eBay's Artificial Intelligence (AI) tools to automate some of the processes around Promoted Listings. eBay's AI can help sellers by automatically adjusting their bids in real-time based on current market conditions, sales data, and other factors. This removes much of the guesswork from the bidding process and ensures that you are always getting the best return on your investment. Sellers who are less comfortable with manual bidding or don't have the time to constantly monitor their campaigns will find AI-driven automation a powerful tool in maximizing their results.

Timing is another critical factor when using Promoted Listings. Sellers often overlook the significance of when they launch their promoted campaigns. In 2025, one of the best practices for eBay sellers is to align their promotions with key shopping events and holidays. By strategically running promotions during peak buying seasons, such as Black Friday,

Cyber Monday, or back-to-school sales, you can take advantage of the surge in buyer activity. Additionally, analyzing customer behavior on eBay during these times and adjusting your bids and listings accordingly can result in better visibility and higher sales. You can also experiment with different bid amounts based on the time of day or week, as shopping patterns can vary depending on when customers are most likely to browse and purchase.

One important point to consider is the relationship between Promoted Listings and your overall seller performance metrics. eBay closely monitors your seller performance, which includes factors such as feedback, shipping time, return rates, and overall customer satisfaction. A higher-performing seller is more likely to benefit from the Promoted Listings system because eBay rewards good sellers with better placement. In contrast, sellers who have poor performance metrics may see their promoted listings pushed lower in search rankings, even if they are bidding competitively. Therefore, maintaining a strong overall seller reputation is just as important as optimizing individual listings for promotion.

For advanced sellers looking to maximize the impact of their Promoted Listings campaigns, consider experimenting with A/B testing. A/B testing allows sellers to create two versions of a promoted listing with slight variations, such as different titles, images, or promotional offers. By running both versions simultaneously, you can gather data on which version performs better in terms of clicks and conversions. This enables you to fine-tune your listings for optimal performance and continually improve your promotional strategy.

Additionally, consider diversifying your promotional approach by using multiple channels. Promoted Listings can be particularly effective when combined with other marketing tactics, such as email marketing, social media campaigns, or even external advertising on platforms like Google or Facebook. A multi-channel marketing approach helps increase the overall visibility of your listings and drives more traffic to your eBay store. Sellers who incorporate a cohesive strategy that spans multiple platforms often see higher returns on their advertising investments.

Mastering Promoted Listings is about finding the right balance between investing in promotions and controlling costs. While it can be tempting to pour a large portion of your budget into these paid listings, the goal is to ensure that the cost of promoting your listings doesn't exceed the profit you stand to gain. By setting clear goals, tracking your ROI, and adjusting bids based on performance data, you can ensure that your promotional campaigns are not only effective but also sustainable in the long run.

Mastering Promoted Listings is a powerful strategy for sellers looking to gain a competitive edge in eBay's crowded marketplace. By carefully selecting the right products, optimizing your listings, leveraging eBay's reporting and AI tools, and strategically timing your campaigns, you can significantly increase your visibility and sales. Advanced sellers who can fine-tune their bidding strategies, use automation tools, and align their promotions with key shopping events will be well-positioned to capitalize on the full potential of eBay's Promoted Listings system. With the right approach, this feature can become a cornerstone of a successful eBay business in 2025 and beyond.

CREATING AND MANAGING EBAY STORE SUBSCRIPTIONS (IF APPLICABLE)

Creating and managing eBay store subscriptions is an essential strategy for sellers looking to establish a professional online presence while maximizing their visibility and sales potential. eBay offers various store subscription options tailored to different seller needs, allowing individuals to scale their businesses effectively. Whether you are a hobbyist seller with a few items or a serious entrepreneur with hundreds or thousands of products, the right store subscription can make a significant difference in your ability to grow your eBay business.

The first step in navigating eBay store subscriptions is understanding the different types of store plans available. eBay offers several tiers of subscriptions, each with distinct benefits, features, and pricing structures. These plans include the Basic Store, Premium Store, and Anchor Store, each designed for sellers with different levels of inventory and sales volume. The Basic Store is ideal for smaller sellers with fewer than 100 items, offering a low monthly fee and a moderate number of free listings. As you move up the scale, the Premium Store is better suited for sellers with a higher volume of listings, typically between 100 and 1,000 items, providing more robust features and additional benefits. For high-volume sellers with extensive inventories, the Anchor Store offers the most comprehensive benefits, such as the highest number of free listings, exclusive promotions, and premium support services.

Once you've chosen the right store subscription for your business, it's time to focus on how to create and manage the store efficiently. Setting up an eBay store is a straightforward process, but there are some key decisions to make to ensure that your store is optimized for success. The first step is selecting a name for your store, which should reflect your brand and the type of products you sell. Ideally, your store name should be memorable, easy to spell, and relevant to your niche. Avoid using generic names that don't convey any meaning about what you offer. Instead, aim for a unique name that helps to establish your business's identity and makes it easy for customers to find you.

Once your store name is established, you can customize your store layout and design. eBay offers various themes and templates that allow you to create a visually appealing storefront that reflects your brand identity. It's important to keep the design professional, clean, and easy to navigate. A well-organized store layout with clear categories can help customers find what they're looking for quickly, increasing the likelihood of conversions. Additionally, having a polished and cohesive design can enhance your credibility and attract repeat customers.

Managing your store subscription involves more than just setting up the store initially. Ongoing management is key to ensuring that your eBay store remains effective and competitive. Regularly reviewing and updating your listings is an essential part of maintaining a successful store. This includes optimizing your product descriptions, ensuring that titles are clear and keyword-rich, and updating images as needed to reflect the current condition of your inventory. By keeping your listings fresh and up to date, you improve your store's visibility and attract potential buyers who are searching for the latest products.

Another important aspect of managing an eBay store is inventory control. The more products you sell, the more important it becomes to stay on top of stock levels and avoid overselling. eBay's store management tools allow you to track your inventory in real time, so you always know what items are in stock and what needs to be restocked. This helps to prevent customer frustration due to out-of-stock items and ensures that you are consistently meeting demand. Setting up automated alerts for low stock or creating custom inventory reports can streamline this process and save time.

In addition to maintaining your inventory, managing promotions is a crucial part of growing your eBay store. eBay offers a variety of promotional tools that allow you to highlight special offers, discounts, and limited-time sales. You can create markdowns, set up promotional campaigns, and offer volume discounts to attract more buyers. When running a promotion, be sure to advertise it within your store and across other eBay platforms to ensure maximum visibility. Running regular promotions helps to keep your store dynamic and engaging, drawing in new customers while encouraging repeat purchases from existing ones.

One of the key benefits of having a store subscription on eBay is access to advanced selling tools. These tools are designed to help you manage and grow your business more efficiently. The eBay Seller Hub provides a centralized location where you can access everything from sales reports and performance analytics to order management and customer feedback. These insights can help you make data-driven decisions about your store, such as which products are selling well, which need improvement, and which ones may be underperforming. By analyzing these metrics, you can fine-tune your store's offerings, adjust pricing strategies, and optimize your marketing efforts.

An additional feature for store subscribers is the ability to list in bulk, which is an invaluable tool for sellers with large inventories. Bulk listing allows you to upload multiple listings at once, saving time and ensuring consistency across your product offerings. Whether you are adding new products or updating existing ones, bulk listing streamlines the process and makes it more efficient. You can also create custom templates for your listings, making it easier to manage similar products with consistent formatting and descriptions.

As your store grows, it's important to invest in customer service and communication. A great customer experience can set your store apart from competitors and encourage positive feedback and repeat business. eBay offers store owners tools to manage customer communication efficiently, such as automated responses to frequently asked questions and customizable templates for messages. Timely and personalized responses to inquiries can help build trust with your customers and enhance their shopping experience. Providing excellent customer service, including fast shipping and hassle-free returns, can increase your chances of receiving positive reviews and higher ratings, which are crucial for maintaining a good standing within eBay's search rankings.

Another aspect of managing your eBay store subscription is staying updated on eBay's policies and fees. As a store owner, you are required to adhere to eBay's rules and regulations regarding listings, payment processing, shipping, and returns. Failure to comply with these policies can result in penalties, including suspension or termination of your store. Keeping yourself informed about eBay's updates and changes to policies will ensure that your store operates smoothly and avoids any disruptions in your selling activities.

Managing your eBay store subscription also involves understanding and controlling your costs. Each subscription plan comes with its own set of fees, which can include monthly subscription fees, listing fees, and final value fees. It's essential to track your expenses carefully and factor these costs into your pricing strategy. Sellers with larger inventories or more expensive items may benefit from higher-tier subscriptions, such as the Premium or Anchor plans, which offer additional benefits and free listings. By understanding the costs associated with each store subscription, you can choose the plan that best aligns with your business goals and budget.

As you continue to grow your store, consider experimenting with new strategies and expanding your product offerings. Use eBay's advanced analytics to track trends and identify new opportunities for growth. For example, consider adding new categories or branching into complementary products that align with your current inventory.

Expanding your range of products can attract new customers and help you tap into new markets.

Creating and managing an eBay store subscription requires careful planning, ongoing attention, and an understanding of the various tools and features available. By selecting the right store plan, customizing your store design, maintaining inventory control, running promotions, and utilizing advanced selling tools, you can create a successful and scalable eBay business. The right subscription can help streamline your operations and position your store for long-term growth and success. As the eBay marketplace continues to evolve, sellers who invest time and effort into managing their stores effectively will have a competitive edge in a dynamic and ever-changing online marketplace.

UTILIZING EBAY'S SALES EVENTS AND PROMOTIONS

eBay's sales events and promotional tools are a powerful resource for sellers looking to boost their sales, increase visibility, and attract more customers to their listings. By taking advantage of these events and using eBay's promotional features strategically, you can elevate your online business and achieve long-term success. Understanding how to navigate and effectively utilize eBay's sales events and promotional tools is crucial for any seller seeking to grow their presence on the platform.

One of the most notable promotional opportunities on eBay is the regular sales events hosted by the platform itself. These sales events are typically centered around specific holidays, shopping seasons, or special occasions such as Black Friday, Cyber Monday, eBay's own promotional events, and seasonal sales like Back to School or Winter Clearance. These sales events are designed to drive a high volume of traffic to the site, providing sellers with an invaluable opportunity to capitalize on the influx of buyers looking for deals. Participating in eBay's sales events can significantly enhance your visibility, particularly if your products are part of the event's featured categories or themes.

When you choose to participate in one of eBay's sales events, you are often given the option to include your listings in the event's promotional categories. These categories are highly visible, attracting many potential buyers who are actively browsing for discounted or specially promoted items. By including your listings in these categories, you gain the advantage of exposure to a much wider audience than you might receive through regular listings alone. Additionally, eBay often provides sellers with specific tools to help them advertise their participation, such as banners and promotional materials to showcase your discounted items.

To get the most out of eBay's sales events, it's important to ensure that your listings are optimized for success. First and foremost, you'll want to set competitive prices that align with the expectations of the event. For example, during a holiday or clearance event, buyers are often looking for significant discounts. Offering compelling deals and price reductions will help your listings stand out in the crowded marketplace. Another essential strategy is to use effective and accurate keywords in your item descriptions. By doing so, you make sure that your products are easily discoverable by shoppers searching for specific items or deals during the event. Well-crafted listings that speak to the value of your products can help you generate more sales and take advantage of the increased traffic.

In addition to the regular sales events hosted by eBay, there are various promotional tools that you can use year-round to further enhance your sales efforts. eBay's Promoted Listings is one of the most effective features for driving additional visibility to your products. This tool allows you to promote specific listings by paying a small fee to boost their visibility in search results. The promoted listings are placed at the top of search results or in other prime locations on eBay, making them more likely to be seen by potential buyers. This type of advertising is based on a cost-per-click model, meaning you only pay when a buyer clicks on your promoted listing. It's a highly cost-effective way to increase traffic to your products without committing to a flat-rate advertising fee.

To make the most of Promoted Listings, you'll need to choose which listings to promote based on several factors. High-demand items or products with the potential for high margins are good candidates for promotion. By boosting the visibility of these listings, you can maximize your chances of converting views into sales. Additionally, it's important to monitor the performance of your promoted listings regularly. eBay provides detailed analytics to help you track which listings are performing well and which might need adjustments to their promotional strategy. This data-driven approach allows you to fine-tune your advertising efforts and ensure you're investing in the listings that offer the greatest return on investment.

Another valuable promotional tool offered by eBay is the ability to create and manage custom sales events tailored to your store's offerings. For instance, you can create your own flash sales, bundle discounts, or specific promotions for holidays, special occasions, or even new product launches. These types of sales events allow you to engage directly with your target audience and create a sense of urgency around your products. For example, offering a limited-time discount or free shipping for a specific period can create excitement and encourage potential buyers to make a purchase before the promotion expires.

When setting up your custom sales events, it's important to create clear, eye-catching promotions that communicate the value of your offer.

Use eBay's promotion management tools to set up discounted pricing, apply coupon codes, and configure free shipping options. Make sure to promote your sale across various eBay platforms, including social media and your eBay store's homepage. The more visibility your promotion receives, the greater the chances of attracting buyers. Additionally, always monitor the performance of your sales event to assess its success. Pay attention to metrics such as sales volume, traffic, and customer engagement to evaluate how well your promotion is performing. This allows you to refine your promotional strategies for future sales events.

A key benefit of eBay's promotional tools is that they are not limited to major sales events or single promotions. You can also run ongoing promotional campaigns that allow you to engage with your customers on a regular basis. For example, you can offer volume discounts or set up a Buy More, Save More deal where customers receive a discount when they purchase multiple items from your store. This not only incentivizes larger orders but also encourages repeat business. Offering free shipping on orders over a certain amount or bundling related items can also be effective strategies to increase sales and keep your customers coming back.

Managing your promotional efforts effectively requires consistency and careful planning. By regularly running promotions and participating in eBay's sales events, you can establish your store as a go-to destination for deals and discounts. Be sure to take advantage of eBay's analytics tools to measure the impact of your campaigns. These insights can help you make data-backed decisions and identify the types of promotions that generate the most engagement and sales.

Another important factor to consider when participating in eBay's sales events and using promotional tools is customer experience. Ensure that your products are accurately represented and that your descriptions clearly communicate the value of your offer. Providing exceptional customer service, including fast shipping and hassle-free returns, is key to maintaining a positive reputation and generating repeat business. Shoppers are more likely to return to your store if they feel valued and have a smooth, enjoyable shopping experience.

Lastly, keep in mind that eBay's sales events and promotions are not just for driving sales; they are also an opportunity to build your brand and establish customer loyalty. By consistently offering great deals, running engaging promotions, and maintaining a high level of customer satisfaction, you create a positive impression of your store. Customers who have a good experience are more likely to leave positive feedback, recommend your store to others, and return for future purchases.

eBay's sales events and promotional tools offer sellers a wealth of opportunities to boost their visibility, increase sales, and foster long-term customer loyalty. Whether you are participating in eBay's seasonal events, running your own custom sales, or using promoted listings, these tools can significantly enhance your online business. By strategically utilizing these resources and optimizing your listings, pricing, and customer experience, you can ensure that your eBay store remains competitive and successful in a crowded marketplace.

EXPLORING EXTERNAL MARKETING STRATEGIES TO DRIVE TRAFFIC

Building a successful eBay business doesn't only rely on optimizing your listings and taking advantage of eBay's internal tools; external marketing strategies play a crucial role in driving traffic to your store and increasing visibility. While eBay's platform offers many built-in promotional options, there is a vast array of external strategies that can help you reach potential buyers who may not be actively searching on eBay. By tapping into various channels like social media, email marketing, search engine optimization (SEO), and partnerships, you can significantly enhance the exposure of your eBay store, attracting more traffic and ultimately driving more sales.

One of the most powerful external marketing strategies is social media marketing. Social media platforms such as Facebook, Instagram, Twitter, and Pinterest offer a unique opportunity to directly connect with potential customers and showcase your products in a more personal, engaging way. These platforms allow you to build a community of followers who are interested in your products and brand. Sharing posts that feature your products, behind-the-scenes glimpses of your business, and special promotions can help foster trust and interest among your audience. Social media also enables you to run targeted ads that reach a highly specific demographic based on factors like age, location, and interests, which increases the chances of converting viewers into buyers.

On platforms like Instagram and Pinterest, visual content is king. High-quality photos of your products in use or styled in appealing settings can attract customers and encourage them to visit your eBay store. Since these platforms are image-centric, it's important to invest time and effort into producing eye-catching, professional-looking visuals that capture the essence of your products. Hashtags are another vital tool in the social media world. Using relevant hashtags allows you to reach a broader audience, including people who are searching for specific types of products or who follow similar interests. By engaging consistently with your followers and using trending hashtags, you can organically grow your audience and drive traffic to your eBay listings.

Facebook, in particular, offers opportunities to engage with potential customers through groups and pages. You can join or create niche-specific groups related to the products you sell, participate in discussions, and subtly promote your store. This approach not only helps build brand awareness but also establishes your reputation as an authority in your niche. On top of organic engagement, Facebook's targeted advertising allows you to reach users who may not yet know about your business but are likely to be interested in your products. The platform provides a variety of ad formats, from carousel ads showcasing multiple products to dynamic ads that tailor the content to individual users based on their browsing behavior.

Another highly effective external marketing strategy is search engine optimization (SEO). SEO is the practice of optimizing your content so that it ranks higher on search engines like Google, driving organic traffic to your store or listings. While eBay itself has its own internal search engine, much of your traffic will come from Google and other search engines when users search for products outside of eBay. This makes SEO an essential element of driving traffic to your eBay business.

When optimizing your listings for SEO, one of the most important elements is keyword research. Understanding the words and phrases your target customers use when searching for products similar to yours will help you optimize your titles, descriptions, and other listing details. Tools like Google Keyword Planner, Ubersuggest, or even eBay's own search bar can help you discover relevant keywords that you can incorporate into your listings. Additionally, creating a blog or content that is related to your niche can help you rank for long-tail keywords that might not be as competitive but still bring in highly targeted traffic.

Beyond product listings, creating valuable content related to your niche can significantly enhance your SEO efforts. For example, if you sell kitchen gadgets on eBay, consider writing blog posts, guides, or even creating videos that offer helpful tips on using these products or share recipes using your items. By offering valuable content that answers common questions or provides solutions to problems, you can drive traffic from search engines to your site, where potential buyers may also visit your eBay store.

Another valuable tool for driving external traffic to your eBay store is email marketing. While email may seem like an outdated tactic, it remains one of the most effective ways to engage with customers and encourage repeat business. Building an email list is critical for staying in contact with your existing customers and enticing them back for future purchases. You can collect email addresses by offering incentives like discounts, giveaways, or exclusive access to sales events in exchange for subscribing to your newsletter.

Once you have a list of subscribers, you can send regular newsletters that feature your latest products, promotions, or even highlight items on sale. Personalized emails based on customer preferences, previous purchases, or browsing history can also help you target the right audience with the right message. Email marketing allows you to directly communicate with people who have already shown interest in your products, making it a highly effective strategy for driving traffic and encouraging conversions. Additionally, setting up automated email campaigns for abandoned cart reminders or follow-ups after a purchase can help recover lost sales and further increase traffic to your eBay store.

One of the most impactful external marketing strategies for eBay sellers is collaboration and partnership marketing. Partnering with influencers, bloggers, or other businesses in your niche can significantly increase your brand's exposure. Influencer marketing, in particular, has become a go-to tactic for many eBay sellers. By collaborating with influencers who have an established following, you can leverage their credibility and audience to drive traffic to your store. Influencers can review your products, create sponsored content, or simply showcase your products in a post or video. It's important to work with influencers whose audience aligns with your target market, ensuring that the partnership results in genuine interest and engagement with your eBay store.

Collaborating with bloggers is another effective way to drive traffic to your eBay listings. Many bloggers review products in exchange for a fee or free products. By sending your products to relevant bloggers and asking them to write reviews or feature your items in their content, you can attract their readers and drive traffic to your store. Similarly, partnering with other small businesses that complement your products can create mutually beneficial promotional opportunities. For example, if you sell handmade jewelry, partnering with a clothing boutique could result in cross-promotional content, giving both businesses exposure to each other's customer base.

Paid advertising is another external strategy that can generate targeted traffic for your eBay business. Beyond social media ads, Google Ads is a powerful tool for driving traffic to your eBay store. With Google Ads, you can create text, display, or shopping ads that appear in search results when users look for products you sell. Google Ads offers powerful targeting options, allowing you to refine your audience by keywords, demographics, and even location. If managed correctly, paid ads can be an excellent way to drive traffic to your eBay listings and significantly boost sales.

Participating in relevant online communities and forums can also drive traffic to your eBay store. Whether it's joining niche-specific subreddits, Facebook groups, or online forums, these communities allow you to connect with potential customers and engage in discussions related to your products. By offering helpful advice, answering questions, and providing useful resources, you can position yourself as an expert in your field. With time, your participation can drive traffic to your eBay store and establish trust with potential buyers.

While eBay offers various internal promotional tools, external marketing strategies are just as crucial for driving traffic and expanding your online business. By harnessing the power of social media, SEO, email marketing, collaborations, paid ads, and online communities, you can significantly increase the visibility of your eBay store. Implementing a combination of these strategies will not only drive more traffic but also build brand loyalty, engage with potential customers, and ultimately result in increased sales.

UNDERSTANDING EBAY'S ADVERTISING OPTIONS

Advertising plays a pivotal role in driving traffic to your eBay listings and helping your products stand out in a crowded marketplace. With millions of sellers and products available, it's easy for new listings to get lost in the shuffle. This is where eBay's advertising options come into play, offering sellers a range of tools to enhance visibility, increase sales, and boost their brand recognition. By understanding how these options work and how to effectively implement them, you can significantly improve the performance of your eBay business.

One of the most widely used advertising options on eBay is the Promoted Listings feature. Promoted Listings allows you to pay to boost the visibility of your listings, helping them appear higher in search results. When a potential buyer searches for a product, listings that are promoted often appear in prominent positions, including at the top of search results or in the "sponsored" section of the page. This increased visibility is especially important for new sellers who may not have the same established reputation or ranking as more experienced competitors.

Promoted Listings works on a cost-per-click (CPC) model, meaning that you only pay when a buyer clicks on your promoted listing. This makes it a performance-based advertising option, allowing you to control your costs and only pay for actual engagement with your listings. Setting up Promoted Listings is relatively simple: you select the products you want to promote, choose a percentage of the final sale price as your ad rate, and then let eBay do the rest. The higher the ad rate, the more likely it is that your listing will be shown in top positions, but it's important to balance this with your profit margins to ensure you're not over-spending.

One of the most powerful aspects of Promoted Listings is the ability to reach customers outside of eBay's organic search results. As an eBay seller, you're competing against thousands of other listings, and it's not always easy to get noticed. By promoting your listings, you can ensure that your products are being seen by a wider audience, which can lead to increased clicks, higher conversion rates, and ultimately more sales. This is especially beneficial for sellers in highly competitive categories or those who are just starting out and may not have a significant number of reviews or sales history to help their listings rank organically.

In addition to Promoted Listings, eBay offers another advertising tool known as Promoted Listings Advanced. This option offers more advanced targeting and bidding options, allowing you to have greater control over where and how your ads are shown. With Promoted Listings Advanced, you can choose specific keywords related to your listings, target certain customer demographics, and even advertise your products on external websites that eBay partners with. This expanded reach is ideal for sellers who want to diversify their marketing strategy and attract a broader audience.

The bidding process in Promoted Listings Advanced works similarly to that of Google Ads, where you can set your bids based on keywords or audience segments. The platform then uses an auction system to determine which listings will appear in prime positions. You can optimize your campaigns by adjusting your bids for specific keywords or categories that are most relevant to your products. This allows for a more tailored and focused approach to advertising, ensuring that you're targeting the right customers at the right time.

In addition to the CPC-based advertising options, eBay also provides other forms of promotional tools to enhance your visibility. One of these tools is the eBay Deals feature, where eBay promotes certain products on its homepage and in a dedicated section to shoppers who are looking for discounts. To participate in eBay Deals, sellers must apply for inclusion and meet certain criteria, such as offering products at competitive prices and providing free shipping. This promotional tool is ideal for sellers who want to clear inventory, offer special promotions, or simply attract a larger audience to their store.

eBay also offers a free promotion tool known as the Markdown Manager, which allows you to run sales events for specific products or your entire store. This feature allows you to discount selected items for a limited time and display those discounts prominently in search results, on your store page, and in other key areas of the eBay platform. Markdown events are a great way to increase traffic and generate interest in your products, especially during peak shopping seasons such as holidays or special shopping days like Black Friday or Cyber Monday.

Another advertising option available to eBay sellers is the use of coupon codes. Coupon codes are a great way to provide incentives for customers to make a purchase. As a seller, you can create custom coupons for your store that offer discounts on specific items or your entire inventory. When buyers use these codes at checkout, they receive a discount, and you have the potential to increase your conversion rate and boost sales. Coupons can be distributed through various channels, including social media, email marketing, and eBay's own promotional messaging. By offering time-sensitive discounts, you can create a sense of urgency that encourages buyers to take action.

While eBay offers several tools to help you promote your listings and increase visibility, it's also important to consider integrating your eBay advertising strategy with external marketing tactics. Social media marketing, for example, can be a highly effective way to drive traffic to your eBay store. By leveraging platforms like Instagram, Facebook, and Pinterest, you can create posts and ads that link directly to your eBay listings. Sharing high-quality images of your products, running contests, and collaborating with influencers can help generate buzz around your store and encourage more visitors to click through to your eBay listings.

Email marketing is another valuable external marketing strategy that can complement your eBay advertising efforts. By building an email list of customers and interested buyers, you can send personalized offers, product updates, and promotions directly to their inbox. These emails can include exclusive discounts, reminders about items left in shopping carts, or notifications about new listings. Engaging with your customers through email helps build loyalty and encourages repeat business, which can increase your eBay sales over time.

When it comes to optimizing your eBay advertising efforts, data analysis is key. eBay provides detailed analytics for your Promoted Listings campaigns, allowing you to track performance metrics such as clicks, impressions, and sales generated from your ads. By analyzing this data, you can determine which products are performing the best, which keywords are driving the most traffic, and whether your ad spend is yielding a positive return on investment (ROI). This data can inform future advertising decisions, helping you refine your strategy and allocate your budget to the most effective campaigns.

Ultimately, the key to success with eBay advertising is to experiment, test, and optimize. What works for one seller may not work for another, and it's important to continuously monitor and adjust your campaigns to find the best combination of ad formats, bidding strategies, and promotional tools. Whether you're using Promoted Listings to increase visibility, running markdown sales to attract shoppers, or offering coupons to incentivize purchases, eBay's advertising options provide powerful tools to help you grow your business and reach new customers. With the right approach, eBay advertising can be a highly effective way to drive traffic, boost sales, and enhance the overall success of your eBay store.

CHAPTER 12

MANAGING YOUR FINANCES AND TRACKING YOUR PERFORMANCE

SETTING UP EFFECTIVE FINANCIAL TRACKING SYSTEMS

Setting up an effective financial tracking system is crucial for any eBay seller aiming to build a successful and sustainable business. Whether you're selling as a side hustle or as your primary source of income, keeping an organized record of your income, expenses, and profits ensures that you stay on top of your finances and avoid costly mistakes. Additionally, a well-maintained financial tracking system will help you make informed decisions, improve your cash flow, and ensure that you meet your tax obligations. In this section, we will explore how to set up a robust financial tracking system for your eBay business, touching on various tools, techniques, and best practices to ensure that your financial records remain organized and accessible.

At the heart of an effective financial tracking system is the ability to accurately record all business-related transactions. Every sale, return, refund, and expense should be documented to give you a clear understanding of how much money is flowing in and out of your business. Without this level of detail, it can be difficult to assess the profitability of your eBay business or to make decisions that will help you grow in the long term. Tracking your finances begins with setting up a dedicated account that's separate from your personal finances. This not only helps keep things organized but also simplifies tax filing and reporting.

To track your financial activities, you will need reliable accounting tools. One of the most popular options for small business owners is accounting software. Programs like QuickBooks, Xero, and FreshBooks are designed to streamline financial record-keeping by automatically syncing with your bank accounts, credit cards, and payment platforms like PayPal. These tools allow you to record income and expenses, generate financial reports, track inventory, and even manage invoices. Many of these platforms also offer features that integrate with eBay, allowing you to import sales data directly into your financial system. This integration eliminates the need for manual entry, reducing the chance of errors and saving you valuable time.

When setting up your accounting software, be sure to categorize your transactions properly. Common categories for eBay businesses include income from sales, shipping costs, eBay fees, inventory costs, marketing expenses, and office supplies. If you have employees or hire contractors for specific tasks, such as photography or packing, their wages or fees should also be tracked separately. By organizing your finances into clear categories, you can easily review where your money is coming from and where it's going, which is essential for making decisions about pricing, inventory, and scaling your business.

Another critical aspect of setting up an effective financial tracking system is managing inventory. As an eBay seller, your inventory represents a significant portion of your investment. Whether you're selling physical goods that you source from suppliers or items you've purchased wholesale, tracking your inventory costs is vital for calculating profit margins. You need to know how much you've spent on acquiring your products and how that compares to the revenue generated from their sale. Accounting software typically includes inventory management features that allow you to track the cost of goods sold (COGS) and automatically update your inventory levels as sales are made.

In addition to inventory tracking, it's important to monitor other variable expenses such as packaging, shipping, and transaction fees. Packaging materials, such as boxes, bubble wrap, and tape, can add up over time, especially if you're selling high volumes of products. Shipping fees are another significant cost, and these vary depending on the size, weight, and destination of your products. By tracking these expenses carefully, you can adjust your pricing strategy to ensure that these costs are covered by your sales revenue. For example, if shipping fees are consistently higher than anticipated, you may decide to increase the price of your products or offer free shipping, factoring the cost into your overall pricing structure.

eBay also charges various fees that must be accounted for in your financial system. These include listing fees, final value fees (a percentage of the total sale price), and fees for using additional services like Promoted Listings or international shipping options. It's essential to keep track of these fees, as they directly affect your profit margins. Some accounting software, as mentioned earlier, can automatically import these fees from your eBay account, so you don't have to manually calculate them each time you make a sale.

For many eBay sellers, managing cash flow is a key challenge. Cash flow refers to the movement of money in and out of your business, and ensuring that you have enough cash on hand to cover your operating expenses is crucial for the health of your business. To maintain a positive cash flow, it's important to track not only your sales revenue but also your outstanding invoices, expenses, and pending payments. You should also be mindful of your sales cycles, which refer to how long it takes for inventory to sell and for payments to be processed. If you experience delays in receiving payments or have to wait for inventory to move, it can impact your ability to pay bills, restock products, or invest in marketing. By understanding your sales cycles and planning your cash flow accordingly, you can ensure that you have the funds necessary to keep your business running smoothly.

One way to ensure that you stay on top of your financial situation is to regularly review your financial statements. These reports provide a snapshot of your business's financial health and can be used to assess your profitability, identify areas of improvement, and track your progress toward your financial goals. Common financial statements include income statements, balance sheets, and cash flow statements. An income statement shows your revenue, costs, and expenses over a specific period, giving you insight into your profitability. A balance sheet provides an overview of your business's assets, liabilities, and equity, while a cash flow statement tracks the inflow and outflow of cash in your business. Regularly reviewing these reports will help you understand how well your business is performing and where adjustments need to be made.

Tax planning is another critical consideration for eBay sellers. Keeping accurate records of all your financial transactions ensures that you can easily calculate your tax obligations at the end of the year. Whether you're required to pay income tax, sales tax, or other business-related taxes, having well-organized financial records will make it much easier to file your taxes and avoid penalties. Many accounting tools also offer tax-related features, such as automatic tax calculations, which can help ensure that you stay compliant with local tax laws. It's also advisable to set aside a percentage of your income for taxes throughout the year, rather than waiting until tax season to pay, so that you are not caught off guard by a large bill.

To further streamline your financial tracking system, consider using spreadsheets as an additional tool for organizing your finances. While accounting software is a powerful solution, spreadsheets can be useful for tracking specific metrics that may not be covered in your primary accounting system. For example, you might use a spreadsheet to track the performance of specific products or monitor the impact of seasonal promotions on your sales. Excel or Google Sheets can also be used for budgeting, forecasting, and managing large volumes of data.

As your business grows, you may want to consider hiring a professional accountant or bookkeeper to help manage your finances. While software tools can automate much of the process, there are still complex financial considerations that may require expert guidance. An accountant can help you optimize your financial system, minimize your tax liability, and ensure that you are compliant with any legal or regulatory requirements.

Setting up an effective financial tracking system for your eBay business is essential for staying organized, making informed decisions, and ensuring long-term success. By using the right tools, tracking all income and expenses, monitoring cash flow, and reviewing financial statements regularly, you'll be better equipped to manage your finances and grow your business. With careful attention to detail and consistent monitoring, your financial system will be a valuable asset in achieving your business goals and maintaining a profitable eBay store.

UNDERSTANDING EBAY FEES AND CALCULATING PROFIT MARGINS

Understanding eBay fees and calculating profit margins is a critical aspect of managing a successful online business. As an eBay seller, comprehending the various fees associated with selling on the platform and knowing how to calculate your profit margins can help you make informed decisions about pricing, sourcing, and overall business strategy. A clear understanding of these concepts will empower you to maximize profits and avoid common pitfalls that can erode your earnings.

When you list a product on eBay, there are several types of fees that may apply. The most common fees include listing fees, final value fees, PayPal fees, and additional service fees for options such as Promoted Listings or international shipping. Each of these fees plays a role in determining the true cost of selling on eBay and must be factored into your pricing strategy to ensure that you are not only covering expenses but also making a profit.

The first type of fee you will encounter as a seller is the listing fee. eBay allows you to list a certain number of items for free each month, but beyond that, you will incur a listing fee for every additional item you choose to sell. The listing fee is typically a fixed amount per item and is charged regardless of whether the item sells. If you're using an auction-style listing, the listing fee is usually the same regardless of the starting bid, but for fixed-price listings, the fee may vary depending on the price at which you set the item. It's important to consider this fee when deciding how to price your products and whether the potential for sales justifies the cost of additional listings.

The second major fee to understand is the final value fee. This fee is charged when an item sells, and it's calculated as a percentage of the total selling price, including shipping costs. The percentage varies depending on the category of the item being sold, with categories like electronics and clothing generally attracting higher final value fees than other categories. This fee is one of the most significant costs associated with selling on eBay and can significantly affect your profit margins. As a seller, you need to account for this fee when setting your prices, as it reduces the amount of money you receive after a sale.

PayPal fees are another important cost to consider. While eBay now offers its own payment processing system called Managed Payments, many sellers still use PayPal to receive payments, especially for international sales. PayPal charges a fee for each transaction, which is typically a percentage of the total transaction amount plus a fixed fee. For example, PayPal's fee is generally around 2.9% of the total sale price, plus a fixed amount based on the currency received. These fees can add up quickly, particularly if you sell high-ticket items, so it's essential to factor them into your cost calculations. Even if you're using eBay's Managed Payments system, be aware that eBay also charges a small processing fee for payments, which you will need to account for.

In addition to these standard fees, eBay offers several paid services that can increase visibility and potentially lead to more sales, but they also come at an additional cost. One of the most popular of these services is Promoted Listings, which allows you to pay eBay to advertise your items and increase their chances of being seen by potential buyers. When you use Promoted Listings, you set an advertising fee, which is a percentage of the final sale price. This fee is only charged if your item sells through the promoted listing, but it's important to remember that this is an extra cost that needs to be factored into your overall pricing strategy.

For sellers offering international shipping, eBay also provides an International Shipping Program, which may involve additional fees for shipping items to international buyers. These fees are typically for shipping services provided by eBay's partner carriers, and they may vary depending on the destination country. While international shipping can expand your potential customer base, the associated fees can eat into your profit margins, so it's important to factor them into your pricing.

Now that we have covered the various eBay fees, the next step is understanding how to calculate profit margins. Profit margin is a key metric that helps you determine how much money you are making after covering all your costs. To calculate your profit margin, you need to consider all of the expenses associated with selling a product on eBay, including the cost of the product itself, eBay fees, PayPal or Managed Payments fees, shipping costs, and packaging materials. The formula for calculating your profit margin is as follows:

Profit Margin = (Selling Price - Total Costs) / Selling Price * 100

In this formula, the selling price is the amount the buyer paid for the item, including shipping costs. The total costs include the cost of the product, any eBay fees, PayPal fees, shipping, and packaging costs. By subtracting the total costs from the selling price and dividing the result by the selling price, you get the percentage that represents your profit margin.

For example, let's say you're selling a product for $50. The cost of the product is $20, and the eBay final value fee is 10%. PayPal charges a fee of 2.9% plus $0.30 per transaction. Shipping costs you $5, and packaging materials cost you $1. Your total costs would be:

- Product cost: $20
- eBay final value fee (10% of $50): $5
- PayPal fee (2.9% of $50 + $0.30): $1.80
- Shipping cost: $5
- Packaging: $1

Total costs = $20 + $5 + $1.80 + $5 + $1 = $32.80

Now, using the formula for profit margin:

Profit Margin = ($50 - $32.80) / $50 * 100 = 34.4%

In this example, your profit margin is 34.4%. This means that after all fees and costs are deducted, you are making 34.4% of the selling price as profit. Understanding your profit margin is crucial because it allows you to assess whether the product is worth selling at the price you've set and whether it aligns with your financial goals.

It's also important to regularly review your profit margins and adjust your pricing strategy accordingly. Over time, as your eBay business grows, you may find that certain products have higher margins than others, or that specific fees increase due to eBay's changes in policies or shipping costs. By consistently tracking your costs and adjusting your pricing, you can ensure that you are maximizing your profit potential.

In addition to reviewing individual product margins, it's also important to monitor your overall business profitability. This means looking at your total sales, expenses, and net profits across all your listings. You can use accounting software to generate profit and loss statements, which will give you a clear picture of your business's financial health. If you find that your overall profit margins are too low, you may need to reconsider your product sourcing, improve your marketing efforts, or adjust your pricing strategy.

It's essential to stay informed about eBay's fee structure and any changes that may affect your business. eBay regularly updates its fee policies, and these updates can have a significant impact on your bottom line. By staying up to date with fee changes and adjusting your business practices accordingly, you can ensure that you continue to operate profitably.

Understanding eBay fees and calculating profit margins are vital for any seller aiming to build a successful eBay business. By accurately accounting for all fees and costs, and by regularly calculating your profit margins, you can make informed decisions that will help you maximize your earnings and grow your business over time. With the right knowledge and tools, you can ensure that every sale is a step toward greater profitability and long-term success.

MANAGING TAXES AND RECORD-KEEPING FOR YOUR BUSINESS

Managing taxes and maintaining accurate records for your online business is crucial for long-term success and compliance. When running an eBay store, it's easy to get caught up in the excitement of making sales and growing your customer base, but overlooking tax responsibilities and the importance of proper record-keeping can quickly lead to trouble. Whether you're selling part-time as a side hustle or operating a full-fledged e-commerce business, understanding the basics of taxes and developing a solid system for tracking your finances is essential.

First and foremost, it's important to understand that selling on eBay is considered a business activity, which means you are required to report your earnings and pay taxes accordingly. The specific tax requirements you face depend on a number of factors, including your location, how much you sell, and the overall structure of your business. In many cases, taxes can be one of the most complicated aspects of managing an eBay store, but with the right knowledge and organization, you can navigate the system effectively.

In the United States, the Internal Revenue Service (IRS) requires all business owners to report their income, and that includes any sales made through eBay. Even if you're selling casually or occasionally, the IRS expects you to pay taxes on any profits. The first thing you should understand is the difference between income and sales tax. Income tax is what you owe on the profits from your eBay business, while sales tax is collected from buyers in certain states. You'll need to track both, and each requires a slightly different approach.

Income tax is based on the net profit you make from your eBay sales. This means you only pay taxes on the money you earn after deducting expenses such as the cost of the product, shipping fees, eBay listing fees, packaging materials, and other business-related expenses. When you calculate your profits, it's essential to subtract these expenses from your revenue to determine your taxable income. For example, if you sell an item for $50, but it cost you $30 to purchase the product, $10 for shipping, and $5 for eBay fees, your taxable income from that sale would be $5. The IRS uses this net income figure to determine how much tax you owe.

In terms of filing taxes, if you operate as a sole proprietor (the most common structure for small eBay businesses), you will report your income and expenses on a Schedule C form attached to your individual tax return (Form 1040). The Schedule C allows you to report all the earnings you made from your eBay sales, as well as the expenses you incurred in running your business. This form is crucial for determining your net profit and, subsequently, your tax liability. If you're running your eBay store as a part-time business or as a hobby, you may not have to pay self-employment taxes unless your income exceeds a certain threshold. However, if your business grows and your eBay sales become substantial, you'll likely need to pay self-employment taxes in addition to income taxes.

Self-employment tax, which covers Social Security and Medicare taxes, applies if your net earnings from your eBay business exceed $400 in a year. You'll pay this tax on top of any income tax you owe. The rate for self-employment tax is approximately 15.3%, so it's essential to factor this into your financial planning. In addition, if your income is substantial, you may want to consider making quarterly estimated tax payments to avoid a large tax bill when it's time to file your annual return.

Sales tax is another important consideration for eBay sellers. In recent years, the collection of sales tax has become more complex due to changes in state laws and the introduction of the Marketplace Facilitator laws. These laws require eBay to collect and remit sales tax on behalf of sellers for orders shipped to buyers in certain states. As a seller, you are generally not responsible for collecting and remitting sales tax directly to the state, but you must be aware of how these taxes are applied in your region and understand the implications for your business. eBay handles the collection of sales tax for most states, but it's still important to ensure that your listings are accurate and that you are following all applicable tax rules in your location.

Given the complexity of sales tax, it's essential to stay up to date with any changes to eBay's tax policies and ensure that you are in compliance with local regulations. You can review your tax settings in eBay's "Sales Tax" section, where you can view the states where eBay will automatically collect sales tax. For states not covered by this system, you may be required to collect and remit sales tax yourself. If you're selling in multiple states or internationally, it's a good idea to consult a tax professional to help you navigate these regulations.

One of the most important aspects of managing taxes is keeping accurate records of your sales and expenses. Good record-keeping helps you track your profits, identify deductions, and ensure that you are paying the correct amount of tax. It's essential to maintain detailed records of every transaction, including the cost of the items you're selling, any fees you pay to eBay or PayPal, shipping expenses, and the income you earn. These records will serve as the foundation for your tax filings and will also be useful in case you ever get audited by the IRS.

To keep things organized, you can use a combination of digital tools and manual tracking methods. Many sellers use accounting software or spreadsheets to track their income and expenses. eBay also provides a transaction history feature that allows you to view detailed records of your sales, including the cost of each item, shipping fees, and any applicable fees. These transaction histories can be exported to a spreadsheet, making it easier to track your earnings and expenses in one place. Additionally, PayPal provides transaction reports that can help you keep track of payment fees and income, which can be particularly useful if you're using PayPal for international sales or if your sales volume is high.

In addition to sales records, it's important to keep receipts for any business-related purchases, such as inventory, shipping materials, and packaging supplies. These receipts can serve as evidence of your business expenses and will be necessary for claiming tax deductions. You should also keep a record of any business-related mileage, office supplies, or home office expenses, if applicable. As you continue to grow your business, you may want to consider setting up a separate business bank account to make it easier to track your business expenses and income. A dedicated account can also help ensure that your personal finances and business finances remain separate, which is important for tax and legal purposes.

While keeping accurate records is essential for tax purposes, it also helps you monitor the health of your business. By tracking your expenses, you can identify areas where you may be overspending or where you could improve efficiency. Additionally, having detailed financial records allows you to calculate your profit margins and make more informed decisions about your pricing and sourcing strategies.

Lastly, as your business grows, you may want to consider working with a tax professional or accountant to ensure that you are staying compliant with all relevant tax laws and making the most of any available deductions. A professional can help you understand complex tax regulations, file your taxes, and provide advice on how to optimize your business's financial strategy.

Managing taxes and record-keeping are fundamental components of running a successful eBay business. By understanding the basics of income and sales taxes, staying organized with your records, and utilizing accounting tools, you can ensure that you're paying the correct amount of tax while maximizing your profitability. Regularly reviewing your financials and working with a tax professional will help you maintain compliance and optimize your business operations, setting you up for long-term success.

ANALYZING YOUR SALES DATA AND IDENTIFYING AREAS FOR IMPROVEMENT

Analyzing your sales data is a crucial step in refining your eBay business and driving long-term success. Understanding how your store performs allows you to make informed decisions that enhance your strategies, improve customer satisfaction, and maximize profitability. Without examining your sales data closely, you could miss key insights that could make the difference between just getting by and truly thriving in the eBay marketplace. When done correctly, this analysis helps you pinpoint strengths and weaknesses, uncover trends, and identify areas for improvement that will elevate your business to new heights.

The first step in analyzing your sales data is to have a clear understanding of the key metrics that impact your eBay store's performance. These metrics include your sales volume, average order value, conversion rate, inventory turnover, and customer feedback. Each of these data points tells you something important about how well your store is doing, how efficiently it operates, and what areas need attention. For example, a low conversion rate might suggest that your listings are not compelling enough or that your prices are uncompetitive, while a high return rate could indicate problems with the quality or description of the items you're selling.

One of the most valuable tools for analyzing sales data on eBay is the "Seller Hub," which provides an overview of your sales performance, customer feedback, and more. The Seller Hub dashboard allows you to see all your key metrics in one place, including total sales, sales trends, and buyer activity. From here, you can break down your performance by individual items, categories, and even specific time frames. This data can help you identify patterns that may not be immediately obvious and help you uncover areas where you can improve your approach.

Start by looking at your overall sales trends over time. Do your sales spike during certain times of the year, or do they remain steady? If you notice seasonal fluctuations, it might be worth adjusting your inventory or marketing efforts to capitalize on peak shopping periods. For example, if you see that your sales tend to increase in the lead-up to holidays like Christmas, you may want to focus on promoting certain products during those months or offering special promotions. Conversely, during slower periods, you can analyze which products are still selling and explore ways to increase interest, such as running sales, optimizing listings, or reaching out to your existing customer base.

Another key metric to evaluate is your average order value (AOV). AOV is calculated by dividing your total sales by the number of orders you've received. This figure can give you an indication of how much each customer is spending, which can be useful for setting pricing strategies. If your AOV is low, consider exploring ways to encourage customers to spend more per transaction. You might offer bundle deals, discounts on larger quantities, or free shipping for higher-value purchases. These strategies not only increase AOV but also provide more value to your customers, encouraging them to buy more from you.

Conversion rates are another critical piece of the puzzle. Your conversion rate is the percentage of people who visit your listing and actually make a purchase. A low conversion rate could mean that your listings are not persuasive enough, that your pricing is off, or that your product images or descriptions are not clear. Conversion rate optimization (CRO) is a process that involves tweaking your listings to improve this figure. To start, ensure that your product titles, descriptions, and images are optimized with the right keywords to make your products more visible and attractive to potential buyers. Additionally, examine whether your product prices are competitive compared to similar listings, as price can often be a deciding factor for buyers.

Customer feedback and reviews are also invaluable when it comes to analyzing your sales data. High ratings and positive feedback are essential for building trust with buyers, while low ratings or negative comments can damage your reputation and hurt future sales. Take time to read through your reviews regularly, paying attention to any patterns or recurring themes. For example, if multiple customers mention the same issue with a product's quality or description, you may need to address that specific concern in your listings or product offerings. Negative feedback, while discouraging, can also be a valuable learning opportunity. Address any complaints promptly and professionally, and work on resolving the underlying issues so that you can prevent similar complaints in the future.

In addition to examining individual sales and customer feedback, it's essential to analyze your inventory turnover. Inventory turnover refers to how quickly you're selling through the products you've listed. If certain items are sitting in your store without selling, it may be time to revisit your pricing, product descriptions, or marketing strategies. A slow-moving inventory could indicate that there is little demand for a particular product, or it could simply mean that your listing isn't reaching enough potential buyers. On the flip side, if you have items that sell quickly, you might want to consider increasing your stock of these products or promoting them more aggressively to capitalize on their popularity.

Once you've reviewed your sales data and identified trends and patterns, the next step is to pinpoint specific areas for improvement. One key area to consider is your product listings. If you notice that some of your listings aren't converting well, it's time to examine those pages more closely. Start by looking at the quality of the product images. Are they clear, professional-looking, and well-lit? Are you showcasing the product from multiple angles to give buyers a comprehensive view? High-quality images can significantly increase conversion rates. Next, review the product descriptions. Are they detailed and informative? Do they clearly outline the benefits of the product and address any potential concerns a buyer may have? Well-crafted descriptions that highlight the key features of your product and address common questions or objections can be the difference between a sale and an abandoned cart.

Another area for improvement could be your pricing strategy. If you're noticing that your products aren't selling as quickly as you'd like, it may be time to revisit your prices. Are your prices competitive compared to other sellers offering similar items? If your products are priced too high, potential buyers might pass on your listings in favor of more affordable options. On the other hand, pricing too low might lead to missed profit opportunities. You may want to experiment with different pricing strategies, such as offering discounts, running limited-time promotions, or testing higher prices to see how it affects demand.

Shipping is also a significant factor that can impact your sales. High shipping costs or slow delivery times can deter customers from making a purchase, especially if your competitors offer better shipping options. Review your shipping policies and costs regularly to ensure that you're providing the best possible service. Offering free shipping, for instance, can increase your chances of attracting buyers, as it's often seen as a more attractive option. Additionally, consider offering faster shipping methods or implementing better packaging techniques to ensure that your customers receive their products in a timely and professional manner.

Customer service plays a vital role in analyzing your sales performance. If you notice that your reviews aren't as positive as you'd like, consider how you can improve your customer service interactions. Responding promptly to inquiries, offering solutions to problems, and being proactive in addressing issues can greatly improve customer satisfaction and encourage repeat business. Developing a reputation for excellent customer service will set you apart from your competitors and lead to higher sales and better customer retention.

Analyzing your sales data is an essential part of growing a successful eBay business. By regularly reviewing your key metrics, you can uncover trends, identify areas for improvement, and implement strategies that will help you increase sales, improve customer satisfaction, and optimize your operations. Whether it's tweaking your listings, adjusting your pricing, enhancing your shipping policies, or providing better customer service, taking the time to analyze your data and make informed decisions will give you a competitive edge and set you up for long-term success.

REINVESTING PROFITS FOR GROWTH

Reinvesting profits is one of the most powerful strategies for driving the growth of any business, including your eBay store. When you first start selling on eBay, it can be tempting to treat your profits as disposable income or to spend them immediately on other expenses. However, reinvesting those profits wisely can help scale your business, enhance your operations, and increase your overall profitability in the long term. By using your earnings to make smart investments back into your business, you position yourself for continuous growth and success.

One of the key areas where you can reinvest profits is in expanding your product offerings. When you first launch your eBay store, you may start by selling a small selection of items. As you gain more experience and learn what works well in your store, you'll likely start identifying other products that could complement your existing inventory or appeal to your target market. By using the profits from your initial sales to purchase additional products, you can expand your catalog and cater to a broader customer base. This expansion can result in more visibility for your eBay store and an increased likelihood of generating higher sales volumes.

When selecting new products to invest in, it's important to research the demand and competition for those items. Market research is key to ensuring that your reinvested profits are spent on products with strong demand and low competition. By using eBay's search functions, examining trending products, and monitoring competitor listings, you can identify lucrative opportunities that align with your business strategy. Additionally, you should consider diversifying your product offerings. This allows you to tap into multiple customer segments and reduce the risk of relying on just one category of products. For instance, if you sell clothing, you might explore adding accessories or home decor items to your inventory, thereby increasing the potential for cross-selling and repeat business.

Another area where reinvesting profits can have a significant impact is in improving the quality of your listings. One of the most important factors in eBay sales success is having well-optimized listings that stand out from the competition. Investing in high-quality photography, professional product descriptions, and keyword optimization can make your listings more appealing to buyers and increase your chances of making a sale. High-quality images, in particular, can have a profound effect on conversion rates. If your product images are clear, well-lit, and taken from multiple angles, potential buyers are more likely to trust the quality of the product and feel confident making a purchase.

Professional product descriptions are equally important. By investing in copywriting services or taking the time to write compelling, well-structured descriptions, you can highlight the benefits and features of your products in a way that resonates with customers. A detailed, informative description that addresses common questions or concerns can help buyers make more informed purchasing decisions, which often leads to higher sales.

In addition to improving the visual and written aspects of your listings, you can also reinvest profits into eBay's promotional tools to increase visibility. eBay offers various options for promoting your listings, such as Promoted Listings and eBay Ads, which can give your products a boost in search results. While these promotional tools require an upfront investment, they can pay off in the form of higher visibility, increased traffic, and ultimately, more sales. By strategically reinvesting your profits into advertising campaigns for your most popular or high-margin products, you can drive more qualified traffic to your listings, which increases the likelihood of making a sale.

As your eBay business grows, your operational needs will also expand. Reinvesting profits into improving your business infrastructure can streamline your operations and make your business more efficient. This includes investing in better inventory management tools, upgrading your shipping processes, and automating aspects of your business. For example, if you find that you're spending a lot of time tracking inventory manually, you might invest in an inventory management system that can automatically track your stock levels, manage restocking, and alert you when products are running low.

Upgrading your shipping process is another important area where reinvestment can yield significant returns. Faster shipping options, better packaging materials, and more reliable couriers can improve your customer satisfaction and potentially reduce return rates. Investing in quality packaging can also help protect your products during transit, reducing the risk of damage and the associated costs of returns or replacements. If you're still handling shipping on your own, consider automating parts of the process to save time, such as using shipping software that can automatically generate labels and track shipments.

Additionally, reinvesting profits into business tools that automate tasks, such as invoicing, customer communication, and email marketing, can free up more time for you to focus on other aspects of your business. Using tools like customer relationship management (CRM) systems, automated email marketing campaigns, and bulk listing software can allow you to scale your operations more effectively while maintaining a high level of customer service.

Another strategic way to reinvest profits is by enhancing your brand identity. If you've been selling on eBay for a while, you may notice that building a recognizable brand can foster customer loyalty and increase repeat business. Reinvesting profits into branding efforts, such as designing a professional logo, creating a cohesive brand style, or even developing a dedicated eBay store, can help set your business apart from the competition. A strong brand identity can instill trust in buyers, making them more likely to return to your store when they need to purchase more products. Consider investing in a professional design service to create a visually appealing and user-friendly store layout or invest in branded packaging that leaves a lasting impression on your customers.

Another important area for reinvestment is customer service. Providing excellent customer service can set your eBay business apart from others and build long-term relationships with your customers. Reinvesting profits into improving your customer service operations could include training for you or your team to better handle customer inquiries, resolve issues more effectively, or offer exceptional post-purchase support. Many eBay sellers find that offering an extended return policy or a more personalized customer experience can lead to higher customer satisfaction and positive feedback, which in turn boosts your store's reputation and sales.

It's important to reinvest profits in your own personal development. As your business grows, you may find that you need to acquire new skills or knowledge to continue to scale. Consider taking courses on advanced eBay selling techniques, learning about digital marketing strategies, or improving your financial literacy to better manage your business's finances. These investments in your education can ultimately pay off by helping you make smarter business decisions, improve your efficiency, and increase profitability in the long run.

Reinvesting profits is an essential part of growing and scaling a successful eBay business. Whether you choose to invest in new products, improve your listings, enhance your operations, or boost your marketing efforts, every reinvestment decision should be aimed at creating long-term value for your business. By strategically reinvesting your profits, you can not only improve the customer experience but also enhance your competitive position and continue to build a business that generates sustainable revenue. As you progress, keep an eye on the areas that provide the highest return on investment and adapt your strategy as your business evolves. The power of reinvestment lies in its ability to propel your business to new levels of success, allowing you to achieve sustainable growth and financial freedom.

CHAPTER 13
EXPANDING YOUR BUSINESS: SCALING AND AUTOMATION

EXPLORING DROPSHIPPING AND OTHER FULFILLMENT METHODS IN MORE DETAIL

Exploring dropshipping and other fulfillment methods in detail is crucial for any eBay seller looking to scale their business and optimize their operations. Fulfillment methods are the backbone of any e-commerce business, as they directly impact how quickly products reach customers and how efficiently a business operates. Dropshipping, among other fulfillment models, has become increasingly popular due to its ability to eliminate the need for inventory management and the upfront costs associated with stocking products. However, it's important to fully understand the pros, cons, and alternatives to dropshipping in order to make an informed decision about which method best suits your business goals and resources.

Dropshipping is a fulfillment method where the seller does not hold inventory themselves. Instead, when a customer makes a purchase, the seller forwards the order to a third-party supplier, who then ships the product directly to the customer. The key appeal of dropshipping is its low barrier to entry. Sellers don't need to invest in purchasing large quantities of inventory upfront, which can be a significant financial burden. Additionally, since the supplier handles the packaging and shipping, sellers can focus on other aspects of their business, such as marketing, customer service, and growing their brand.

The biggest advantage of dropshipping is the minimal risk and upfront investment required. Since you're not purchasing products in bulk, there's no need to worry about unsold inventory or overstock. This makes it easier to test out new products without committing to large orders. You can experiment with different product categories, target various customer segments, and adjust your offerings based on demand without worrying about excess stock. This flexibility is especially appealing to new eBay sellers who want to explore multiple niches without large financial risks.

However, dropshipping also comes with its own set of challenges. One major drawback is the low-profit margin. Since dropshipping suppliers typically charge higher prices to cover their costs and services, the price you can charge customers may be higher than what you would pay if you were buying inventory in bulk. This means that your profit margin will likely be thinner, making it necessary to focus on driving high volumes of sales to remain profitable. Additionally, because you have less control over the fulfillment process, you may experience longer shipping times and less control over product quality. Delays or mistakes in shipping can lead to customer dissatisfaction, and since you don't handle the inventory yourself, any issues with product quality or defects may result in disputes that are harder to resolve.

Another potential challenge with dropshipping is intense competition. Since the barriers to entry are low, many sellers may choose the same suppliers, leading to oversaturated markets. As a result, it may be harder to differentiate your offerings and stand out among the competition. Additionally, relying heavily on a dropshipping supplier means your success is tied to their reliability and performance. If they run out of stock, delay shipments, or increase their prices, it directly impacts your business. To mitigate these risks, it's essential to choose reliable suppliers, ideally those who have a proven track record of fulfilling orders on time and providing quality products.

For sellers who want to avoid the challenges of dropshipping but still prefer not to handle inventory themselves, there are other fulfillment methods available. One alternative is using third-party fulfillment centers. This method involves working with a third-party logistics (3PL) provider who stores, picks, packs, and ships products on your behalf. With 3PL fulfillment, you're responsible for purchasing and stocking the products, but once they arrive at the warehouse, the fulfillment center takes care of the rest. The main advantage of 3PL is that you gain more control over the process while still outsourcing the time-consuming tasks of packaging and shipping.

3PL can provide faster shipping times than dropshipping since you can store products closer to your customer base, which reduces shipping costs and delivery times. Additionally, using a fulfillment center allows you to focus on other aspects of your business, such as marketing and customer acquisition, while ensuring that your products are shipped efficiently and consistently. However, the trade-off is that you must invest in purchasing and storing inventory upfront, which can be costly, especially for new businesses. Additionally, you'll need to factor in the storage and fulfillment fees charged by the provider, which can eat into your profit margins.

Fulfillment by Amazon (FBA) is another alternative that has gained popularity in recent years. Although it's most commonly associated with Amazon sellers, FBA can be used to sell products on eBay as well. FBA works similarly to 3PL, with the added benefit that Amazon handles all of the storage, picking, packing, and shipping. When you use FBA, your products are stored in Amazon's fulfillment centers, and when a customer places an order, Amazon fulfills it using their extensive logistics network. This can provide several benefits, such as access to Amazon's customer base, fast and reliable shipping, and the ability to offer Amazon's customer service and returns processing.

The key difference between FBA and dropshipping or 3PL is that FBA is specifically tied to Amazon's platform, which means you may have to navigate the complexities of selling on both eBay and Amazon simultaneously. This can be challenging, especially when it comes to managing pricing, inventory levels, and customer service. However, FBA is a good option for sellers who want to focus on expanding their business while taking advantage of Amazon's vast infrastructure and logistics capabilities.

Another fulfillment option worth exploring is self-fulfillment, where you handle all aspects of inventory management, order picking, packing, and shipping yourself. This method requires more time, effort, and storage space, but it gives you full control over the fulfillment process. By keeping inventory on hand and handling everything in-house, you can ensure that products are shipped quickly and that you can provide a personalized customer experience. The downside is the time commitment and the need for sufficient storage space. You also assume full responsibility for any shipping or fulfillment mistakes, which could lead to costly delays or customer dissatisfaction.

In addition to these methods, hybrid models are becoming increasingly popular. For example, some sellers combine dropshipping and self-fulfillment by sourcing some products from dropshipping suppliers and others from their own inventory. This allows sellers to benefit from the low-risk, flexible nature of dropshipping while still maintaining some control over the shipping process for products they stock themselves. Hybrid fulfillment models require careful planning and inventory management but can offer a balanced approach to running an eBay business.

Ultimately, the fulfillment method you choose will depend on your business goals, budget, and resources. Dropshipping offers a low-risk way to start selling online, but it comes with challenges such as lower profit margins and competition. Third-party fulfillment and FBA provide more control and faster shipping times but require upfront investment in inventory. Self-fulfillment gives you full control but can be time-consuming and space-demanding. By understanding the strengths and weaknesses of each fulfillment method, you can make a more informed decision that aligns with your long-term strategy and helps your business grow effectively.

CONSIDERING HIRING HELP OR OUTSOURCING TASKS

As an eBay seller working to build a successful business, the idea of hiring help or outsourcing tasks can be a game-changer. At the beginning of your entrepreneurial journey, it's likely that you'll handle every aspect of the business yourself, from listing products to managing customer service. However, as your business grows, you'll quickly find that it becomes more difficult to juggle everything. The demands of managing inventory, fulfilling orders, handling customer inquiries, and promoting your store can be overwhelming. At this stage, considering hiring help or outsourcing specific tasks could not only relieve your stress but also contribute to your long-term business success.

When you first start selling on eBay, you may be working with a limited budget, which makes outsourcing tasks seem like an unattainable luxury. However, many tasks within your business can be outsourced affordably and effectively, often providing more value than if you attempted to manage everything yourself. The key is understanding which tasks can be delegated and where your time is best spent. For instance, while you may be skilled at product research and listing optimization, tasks like customer service, bookkeeping, or social media management might not be areas you are passionate about or particularly proficient in. Outsourcing these tasks allows you to focus on the activities that directly contribute to growing your business.

One of the most common tasks that eBay sellers outsource is customer service. As your business grows, you will undoubtedly encounter a higher volume of customer inquiries and requests. Responding to customer messages, handling returns, and dealing with complaints can become time-consuming, especially if you're striving to maintain a high level of customer satisfaction. Rather than spending hours each day answering messages, you might find it beneficial to hire a virtual assistant (VA) to handle customer support on your behalf. Virtual assistants are often skilled in managing emails, live chats, and customer communications, and they can even provide after-sales support. Outsourcing customer service can free up your time so that you can focus on more strategic tasks like marketing and product development.

Similarly, managing returns and resolving customer issues can become a full-time job in itself. Depending on the size and nature of your business, a dedicated customer service representative can manage these tasks, ensuring that your buyers receive prompt and helpful responses. Outsourcing this part of your business allows you to maintain a positive reputation on eBay, as customers appreciate timely and efficient service. By outsourcing customer service, you can avoid burnout and create a more streamlined process for handling disputes, returns, and inquiries.

Another area where outsourcing can be highly beneficial is product listing and optimization. Writing effective product descriptions, creating engaging titles, and taking professional-looking photos are essential elements of running a successful eBay store. However, these tasks can be time-consuming, especially when you have a large inventory or need to update listings regularly. By hiring a freelance copywriter or product photographer, you can ensure that your listings are optimized for eBay's search engine, have high-quality images that attract buyers, and include compelling descriptions that boost conversions. A professional product description writer understands how to incorporate the right keywords, highlight product features, and make the listing stand out in a crowded marketplace. Professional photographers, on the other hand, know how to present products in the most flattering light, ensuring they look their best to potential buyers.

Outsourcing inventory management is another consideration as your eBay business scales. Depending on the volume of products you're selling, keeping track of stock levels, order fulfillment, and supplier communications can become overwhelming. Third-party logistics (3PL) companies or fulfillment centers can handle your inventory and shipping, allowing you to focus on marketing and business strategy. These services can store your products, pack and ship orders, and even handle returns. While this may come with additional costs, it can save you time and reduce the risk of inventory mismanagement, particularly if you sell in large quantities. By outsourcing fulfillment, you can improve your shipping times, reduce overhead costs related to warehousing, and improve the overall efficiency of your operations.

When it comes to marketing your eBay store, there are numerous tasks that can be outsourced to experts. For instance, social media management is crucial for driving traffic to your listings, but many sellers find it difficult to maintain an active social media presence due to time constraints. Hiring a social media manager or a digital marketing specialist can help you increase your online visibility and engagement. These professionals can create content, schedule posts, and run paid advertising campaigns, such as Facebook Ads or Google Ads, to attract potential customers to your eBay store. A well-executed social media strategy can lead to increased sales, improved brand awareness, and greater customer loyalty.

In addition to social media, search engine optimization (SEO) is another area where hiring help can be advantageous. Optimizing your eBay listings for search engines like Google and eBay's internal search system is essential for getting your products in front of more buyers. SEO experts can analyze your product listings, identify relevant keywords, and improve your content to boost visibility in search results. Hiring an SEO specialist ensures that your listings are more likely to rank higher on eBay and search engines, leading to increased traffic and better sales performance.

While hiring help or outsourcing tasks offers numerous benefits, it's important to weigh the costs against the potential return on investment (ROI). Some tasks, such as customer service, can be outsourced to virtual assistants at a relatively low cost, while others, such as professional photography or SEO services, may come with higher fees. As a new seller, it's important to prioritize outsourcing based on the tasks that will have the most significant impact on your business growth. For example, if you're not skilled in photography, hiring a professional to take high-quality images of your products could be a worthwhile investment, as it will make your listings stand out from competitors. However, you may choose to handle other aspects, such as social media posting, yourself if you feel comfortable doing so.

Ultimately, the decision to hire help or outsource tasks should be based on your business goals, budget, and the time you have available to devote to your eBay store. As your business grows, you'll find that outsourcing certain tasks becomes not only a time-saver but a key strategy for scaling your operations. By freeing up your time from administrative tasks, you can focus on growing your product range, enhancing your marketing efforts, and providing excellent customer service. Whether you choose to hire a full-time employee, a part-time virtual assistant, or outsource specific services to freelancers, the goal is to create a more efficient, streamlined process that allows your business to thrive in the competitive eBay marketplace.

Considering hiring help or outsourcing tasks is an essential step for any eBay seller looking to expand their operations. By delegating certain responsibilities, you can focus on high-priority tasks that drive growth and success for your business. It's important to assess your needs, budget, and growth potential to determine which tasks to outsource. With the right support in place, you can elevate your business, improve efficiency, and position yourself for long-term success.

UTILIZING EBAY AUTOMATION TOOLS FOR EFFICIENCY

Running a successful eBay store requires managing a multitude of tasks, ranging from listing products to customer service, inventory management, and marketing. For many sellers, these responsibilities can become overwhelming, particularly as their business grows. Fortunately, eBay offers various automation tools that can help streamline these tasks, allowing sellers to save time, reduce errors, and improve overall efficiency. Understanding and utilizing these automation tools is essential for any eBay seller looking to scale their business and focus on the aspects that matter most, such as product sourcing and customer engagement.

One of the most powerful ways to automate your eBay business is by using eBay's built-in automation tools, designed to take care of repetitive tasks. These tools can help you manage your listings, track inventory, schedule promotions, and even handle customer communication—all without the need for constant manual intervention. By leveraging automation, you can reduce the number of hours spent on administrative tasks and increase your productivity.

One of the most essential automation features eBay offers is the ability to schedule product listings. This feature allows you to create and upload listings at a specific time, which can be especially useful when you have a large number of products or want to time your listings for peak hours. Scheduling your listings in advance ensures that your products go live at the right time, even if you're not available to manually post them. Whether you're launching new products or relisting old ones, automating your listing schedule ensures that your inventory is always up-to-date without requiring your constant attention.

Along with listing scheduling, eBay's automated re-listing feature is another useful tool for sellers. When an item is sold or when the listing expires, eBay will automatically relist it for you. This is especially useful for high-demand items or when you have a consistent inventory flow. By automating the re-listing process, you ensure that you don't miss out on potential sales opportunities, and your listings remain visible to buyers, even if you forget to manually renew them. This tool can save time and effort by eliminating the need to manually relist each product, especially if you have many items in your store.

Another key area where automation can make a significant impact is inventory management. For sellers with a large number of products or a diverse range of items, keeping track of inventory levels can become a daunting task. Fortunately, eBay offers integration with third-party inventory management tools that can automatically update stock levels as products are sold. These tools can track inventory across multiple platforms, synchronize quantities in real-time, and alert you when stock is low. This automated inventory management reduces the risk of overselling or running out of stock, ensuring that your listings are always accurate. By automating inventory updates, you can focus on sourcing new products rather than worrying about manual stock tracking.

Automating customer communication is another essential aspect of managing your eBay store efficiently. As your business grows, responding to customer inquiries, processing orders, and managing returns can become time-consuming. To streamline this process, eBay offers automated messaging tools that can send predefined responses to customers based on certain triggers. For instance, you can set up an automatic message to be sent to buyers when they make a purchase, providing them with important information such as shipping details, expected delivery times, or order tracking numbers. Automated messages can also be used to confirm that a return has been received or to provide instructions on how to complete a return process. These tools can help you maintain high levels of customer service without having to manually respond to every message.

In addition to automated messaging, eBay also provides tools for automatically handling feedback requests. Feedback is a vital aspect of your store's reputation, and automation can ensure that feedback requests are sent out promptly after a transaction. Positive feedback is essential for building trust with potential buyers, and by automating the feedback process, you can increase the likelihood of receiving reviews from satisfied customers. Automation tools can also help you track your feedback history, allowing you to quickly identify any issues and address them before they impact your store's ratings.

Promotions are an essential component of any eBay business, and automating promotional campaigns can help you drive traffic and increase sales without dedicating a significant amount of time to managing them manually. eBay offers promotional tools that allow you to schedule and manage sales events, discounts, and special offers. For example, you can create store-wide sales that automatically apply discounts to all eligible items in your inventory or create targeted promotions based on specific categories or buyer behavior. By automating your promotions, you ensure that discounts are applied consistently, and you can reach potential buyers at the right time. These tools can also help you test different promotional strategies to determine which ones work best for your business.

Beyond eBay's built-in tools, there are several third-party automation platforms that can enhance your selling experience. These platforms offer advanced features that integrate with eBay's system and provide additional customization options. For example, there are software programs that can help you manage multiple eBay accounts, track sales data, optimize your listings for better search rankings, and even automate your shipping processes. These platforms can help you scale your business more effectively by providing tools that automate tasks that eBay's native system may not fully address.

For instance, third-party tools can help you automate the process of managing shipping labels and tracking numbers. Instead of manually generating labels for each order, these tools can automatically create and print shipping labels, reducing the chances of errors and ensuring that your orders are shipped promptly. Some automation platforms can even integrate with your inventory and automatically select the best shipping method based on the weight, dimensions, and destination of the package.

This streamlines the fulfillment process, allowing you to focus on growing your business rather than managing logistics.

Advanced analytics and reporting tools can also be automated to give you insights into how your store is performing. By setting up automated reports, you can receive regular updates on key performance metrics, such as sales trends, inventory levels, and customer feedback. These reports can be customized to focus on specific aspects of your business, allowing you to quickly identify areas for improvement or adjust your strategies accordingly. Automated analytics can help you make data-driven decisions and optimize your eBay store for maximum profitability.

Despite the numerous advantages of using automation tools, it's important to note that automation should be used strategically. While automation can save time and reduce manual effort, it should not replace personal interactions with customers. It's important to ensure that automated messages and responses still maintain a human touch and reflect your brand's personality. Automation should complement your efforts, not replace the essential tasks that require your personal attention. Additionally, sellers must regularly monitor their automated systems to ensure that they are functioning correctly and that no errors occur, particularly with customer orders and inventory updates.

Automation tools are a valuable asset for any eBay seller looking to improve efficiency and scale their business. By automating tasks such as listing management, inventory updates, customer communication, and promotions, you can save time, reduce errors, and provide a better customer experience. eBay offers a variety of built-in automation tools, and third-party platforms can enhance these features further. By using automation strategically, you can streamline your operations and focus on the aspects of your business that will drive growth and success.

EXPANDING YOUR PRODUCT LINE AND EXPLORING NEW NICHES

Expanding your product line and exploring new niches is one of the most effective strategies for growing your eBay business. As the online marketplace becomes increasingly competitive, the ability to diversify and target new audiences can set you apart from other sellers. This approach can bring fresh opportunities, reduce dependence on a single product or category, and help you adapt to changing market trends. However, successfully expanding your product line requires careful planning, research, and a thoughtful strategy to ensure that your new offerings complement your existing products and meet the needs of your target audience.

When considering how to expand your product line, it is important to first understand the needs of your current customers. Analyze your existing sales data, customer feedback, and market trends to determine which products are performing well and which categories are underperforming. By understanding what your customers are already buying and what they are asking for, you can identify potential gaps in your product offering. For example, if you sell home decor items and notice that a significant number of your customers are also interested in outdoor furniture, this could be an indication that expanding into the outdoor living niche may be a profitable move. Expanding your product line in this way not only provides more options to your existing customer base but also helps to attract new buyers who are looking for complementary products.

Expanding your product line also means researching new niches. A niche is a specialized segment of the market that focuses on a particular interest, product type, or demographic. Finding the right niche is critical to targeting specific groups of buyers who may be underserved or overlooked by larger retailers. To explore new niches, start by identifying emerging trends and shifts in consumer behavior. Look for industries or categories that are growing rapidly and consider how your business can cater to these needs. For instance, eco-friendly products, sustainable living, and health-conscious goods have been gaining popularity in recent years. By tapping into these growing trends, you can position your business as a trusted source for high-demand products.

A valuable tool in identifying new niches is keyword research. Platforms like Google Trends, eBay's own search function, and third-party tools can provide insights into what customers are searching for in various categories. By analyzing search volume and competition, you can identify underrepresented product categories that present opportunities for growth. For example, if you notice an increase in searches for "vintage leather handbags" or "biodegradable cleaning products," these could be niches worth exploring. Keyword research helps you gauge the level of interest in a niche and determine whether it is viable for your store. It can also help you fine-tune your product descriptions and listings, ensuring that you're reaching the right audience through SEO.

It's important to evaluate the potential profitability of expanding into a new niche before making any investments. While a niche market may seem promising, not all niches are created equal in terms of profitability. Some niches may have a small customer base but high competition, while others may offer significant demand with relatively little competition. Profit margins are also a crucial consideration. Certain niches may involve higher costs for inventory, shipping, or packaging, which could eat into your profits. To evaluate profitability, you'll need to consider factors such as product costs, shipping fees, and potential sales volume. You may also want to assess whether your current suppliers can provide the new products at a competitive price, or if you will need to source new suppliers who specialize in that niche.

Once you've identified a promising niche, it's time to expand your product offerings. However, expanding your product line is not just about adding more items to your store. It's about ensuring that the new products align with your brand, meet quality standards, and appeal to your target customers. If you've built a reputation for selling high-quality products in a specific category, introducing a new line of products should maintain that same level of quality. Consistency in product quality and customer service is key to building a loyal customer base and sustaining long-term growth. Therefore, when expanding, make sure that any new products you introduce are tested and meet your established standards.

Another important factor when expanding your product line is pricing. Competitive pricing is crucial when entering new markets. While you don't want to underprice your products, which can lead to lower profit margins, you also need to ensure that your prices are in line with what buyers are willing to pay. Research your competitors' pricing strategies and consider offering promotions, bundle deals, or discounts for new customers to entice buyers to try your expanded product offerings. However, make sure that any promotional strategies you use still allow you to maintain profitability, especially when factoring in costs like shipping and eBay's fees.

Marketing plays a central role in introducing new products to your eBay store. Whether you're adding a few items or completely shifting to a new niche, your marketing efforts must effectively communicate the value of these products to potential buyers. One effective strategy is to use targeted ads on eBay, Google, and social media platforms. eBay's promoted listings feature allows you to boost the visibility of your new products to a wider audience, helping you reach buyers who may not have found your store otherwise. Additionally, using social media platforms such as Instagram and Facebook can help generate excitement around your new product offerings. Showcase your products with high-quality images, provide descriptions that highlight their unique features, and engage with your followers to build a community around your brand.

Expanding into a new niche may also require rethinking your store's branding and overall customer experience. Your product line and niche will help define your store's identity, so it's important to ensure that your branding and store design align with your new direction. Consider updating your store's logo, banner, and messaging to reflect the new products and categories you're offering. This will help create a cohesive experience for customers as they explore your store. Additionally, consider creating category-specific pages on your eBay store to make it easy for buyers to browse your new product offerings. A well-organized store that highlights your expanded product line will help enhance the customer experience and improve conversion rates.

One of the benefits of exploring new niches is the potential to build relationships with suppliers or manufacturers that specialize in those areas. By diversifying your product offerings, you may be able to access exclusive deals, bulk pricing, or unique products that are unavailable through mainstream retailers. Establishing strong relationships with reliable suppliers is essential for ensuring that you have consistent access to high-quality products at competitive prices. This is especially important when you're venturing into new niches, as you want to be able to source products that meet the demand while maintaining your profit margins.

As you expand into new niches, it's also important to keep an eye on your current product lines. While exploring new markets is exciting, you don't want to neglect your existing customer base or product categories. Make sure that you continue to manage and update your original product listings to ensure they stay relevant and competitive. You may need to tweak your pricing, update descriptions, or refresh your product images to keep your listings performing well.

Expanding your product line and exploring new niches is a vital step in growing your eBay business. It opens up new opportunities for revenue, reduces reliance on a single product, and helps you remain adaptable in a constantly changing marketplace. However, this expansion must be done strategically by conducting thorough market research, evaluating potential profitability, ensuring quality control, and aligning with your brand. By following these steps, you can successfully diversify your product offerings, attract new customers, and continue building a thriving eBay business.

UNDERSTANDING EBAY'S BUSINESS POLICIES FOR LARGER SELLERS

As a seller on eBay, understanding and complying with eBay's business policies is crucial for maintaining a successful and sustainable online business. This is especially important for larger sellers who are scaling their operations and expanding their reach on the platform. As eBay continues to evolve, the policies that govern seller activity become more nuanced, and larger sellers must be keenly aware of the rules to avoid penalties, suspension, or other disruptions to their business. These policies cover a wide range of topics, from product listings and shipping to returns and customer service, each of which plays a pivotal role in ensuring your business runs smoothly.

One of the first things larger sellers must consider when navigating eBay's business policies is the category of items they sell. eBay has a variety of rules in place for different product categories, particularly those that involve sensitive items such as electronics, health products, or collectibles. Sellers are required to familiarize themselves with the specific policies related to the items they list, as each category may have its own set of regulations. For example, certain electronics may require that sellers meet specific criteria to list them, such as providing proof of authenticity, offering a warranty, or ensuring that the product complies with certain safety standards. Larger sellers who deal with high volumes of products in these categories must ensure that their inventory meets all of eBay's requirements to avoid complications such as listing removals, account penalties, or disputes.

In addition to category-specific rules, eBay has broad regulations regarding the general selling experience. Sellers are expected to provide accurate descriptions of their products, ship orders promptly, and offer clear communication with buyers. Larger sellers, with their larger inventory, face greater responsibility in this regard. Misleading listings or failure to adhere to eBay's standards for product descriptions can lead to account suspension. It is important for larger sellers to regularly audit their listings to ensure that all details are correct, updated, and complete. As a larger seller, the volume of orders you process can increase the likelihood of errors, but maintaining the quality of your listings is vital for upholding your reputation and avoiding complaints or negative feedback.

Shipping policies also play a significant role in eBay's overall business policies. Larger sellers are typically responsible for fulfilling a high volume of orders, which means understanding shipping policies and ensuring that the right shipping options are offered is key to staying compliant with eBay's rules. eBay requires that all sellers accurately represent the shipping costs and delivery times in their listings, and they mandate that items be shipped within the time frame promised. Failure to ship promptly can lead to buyer dissatisfaction and result in negative feedback, which impacts a seller's reputation and ranking within eBay's search results. Larger sellers should also be aware of eBay's international shipping policies, especially if they are expanding their market globally. eBay provides a Global Shipping Program (GSP) to simplify international orders, but sellers still need to follow specific guidelines, such as ensuring that customs forms are completed accurately, to avoid delays or issues with cross-border sales.

Another area where larger sellers must be particularly vigilant is eBay's return and refund policies. eBay encourages sellers to offer free returns, as it has been shown to improve buyer confidence and can enhance sales, but this is not mandatory. However, larger sellers must comply with eBay's minimum return requirements, which vary by product category. For example, most items fall under a standard 30-day return window, but certain items may have shorter or longer return periods.

Furthermore, eBay's policies dictate that sellers must provide a full refund to buyers if the item is returned due to defects or misrepresentations, and they must ensure that the return process is smooth and fair. Larger sellers must have clear procedures in place to handle returns efficiently, as a failure to do so can lead to customer dissatisfaction and potential policy violations. In some cases, sellers who fail to adhere to eBay's return policies can face repercussions, such as account restrictions or the removal of their listings from search results.

For larger sellers, maintaining excellent customer service is paramount. eBay has strict policies surrounding communication between buyers and sellers, and these guidelines apply to all sellers, regardless of size. Sellers must respond to buyer inquiries promptly, provide accurate information, and address any concerns in a professional manner. Larger sellers may have customer service teams or support staff to handle inquiries, but even with a team in place, sellers must ensure that all communication meets eBay's standards. eBay expects all communication to be courteous, clear, and helpful, and failure to meet these expectations can lead to poor feedback, which can harm a seller's reputation. Additionally, eBay has an automatic feedback system that impacts a seller's visibility in search results, so maintaining a positive feedback rating is critical for long-term success.

eBay also has a set of performance standards that apply to all sellers, but these standards become even more important for larger sellers who are handling higher sales volumes. eBay evaluates sellers based on factors such as shipping time, buyer satisfaction, and return rates. Larger sellers, who typically have a greater volume of transactions, are at a higher risk of falling below eBay's performance thresholds. To stay compliant, it's essential for larger sellers to monitor their metrics regularly and take corrective action if their performance begins to slip. For example, if a seller's defect rate is too high, indicating that a significant number of buyers have filed complaints or left negative feedback, eBay may suspend or restrict their account. Sellers who consistently meet or exceed eBay's performance standards are rewarded with better search visibility, access to promotional tools, and higher placement in the Best Match search algorithm.

A more nuanced aspect of eBay's business policies is the concept of seller protection. Larger sellers, with their larger customer base, may face disputes or cases of fraud more frequently than smaller sellers. eBay provides protection for sellers in specific situations, such as if a buyer claims an item was not received but tracking information proves otherwise, or if a buyer leaves negative feedback without proper cause. However, in order to qualify for seller protection, sellers must comply with all eBay policies, including shipping requirements, listing accuracy, and customer communication. Larger sellers need to be diligent in maintaining records of all transactions, shipping details, and communications, as these may be required in the event of a dispute.

One of the most important policy considerations for larger sellers is eBay's Seller Protection Program, which is designed to help safeguard sellers from unjust claims and disputes. However, to qualify for protection, sellers must adhere to eBay's policies on shipping, returns, and handling buyer complaints. Sellers who fail to meet these requirements risk losing protection and may be held accountable for returns, chargebacks, or other disputes.

In addition to understanding the specifics of eBay's policies, larger sellers should also stay updated on any changes or updates to the platform's rules. eBay regularly updates its policies, and failure to comply with these updates can result in penalties. Staying informed about eBay's policy changes is essential for maintaining a compliant and successful business.

Overall, eBay's business policies for larger sellers are designed to create a fair and efficient marketplace for both buyers and sellers. By understanding and following these policies, larger sellers can avoid disruptions to their business, maintain positive relationships with customers, and ensure long-term growth on the platform. Complying with eBay's rules, providing excellent customer service, and staying informed about policy updates are all essential components of running a successful eBay business.

PART 5

Staying Ahead in the eBay Marketplace

CHAPTER 14
NAVIGATING EBAY'S POLICIES AND SELLER STANDARDS (2025 UPDATES)

UNDERSTANDING AND ADHERING TO EBAY'S RULES AND REGULATIONS

Selling on eBay can be a lucrative and rewarding endeavor, but it is important to understand and adhere to eBay's rules and regulations. These policies are designed to create a fair, safe, and effective marketplace for both buyers and sellers, and they cover every aspect of selling on the platform—from listing items to handling returns. As a seller, you are responsible for ensuring that your listings, interactions with buyers, and overall business practices comply with these rules. Failing to follow eBay's regulations can lead to penalties, account restrictions, and in some cases, suspension from the platform. Understanding these rules and making them an integral part of your eBay business strategy will help you succeed and minimize any risks or disruptions.

One of the first areas where eBay's rules come into play is with listing items. eBay has specific guidelines that govern how products should be described, what information must be included, and what kinds of items can and cannot be sold. Every item listed on eBay must be accurately described, and it is crucial for sellers to provide clear and truthful information about the products they are offering. This includes disclosing any defects or issues with the product, providing details about the condition, and ensuring that the product complies with all relevant safety standards. Misleading or incomplete descriptions can result in negative feedback, the removal of listings, or even account suspension.

eBay also has rules regarding what types of products can be sold on its platform. There are a number of restricted and prohibited items, including but not limited to counterfeit goods, stolen merchandise, and certain health and safety-related products. Sellers are required to familiarize themselves with these restrictions to ensure that their inventory is in compliance with eBay's policies. Selling prohibited or restricted items can result in immediate account suspension and the permanent removal of all listings. To avoid this, it is essential to regularly review eBay's policies regarding restricted items, especially as these rules can change over time.

Another critical aspect of eBay's rules is the importance of setting appropriate pricing. Sellers must adhere to eBay's pricing policies, which are designed to prevent price gouging and ensure that products are priced fairly and transparently. While eBay allows sellers to set their own prices, there are guidelines in place to protect both buyers and sellers from misleading practices. For example, eBay prohibits sellers from listing products with artificially inflated prices, and it also ensures that shipping charges are reasonable and reflect the true cost of delivery. Sellers should also be mindful of any promotions or discounts they offer, as eBay has rules that govern how these promotions are presented and applied to listings. Misleading pricing or the failure to comply with eBay's pricing rules can result in the removal of listings and negative impacts on seller performance.

Shipping and handling policies are also a central part of eBay's regulations. Sellers are expected to ship items in a timely and efficient manner, and eBay has established strict guidelines regarding shipping times and costs. When listing an item, sellers must provide accurate information about the expected delivery date and the shipping options available. Shipping fees must be clearly stated in the listing, and these fees should reflect the actual cost of shipping. Sellers are required to ship items promptly once a buyer has made a purchase, and failure to do so can lead to customer complaints, negative feedback, and even penalties from eBay. Additionally, eBay encourages sellers to offer tracking information for all shipments, especially for high-value items. This allows buyers to track their orders, provides transparency in case of delivery issues, and helps protect sellers in the event of a dispute over delivery.

Return policies are another important area governed by eBay's rules. eBay requires sellers to have a clear and fair return policy in place, which is designed to protect both buyers and sellers. Sellers are encouraged to offer hassle-free returns, but it is not mandatory. However, sellers must adhere to minimum return policy requirements, which typically include a 30-day return window for most items. Sellers must also clearly state whether they offer free returns or if buyers will be responsible for return shipping. If a buyer returns an item due to defects, inaccuracies in the description, or other issues covered by eBay's buyer protection policies, the seller is typically required to issue a full refund, including the original shipping cost. Understanding eBay's return rules and providing a customer-friendly return experience can help build buyer trust and improve overall seller ratings.

Buyer protection is a cornerstone of eBay's platform, and sellers must understand how to navigate these policies to ensure that they are operating within the rules. eBay's Buyer Protection Program ensures that buyers are protected in case they receive items that are not as described or if they do not receive their orders. In cases where a buyer opens a case against a seller, eBay will review the situation and make a determination. Sellers must follow the dispute resolution process and be prepared to provide evidence, such as tracking information or communication with the buyer, to support their case. Failure to respond to buyer disputes or to cooperate with eBay's resolution process can lead to negative consequences, including the suspension of the seller's account.

Seller performance is another area where eBay enforces strict rules. eBay evaluates sellers based on several performance metrics, including their feedback rating, defect rate, late shipment rate, and the number of returns. Maintaining a high level of performance is crucial for building a successful eBay business, as sellers who consistently meet eBay's standards are rewarded with increased visibility in search results and access to advanced selling tools. Conversely, sellers who fall below eBay's performance standards may face penalties, such as reduced visibility, restrictions on their ability to list items, or even suspension from the platform. Larger sellers with higher sales volumes must be particularly diligent about their performance metrics, as even small issues can have a significant impact on their standing within the eBay community.

eBay's rules also extend to communication between buyers and sellers. Sellers are expected to respond to buyer inquiries in a timely and professional manner, addressing any questions or concerns about the product or transaction. Failure to communicate effectively can lead to buyer dissatisfaction and negative feedback, which can damage the seller's reputation. eBay's communication policies prohibit sellers from engaging in inappropriate behavior, such as using offensive language or sending unsolicited promotional messages to buyers. Sellers should always maintain a courteous and respectful tone in their communications, as maintaining positive buyer relationships is essential for long-term success on the platform.

In addition to understanding eBay's specific rules and regulations, sellers must stay updated on any changes to the platform's policies. eBay regularly revises its guidelines to address new challenges, market trends, and changes in consumer behavior. Sellers should regularly check eBay's policy updates and make any necessary adjustments to their practices in order to remain in compliance. Staying informed about eBay's evolving rules ensures that sellers can continue to grow their businesses while avoiding any risks or penalties associated with non-compliance.

Understanding and adhering to eBay's rules and regulations is an essential part of running a successful eBay business. By following eBay's guidelines for listing items, setting fair prices, managing shipping and returns, maintaining high performance standards, and communicating effectively with buyers, sellers can ensure a smooth and profitable selling experience. Sellers who consistently follow eBay's rules are rewarded with better visibility, higher customer trust, and a greater likelihood of success in the competitive online marketplace.

MAINTAINING HIGH SELLER STANDARDS AND AVOIDING PENALTIES

When running a business on eBay, one of the most crucial factors in achieving long-term success is maintaining high seller standards. As an online marketplace, eBay holds its sellers to a set of expectations designed to ensure smooth transactions, protect both buyers and sellers, and foster a positive community. For newcomers and even seasoned sellers, it's essential to understand the importance of adhering to eBay's rules, providing excellent customer service, and continuously striving for quality and professionalism in all aspects of your business. Sellers who consistently meet eBay's high standards are rewarded with greater visibility, higher search rankings, and increased trust from buyers. Conversely, failing to uphold these standards can lead to penalties, loss of sales, and potentially suspension from the platform.

At the heart of maintaining high seller standards is the consistent delivery of excellent customer service. Every aspect of a transaction, from the moment a buyer clicks on a product listing to the point of delivery, plays a part in shaping the customer's experience. It is important for sellers to provide clear and accurate product descriptions, including high-quality images and detailed specifications. Misleading descriptions or poor-quality photos can lead to buyer dissatisfaction, which in turn could result in negative feedback, return requests, or disputes. Providing accurate information, on the other hand, helps foster trust and increases the likelihood of positive reviews.

Beyond descriptions, communication with buyers is another pillar of high seller standards. eBay's platform thrives on open and respectful communication between buyers and sellers. Responding promptly to buyer inquiries and resolving any issues in a timely and professional manner can make a significant difference in maintaining a strong seller reputation. Many buyers value good communication and will return to sellers who offer timely support. Moreover, positive communication can lead to repeat customers and excellent feedback, both of which can boost a seller's position on eBay. A seller who fails to communicate effectively risks frustrating customers, which may result in disputes, negative reviews, and ultimately penalties.

An essential part of customer service on eBay is managing the fulfillment process—ensuring that items are shipped promptly and securely. Shipping is one of the most important aspects of the buying experience, and a delay in dispatch can quickly lead to buyer frustration. eBay encourages sellers to offer fast and reliable shipping options. In fact, a timely dispatch is often factored into seller ratings. To avoid penalties, sellers should ensure that items are shipped within the promised time frame and that tracking information is uploaded as soon as possible.

Tracking allows buyers to monitor their shipments, providing them with reassurance and reducing the likelihood of misunderstandings.

However, shipping delays can occur from time to time due to factors outside the seller's control, such as issues with couriers or customs. In these instances, it is essential for sellers to proactively communicate with buyers, providing updates on the status of the shipment. Transparency goes a long way in maintaining trust. Additionally, sellers should understand eBay's policies regarding late shipment and the potential consequences of missed deadlines. If a seller consistently fails to ship on time, they may face penalties such as reduced visibility in search results, a lower seller rating, or restrictions on their account.

A fundamental expectation eBay has of its sellers is compliance with the platform's rules regarding returns. Offering a fair and clear return policy is a requirement, and sellers must adhere to their listed return terms. eBay encourages hassle-free returns, as this enhances the buying experience. However, sellers are also allowed to establish their own return policies as long as they are within the guidelines. These policies should be clearly stated in every listing, including the time frame within which returns are accepted and whether buyers are responsible for return shipping. A seller who fails to honor their return policy, such as refusing to issue a refund for an item returned within the designated time frame, risks receiving negative feedback and possibly facing penalties from eBay.

In addition to the fundamental rules related to product descriptions, communication, shipping, and returns, eBay also evaluates sellers based on their performance metrics. These metrics are critical to maintaining high seller standards, as they determine a seller's overall standing in eBay's marketplace. The four main performance metrics eBay uses to assess sellers are feedback score, defect rate, late shipment rate, and the percentage of cases where eBay has sided with the buyer in a dispute. Sellers with a high defect rate, frequent late shipments, or a history of disputes are at risk of facing penalties, such as being downgraded in search results or restricted from listing certain types of items.

To avoid penalties and improve these performance metrics, sellers must focus on consistently meeting eBay's expectations. This includes resolving any buyer complaints quickly and professionally. A seller's feedback score is an essential part of their reputation on eBay, and maintaining a positive score should be a top priority. Positive feedback not only helps establish credibility but also improves a seller's chances of appearing higher in search results, which can lead to more sales. On the other hand, a negative feedback score, especially if it's due to avoidable issues, can severely damage a seller's reputation and sales potential.

While maintaining high seller standards is critical, it's equally important to stay informed about eBay's ever-evolving rules and regulations. eBay frequently updates its policies to address changes in the marketplace, emerging trends, and legal requirements. A seller who fails to stay up to date with these changes may unknowingly violate new rules, leading to penalties or account restrictions. For instance, eBay has strict policies regarding the sale of counterfeit goods, banned products, and misrepresentations of products. Sellers should take the time to review eBay's policies regularly to ensure that their listings comply with the latest guidelines.

Understanding eBay's seller performance standards and how they affect visibility is another key element of maintaining high standards. Sellers who consistently meet or exceed eBay's expectations are more likely to enjoy prominent placement in search results and gain access to additional selling tools. On the contrary, those who fail to uphold these standards may find themselves penalized with reduced visibility, limited access to selling features, or even suspension of their selling privileges.

One of the best ways to maintain high seller standards is by incorporating a mindset of continuous improvement. Sellers should regularly assess their business practices, identify areas for improvement, and implement changes to provide a better experience for buyers. This could involve optimizing product listings for clarity and accuracy, improving shipping processes, refining customer communication, or exploring new ways to enhance customer satisfaction. Staying proactive and consistently seeking to improve will not only help sellers avoid penalties but also ensure that they build a positive, sustainable business on eBay.

Another way to ensure compliance with eBay's rules and maintain high standards is by seeking assistance when needed. eBay provides a wealth of resources, including detailed guides, customer support, and forums where sellers can ask questions and get advice. Engaging with the eBay seller community and utilizing available resources can help sellers navigate the complexities of the platform and avoid common pitfalls.

Maintaining high seller standards is essential for long-term success on eBay. Sellers who consistently adhere to eBay's rules and regulations, provide exceptional customer service, and maintain good performance metrics will be more likely to build a reputable, profitable business. By staying informed, upholding high standards, and seeking continuous improvement, sellers can avoid penalties and position themselves for success in the competitive eBay marketplace.

STAYING INFORMED ABOUT POLICY CHANGES AND UPDATES

As an eBay seller, staying informed about policy changes and updates is crucial for maintaining a successful and compliant business. eBay is a dynamic marketplace, and the platform's policies, rules, and regulations evolve regularly to address changes in technology, consumer behavior, legal requirements, and the competitive landscape. For new and experienced sellers alike, understanding these changes and adapting to them can make the difference between success and failure. Sellers who neglect to stay up to date with policy changes may inadvertently violate new rules, resulting in penalties, account restrictions, or even suspension from the platform.

One of the most important steps in staying informed about policy changes is making it a habit to regularly check eBay's official resources. eBay's Seller Center is a comprehensive hub for all the essential tools and resources that sellers need to manage their businesses. It includes information on everything from listing guidelines and payment policies to customer service best practices and shipping standards. eBay frequently updates this section with important notices about policy changes, system updates, and new features that could impact the way sellers operate. Keeping a close eye on these updates will ensure that you don't miss anything critical that could affect your business.

In addition to the Seller Center, eBay also maintains a dedicated Policy Updates section on its website. This section provides detailed information on the latest changes to eBay's selling policies, fees, and other terms of service. When a new update is published, it typically includes a summary of the changes, their effective dates, and any actions that sellers must take to comply. Reading these updates carefully and understanding their implications can help you avoid common pitfalls that arise when sellers overlook or misunderstand policy changes.

Another effective way to stay informed about policy updates is by subscribing to eBay's newsletters and email notifications. These communications are a great way to receive timely updates on new policies, upcoming promotions, or changes to existing procedures. You can customize the types of notifications you receive to ensure that you only get the most relevant information based on your business needs. For example, if you specialize in a particular product category or sell internationally, you can set your preferences to receive updates specifically related to those areas. Being proactive in subscribing to these notifications ensures that you are always in the loop and can take immediate action when necessary.

In addition to official eBay communications, it is also essential to stay connected with the broader eBay seller community. One of the most valuable resources for learning about policy changes is the eBay community forums. These forums are where eBay sellers share their experiences, ask questions, and offer insights on various aspects of selling on the platform. Often, when policy changes occur, other sellers will discuss the changes in the forums, offering their interpretations, advice, and suggestions for navigating the new rules. While forums should not be your sole source of information, they can provide valuable perspectives and help you understand how other sellers are adjusting to policy updates. Engaging in the forums also provides an opportunity to ask questions, clarify any confusion, and learn from the experiences of others.

Social media is another platform where you can stay informed about eBay's policies. Many eBay sellers, as well as eBay itself, maintain social media accounts where they share updates, tips, and advice. eBay's official social media channels on platforms like Twitter, Facebook, and LinkedIn often post about changes to policies, new initiatives, or upcoming deadlines. Following these channels can keep you updated in real-time, ensuring you are among the first to know about any important changes. Additionally, eBay influencers and successful sellers often share their insights and experiences on social media, which can help you navigate policy changes more effectively.

While relying on eBay's official channels is important, it is also wise to keep track of external news sources that cover e-commerce and online selling trends. Industry blogs, podcasts, and news websites often discuss eBay's changes in greater detail and offer expert analysis on how those changes may affect sellers. These sources can provide a broader perspective on eBay's evolving policies, as well as offer tips on adapting your business to stay compliant and competitive. By staying informed through multiple channels, you can gain a well-rounded understanding of the changes and make more informed decisions about how to adjust your strategies.

It's also important to understand the underlying reasons behind policy changes. eBay's decisions to update or revise its policies are often driven by larger trends in the marketplace, changes in consumer behavior, legal requirements, or improvements in technology. By staying informed about the broader context in which these changes occur, you can anticipate future updates and prepare your business accordingly. For instance, eBay may revise its return policies due to changes in consumer protection laws or introduce new listing requirements to enhance buyer trust and security. Understanding the rationale behind these changes can help you adjust more effectively and remain compliant with eBay's evolving standards.

In addition to being proactive in keeping up with policy updates, it is also important to take action once you are aware of a change. Many policy changes on eBay require sellers to update their listings, modify their business practices, or adopt new tools and processes. When eBay introduces new rules, sellers are typically given a grace period to make necessary adjustments. However, failing to implement these changes within the allotted time frame can result in penalties, such as reduced visibility in search results or restrictions on your account. To avoid these consequences, it's essential to act swiftly and ensure that you are fully compliant with the new policies.

Furthermore, keeping track of policy changes also involves ensuring that your records and documentation are up to date. This includes maintaining accurate tax information, ensuring that your business practices align with eBay's guidelines, and regularly reviewing your account settings to make sure they reflect the latest rules. By staying organized and diligent in your record-keeping, you can avoid misunderstandings and complications down the line. It's also a good idea to periodically review your product listings to ensure they comply with the latest content guidelines and listing standards.

Lastly, even though eBay's policies are generally comprehensive, there may be occasional ambiguities or gray areas that arise. In these cases, don't hesitate to reach out to eBay's support team for clarification. eBay offers various channels for sellers to get in touch with customer service, including live chat, phone support, and email. If you're unsure about how a particular policy change affects your business, contacting eBay directly can provide peace of mind and ensure that you're on the right track.

Staying informed about policy changes and updates on eBay is an ongoing process that requires diligence, engagement, and proactive management. By regularly checking eBay's official resources, subscribing to email notifications, participating in community forums, and leveraging social media, you can stay on top of the latest developments and ensure that your business remains compliant. Understanding the reasoning behind policy changes and taking swift action to adjust your business practices will help you avoid penalties and stay competitive in the ever-changing world of online selling. With a commitment to staying informed, you can continue to build a successful and sustainable business on eBay for years to come.

PROTECTING YOURSELF FROM SCAMS AND FRAUD

In the world of e-commerce, protecting yourself from scams and fraud is a critical aspect of running a successful online business. While platforms like eBay provide some security measures, sellers are still at risk from fraudsters and dishonest buyers. As a seller, your business's integrity, financial security, and reputation depend on your ability to identify and protect yourself from potential threats. Knowing how to recognize scams, take preventive measures, and handle fraud-related issues effectively is essential for the long-term success of your business.

One of the first steps to protecting yourself from scams and fraud is understanding the common types of fraud that occur on eBay. A prevalent scam that many sellers face involves chargebacks. This happens when a buyer disputes a charge with their credit card company or payment provider after they've made a purchase. The buyer may claim that the item was not received or that it was damaged, even if the seller has provided proof of shipment. Chargebacks can be costly, as sellers are typically liable for the amount of the transaction, including shipping fees, and may also face fines or penalties from payment processors.

To prevent chargebacks, always provide accurate tracking information for every shipment and ensure that you have clear communication with your buyers. Additionally, offering a secure return policy and packaging items carefully can reduce the likelihood of disputes. For high-value items, consider requiring a signature upon delivery to verify that the item has been received by the buyer. This extra step can provide protection in case a buyer falsely claims that they never received the product.

Another common scam that can affect sellers is the "item not as described" scam. In this scenario, a buyer may claim that the item they purchased does not match the description or the images provided in the listing, even when it does. The buyer may demand a refund or return the item for an exchange. In some cases, they may even send back a different, less valuable item in place of the original one. This scam can be particularly damaging to sellers, as it undermines their reputation and can result in financial loss.

To protect yourself from this type of scam, always ensure that your listings are as accurate and detailed as possible. Provide high-quality images from multiple angles, and include thorough descriptions of the product's condition, dimensions, and any flaws it may have. Being transparent and honest in your listings not only helps avoid misunderstandings but also builds trust with your buyers. If a buyer claims that the item they received is not as described, request clear evidence, such as photographs, to verify the claim. Document all communication with the buyer to protect yourself in case the situation escalates.

Fraudsters also sometimes attempt to manipulate the system by using fake buyer accounts. These accounts may be created to exploit seller policies, including refund or return processes. In some cases, fraudsters will purchase an item and later file a false claim, hoping to receive a refund without ever returning the item. They may also attempt to manipulate sellers by providing fake shipping addresses or using stolen payment information.

To avoid falling victim to these scams, always verify the buyer's account and their feedback history before proceeding with any transaction. Buyers with poor feedback or newly created accounts may warrant closer scrutiny. Additionally, consider implementing certain security measures, such as requiring PayPal or other secure payment methods. These platforms offer buyer protection, which can help safeguard you in case of fraud. However, they may also impose certain conditions, so it is important to understand the buyer protection policies thoroughly.

Phishing scams are another significant risk for sellers. In these scams, fraudsters impersonate eBay or PayPal representatives and send fake emails or messages attempting to lure sellers into providing sensitive information, such as login credentials, bank account details, or credit card information. These emails often look legitimate, mimicking official eBay or PayPal correspondence, and may contain urgent requests to verify account information or resolve a supposed issue with the seller's account.

To avoid falling victim to phishing attempts, never click on links from unsolicited emails, especially those requesting personal or financial information. Instead, log in to your eBay or PayPal account directly from the official website and check for any alerts or messages. If you receive a suspicious email, report it to eBay or PayPal's customer support, and delete the message immediately. Be cautious of any communication that seems too urgent or asks for information that you would not typically provide through email.

Seller protection programs offered by platforms like eBay can provide an added layer of security. eBay offers a range of protections for sellers, such as coverage for losses resulting from fraudulent claims or disputes. To qualify for seller protection, you must follow specific guidelines, such as providing accurate tracking information, maintaining clear communication with buyers, and adhering to eBay's policies. Being aware of these protections and knowing how to use them can help you resolve disputes and minimize your risk of financial loss due to fraud.

Additionally, setting clear and firm terms and conditions in your listings can act as a deterrent for fraudulent buyers. For instance, if you specify that you do not accept returns on certain items or that you will only ship to verified addresses, you provide yourself with a clear legal stance if a buyer tries to dispute the transaction. Make sure these terms are visible in the listing and clearly communicated to the buyer. This transparency can help reduce misunderstandings and prevent fraudulent activity.

One of the most effective ways to protect yourself from scams is to monitor your account regularly for any suspicious activity. This includes reviewing your feedback score, checking for any unauthorized returns, chargebacks, or negative reviews that may indicate a pattern of fraudulent behavior. If you notice anything unusual, take immediate action to investigate and resolve the issue. Quick responses and proactive management of your account can prevent minor issues from escalating into major problems.

If you suspect that a buyer is attempting to scam you, or if you have already been scammed, it's crucial to report the incident to eBay's customer support immediately. eBay has a robust system in place for handling disputes, fraud claims, and policy violations. By reporting the issue early, you not only protect yourself but also help eBay track and address fraudulent activity across the platform.

While scams and fraud are unfortunate risks of selling on eBay, they can be mitigated with proper precautions, vigilance, and a proactive approach. Protecting yourself from fraud requires a combination of accurate listing practices, effective communication with buyers, adherence to eBay policies, and leveraging available protections such as seller protection programs. By staying informed, practicing caution, and being prepared to address issues quickly, you can safeguard your business and minimize the impact of scams and fraud.

CHAPTER 15

THE FUTURE OF SELLING ON EBAY: TRENDS AND PREDICTIONS FOR 2025 AND BEYOND

EMERGING TECHNOLOGIES AND THEIR IMPACT ON EBAY

Emerging technologies are transforming the way people buy and sell online, and eBay is not immune to these sweeping changes. As digital tools become more intelligent, more connected, and more accessible, sellers who adapt to and adopt these innovations are better positioned to stay ahead in the competitive world of e-commerce. These advancements are reshaping customer expectations, streamlining operations, and opening up entirely new opportunities for those who are willing to embrace them.

One of the most significant technological shifts impacting eBay is the rapid development of artificial intelligence. AI is increasingly being woven into every part of the buying and selling experience. From product listings to customer service, artificial intelligence is helping sellers become more efficient while enhancing the overall shopping experience for buyers. eBay's own platform is now leveraging AI to provide smarter product suggestions, better search filtering, and automated listing optimizations. These tools analyze massive amounts of data to determine what titles, keywords, and photos are likely to perform best based on current trends and historical buyer behavior.

For sellers, this means that instead of relying solely on intuition or trial and error, there are now AI-driven tools that can analyze what sells, how it sells, and who it sells to. Automated listing tools can generate optimized descriptions, recommend pricing strategies based on market demand, and even predict when items are most likely to sell. Some software can track trends and identify profitable niches before they become saturated, giving proactive sellers a powerful edge. Artificial intelligence also plays a critical role in fraud detection, helping eBay identify suspicious activity and protect sellers and buyers from fraudulent transactions.

Another technological frontier making a big impact is machine learning, which is a subset of AI. Machine learning systems can recognize patterns and adapt over time based on new data. This becomes extremely valuable in areas such as dynamic pricing, personalized marketing, and buyer-seller matching. By understanding how different categories of products perform across seasons or among various buyer demographics, machine learning tools help sellers adjust their strategies more precisely and profitably.

Automation technology is also reshaping the day-to-day operations of eBay sellers. Automated inventory management systems now make it possible to sync stock levels across multiple platforms, preventing overselling and reducing the need for manual updates. When a product sells on eBay, the system can automatically update the available quantity, issue a reorder notification, or even place a restocking order with a supplier. This is especially valuable for sellers managing large inventories or using fulfillment centers. With the right tools, a single person can now run an operation that once required an entire staff.

Chatbots and virtual assistants have emerged as another critical innovation. These tools are helping sellers handle customer inquiries around the clock. Buyers expect prompt responses, and chatbots can provide instant answers to common questions, resolve simple issues, and escalate more complex concerns to the seller when necessary. This improves the buyer experience without adding to the seller's workload. Some advanced bots can even interpret sentiment in messages, allowing them to tailor responses based on the customer's tone or urgency.

Mobile technology has also become central to how business is conducted on eBay. As more buyers and sellers operate via smartphones, eBay has invested heavily in optimizing its mobile experience. Sellers can now list, photograph, price, ship, and communicate entirely from their phones. Emerging technologies are enabling high-resolution product photography, barcode scanning for fast item lookup, and voice-to-text descriptions directly from mobile devices. This is making eBay selling more accessible to people who may not have traditional computing setups but want to run a business from anywhere.

Blockchain technology, while still evolving in practical application, is beginning to influence e-commerce in meaningful ways. Though not yet fully integrated into mainstream marketplaces like eBay, blockchain's potential is already drawing attention. Blockchain offers transparency, security, and decentralization—features that could be highly beneficial in the future. For example, blockchain could provide immutable records of transactions, supply chain traceability, and verified authenticity for high-value goods. These features could help eliminate disputes over condition, origin, or ownership, especially in categories such as collectibles, art, luxury goods, and electronics.

As the popularity of cryptocurrencies continues to rise, eBay and similar platforms may find themselves integrating crypto payment options. Although this transition is not fully realized, some sellers are already exploring off-platform sales that accept Bitcoin, Ethereum, or stablecoins. For sellers looking to future-proof their operations, understanding cryptocurrency and blockchain fundamentals could become increasingly important.

Augmented reality is another emerging technology beginning to touch the eBay experience. AR allows buyers to visualize products in their environment before making a purchase. In categories like home decor, furniture, and fashion accessories, this can dramatically reduce returns and increase buyer confidence. Sellers who adopt 3D imaging and AR-friendly formats are better able to showcase their products and stand out in crowded listings. As eBay experiments with these features, sellers should keep an eye on how these capabilities evolve and how they can be integrated into their own listings.

Voice commerce, driven by smart speakers and virtual assistants like Alexa, Siri, and Google Assistant, is growing steadily. Although it's still early days for voice-activated eBay shopping, this trend signals a shift in how consumers search for and purchase products online. As buyers become accustomed to using voice commands to browse and buy, sellers will need to adapt their product listings to include more natural language, voice-optimized keywords, and conversational descriptions. This shift will also place more importance on precise product categorization and clear, intuitive titles.

Even logistics and shipping are being transformed by emerging technology. Smart logistics platforms can now analyze shipping routes, optimize carrier selection, and reduce costs while improving delivery speed. Sellers can access integrated shipping dashboards that recommend the most efficient shipping method based on location, weight, delivery expectations, and cost. Predictive shipping tools can anticipate future sales trends and recommend how much inventory to keep on hand or where to position it, whether in your own warehouse or through a fulfillment partner.

Robotics and warehouse automation are beginning to play a larger role, particularly for high-volume eBay sellers. Automated packing stations, label printers, and robotic picking arms are becoming more accessible, particularly through third-party fulfillment services. These systems speed up order fulfillment, reduce errors, and lower long-term labor costs. While not every seller will invest in this kind of infrastructure, understanding its availability helps you evaluate when outsourcing fulfillment might become a more efficient choice.

Cybersecurity technology is also growing in importance as more business moves online. Sellers must protect sensitive buyer information, payment data, and personal accounts from increasingly sophisticated cyber threats. Multi-factor authentication, encrypted communication, and secure payment gateways are now standard best practices. Investing in up-to-date security tools not only helps prevent loss but also reinforces trust with buyers, many of whom will avoid sellers who seem careless with data or slow to adopt modern security practices.

The role of data analytics cannot be overlooked. Sellers now have access to real-time dashboards and analytics tools that offer insights into buyer behavior, inventory performance, market trends, and profit margins. With the help of machine learning and predictive modeling, these platforms can go beyond basic sales reports to help sellers make informed decisions that drive long-term success. Sellers who understand how to interpret and act on this data are more agile, more strategic, and better equipped to grow their business intelligently.

Ultimately, the impact of emerging technologies on eBay is both disruptive and empowering. It is leveling the playing field by giving even small-scale sellers access to sophisticated tools that were once available only to large retailers. Success in this new era requires a mindset of adaptability and continuous learning. Sellers who keep an eye on technology trends and actively seek out ways to incorporate them into their workflow will not only survive but thrive in the ever-evolving landscape of online commerce.

SHIFTING CONSUMER BEHAVIORS AND EXPECTATIONS

Consumer behavior is never static. It evolves constantly, driven by cultural shifts, economic changes, technological advancements, and global events. For anyone selling on eBay, staying attuned to these changing patterns isn't just helpful—it's vital. The expectations customers bring with them today are far more nuanced and demanding than they were even a few years ago. They no longer simply want to find a product at a fair price. They want speed, transparency, personalization, ethical business practices, and seamless digital experiences. Understanding these shifting behaviors is what separates stagnant sellers from those who consistently thrive.

One of the most significant transformations in recent years has been the rise of the convenience-driven buyer. Today's customers are busy, distracted, and have an ocean of options at their fingertips. They gravitate toward sellers who make the process easy, fast, and intuitive. Long gone are the days when buyers would patiently scroll through multiple pages of listings or tolerate slow response times. Now, they expect near-instant search results, filters that narrow choices precisely, and sellers who respond quickly to messages. Listings that are clear, visually appealing, and easy to scan hold their attention. Those that are cluttered, ambiguous, or incomplete are quickly skipped over.

Shipping expectations have also shifted dramatically. Influenced by e-commerce giants that offer next-day or even same-day delivery, buyers have come to expect faster shipping across the board. Even on platforms like eBay, where many sellers are small businesses or individuals, buyers often assume that items will ship within 24 hours. When delivery estimates are slow or uncertain, buyers hesitate. Sellers who can streamline their fulfillment process—either by managing inventory efficiently or partnering with faster carriers—earn more repeat customers and better feedback.

The modern consumer is also much more informed. They come to a listing with research already done, often knowing what the product should cost, what its features are, and how it compares to competitors. This creates both a challenge and an opportunity. On one hand, sellers can't rely on vague claims or inflated pricing. On the other, by clearly presenting the value of a product, being transparent about condition or features, and offering excellent customer service, a seller can stand out in a crowded market. Trust is a currency more powerful than price, and it is built through clarity, consistency, and responsiveness.

Mobile behavior is another force reshaping how people shop on eBay. More buyers now browse and purchase through their smartphones than through desktop computers. This means listings must be optimized for mobile devices. Images should be high-resolution but load quickly. Descriptions should be concise yet thorough, formatted in a way that's easy to scroll through. Buttons must be clearly visible and interactive elements must function well on small screens. A listing that performs well on mobile is more likely to convert casual browsers into actual buyers.

Today's consumers also care about values and purpose. Many buyers are consciously choosing to support small businesses, environmentally responsible sellers, or those who operate ethically. They may seek products that are locally sourced, recycled, handmade, or produced in low-waste environments. They're interested in the story behind the seller, and many are willing to pay a premium for products that align with their values. Sellers who take the time to share their journey, explain how their products are made, or highlight their commitment to sustainability find themselves resonating with these increasingly conscientious consumers.

There's also a notable shift toward personalization. Buyers now expect tailored experiences even in spaces like eBay, where the marketplace structure makes standardization more common. Still, personalization can show up in many forms. It could be as simple as offering size or color variations based on previous buyer trends, using messaging that reflects a customer's region or past purchases, or sending follow-up messages with thoughtful suggestions. Even the way sellers write their descriptions or thank buyers after a sale can feel personal and build loyalty.

Social proof plays a larger role than ever before. Reviews, ratings, and seller feedback heavily influence purchasing decisions. A seller's reputation can be the deciding factor between one listing and another, even when prices and shipping are identical. As a result, sellers must take every interaction seriously. From ensuring that products are described accurately, to responding to questions promptly, to handling disputes with professionalism, every touchpoint is an opportunity to earn trust and bolster public credibility. This is especially important as buyers increasingly cross-check seller profiles before committing to a purchase.

Another layer of modern consumer behavior involves omnichannel expectations. Shoppers don't compartmentalize platforms the way they used to. They may see something on social media, search for it on Google, compare it with eBay prices, and check reviews elsewhere before buying. As more sellers link their eBay store to Instagram, Pinterest, or their own websites, customers begin to expect consistency across platforms. Listings, brand voice, pricing, and customer service should feel unified, no matter where the interaction begins.

Buyer attention spans have also shortened in the age of instant gratification. People expect to find what they need quickly and move on. This means sellers must think like digital marketers—making sure titles are keyword-optimized, images are compelling, and essential details are presented right up front. Buyers want answers at a glance: What is it? What condition is it in? How much does it cost? When will it arrive? If a listing fails to answer these questions within the first few seconds of viewing, the buyer is likely to move on to another seller.

Customer service expectations are also rising. Buyers no longer consider a slow response or a missed message just a minor inconvenience. It can turn into a negative review or even a lost sale. Sellers must adopt tools and routines that enable fast, consistent communication. This might include using eBay's automated message features, setting clear policies, or having a regular schedule for checking inquiries. Speed, politeness, and clarity are no longer optional—they're essential.

The global nature of eBay's platform has also influenced buyer behavior. Many consumers are now comfortable buying from international sellers, provided the shipping process is transparent and the seller is reputable. Language barriers, currency conversion, and time zones are becoming less of a hurdle as eBay and other tools offer automatic translations and global shipping programs. Sellers who are willing to embrace international buyers by clearly outlining shipping options and setting expectations will tap into a growing customer base that stretches far beyond their region.

Security and data privacy concerns have also become more prominent. Consumers are increasingly cautious about where and how their information is shared. They want to feel confident that their transactions are secure and that sellers are trustworthy. This has led to greater scrutiny over listings that seem vague, sellers with low feedback scores, or profiles that appear inactive. Sellers who maintain consistent branding, use secure payment options, and communicate proactively about shipping and returns help put buyers at ease.

The COVID-19 pandemic further accelerated many of these behavioral changes. It trained millions of people—many of whom had never shopped online before—to expect fast, reliable digital transactions. It normalized contactless shopping, remote work, and a preference for home delivery. Even as the world moves into a post-pandemic phase, these habits are unlikely to reverse. In fact, they've become foundational to how people engage with online marketplaces.

Consumer behavior is no longer just about what people buy—it's about how, when, and why they choose to buy it from one seller instead of another. The expectations are higher, but so are the tools available to meet them. Sellers who pay attention to these shifts, who listen to their buyers, and who evolve their practices accordingly will find themselves not only keeping up with the times but setting themselves apart in a marketplace that rewards adaptability, integrity, and excellence.

ADAPTING YOUR STRATEGIES FOR LONG-TERM SUCCESS

Long-term success in any online business is rarely about a single, grand strategy. Instead, it is rooted in a series of intentional, adaptive decisions that evolve over time. Selling on eBay, like any dynamic business environment, requires a deep awareness of shifting patterns and a willingness to refine your approach continually. The strategies that bring early momentum often need reshaping to accommodate growth, market trends, changing buyer behaviors, or platform updates. In this sense, success is not a fixed destination—it's a moving target that demands resilience, experimentation, and strategic evolution.

At the core of adapting for long-term success is the mindset of growth through change. Sellers who view their business as a living system—capable of learning, adjusting, and thriving in new conditions—are the ones who sustain profitability and relevance. Early in your eBay journey, it's natural to focus on basic tasks: creating listings, making your first sales, managing shipping. But as your store grows, you'll face new decisions about scaling your operations, investing in tools, optimizing your customer experience, and keeping your business model aligned with your larger goals. What worked when you had ten listings may not work when you have a hundred. Systems that supported fifty orders a month might break down when you're handling five hundred. Recognizing the signs that it's time to adapt is the first step toward ensuring continued success.

One key shift often occurs when sellers begin to plateau after their initial burst of sales. This dip doesn't always mean you've done something wrong—it usually means the environment around you has changed. New competitors enter the space. eBay algorithms shift. Buyers start favoring different keywords, formats, or shipping speeds. Sellers who cling rigidly to their old methods risk becoming obsolete. Those who remain curious and data-driven will thrive. Tracking your sales, conversion rates, customer reviews, and inventory turnover allows you to spot patterns and problem areas. If your top-selling product suddenly dips in views, it may be due to seasonality, a change in eBay search rankings, or a flood of new competitors. Instead of guessing, dig into the numbers. Are your prices still competitive? Are your listings optimized for the latest mobile interface? Have buyer expectations changed?

Responding to these insights may mean revising your listings with fresh photos, rewriting descriptions for clarity or keyword strength, or even repositioning products into new categories. As the marketplace matures, refinement is not a luxury—it's a necessity. The most successful sellers rarely coast on autopilot. They treat every quarter as an opportunity to improve their store's performance and relevance.

Adapting also includes evaluating your product mix. What once sold well may no longer be in demand. Consumer interests shift quickly, often influenced by global events, social media trends, or technological innovations. Smart sellers remain attuned to these signals. If a certain category is losing traction, consider testing new inventory in adjacent niches. Maybe you started by selling vintage electronics but noticed increasing demand for modern home tech accessories. Exploring those new opportunities doesn't mean abandoning your core—it means expanding your relevance.

Sometimes adaptation takes the form of stepping back to work on the business rather than just in it. This can mean investing in tools that save time, outsourcing repetitive tasks like packaging, or even hiring help to manage customer service. As your business grows, your time becomes more valuable. Repetitive tasks that were manageable in the beginning can become bottlenecks. Strategic delegation allows you to shift focus to higher-impact activities: sourcing better inventory, marketing your brand, or analyzing trends to stay ahead.

In a constantly changing environment, education becomes one of your greatest assets. Staying informed about platform updates, marketing techniques, and consumer behavior is not optional if you're aiming for long-term viability. Platforms like eBay are never static. They roll out policy changes, algorithm updates, new features, and seller tools that can significantly impact visibility and performance. Keeping yourself informed through seller forums, eBay announcements, webinars, or newsletters keeps you in control. When sellers fail to adapt to platform changes—such as new shipping policies, promotional tools, or search prioritization rules—they often experience declines in traffic or unexpected penalties. Those who proactively learn and respond stay ahead of the curve.

Equally important is the need to cultivate and nurture your brand identity. In the beginning, it may be enough to simply be a seller of a certain type of product. But as competition increases, buyers start looking for more. They want consistency, trustworthiness, and a reason to return. Creating a recognizable and professional identity—from your store name and logo to your tone of communication and packaging presentation—helps you stand out in a sea of generic listings. Long-term success often hinges on repeat business, and repeat customers return when they feel they know who you are and what to expect.

Adapting your strategies over time also involves managing your finances differently. When you start out, profit may be reinvested into purchasing more stock or basic supplies. As your store matures, you'll want to shift toward a more sophisticated budgeting approach that accounts for taxes, platform fees, returns, marketing costs, and emergency reserves. Proper financial planning ensures that temporary slumps don't become long-term crises. It also gives you the clarity to make big moves—like investing in a high-demand product line or upgrading your warehouse space—without guessing whether you can afford it.

Another aspect of long-term adaptation is building resilience into your business model. Online selling comes with inherent uncertainties. Supply chains may get disrupted. A negative review can sting. An unexpected return policy change can impact your margins. Sellers who rely on a single product, a single supplier, or a single strategy are vulnerable to setbacks. Diversifying your product base, sourcing from multiple suppliers, and maintaining a cushion of cash flow are all ways to reduce your risk and build staying power. You want your business to survive not just in good seasons, but when things go wrong.

Customer relationships become even more critical the longer you operate. Early on, you may be focused on attracting new buyers. Over time, however, a major advantage lies in building loyalty and positive word-of-mouth. This requires consistent follow-through on your promises: shipping when you say you will, describing items accurately, and resolving complaints with empathy and professionalism. When buyers feel taken care of, they remember—and they come back. Positive experiences multiply. They become your reviews, your reputation, and your best marketing.

Lastly, adapting for long-term success also means aligning your business with your personal goals and lifestyle. As your eBay store becomes more successful, you may find it taking over more of your time or energy. What began as a side hustle could evolve into a full-time income stream—or, conversely, become unsustainable without better systems in place. Periodically stepping back to evaluate what you want from your business ensures that it continues to serve you, not the other way around. Do you want more freedom? More revenue? Less stress? Your strategies should reflect those evolving priorities.

In a world where change is the only constant, the sellers who succeed over the long haul are not necessarily the most skilled or well-funded. They're the ones who are most adaptable. They listen to the data, they learn from experience, and they're never afraid to evolve. Success on eBay is not about a single breakthrough moment. It's about a steady, ongoing commitment to growth, refinement, and resilience. That's how great sellers become lasting ones.

RESOURCES FOR STAYING UPDATED ON EBAY TRENDS

In today's fast-paced digital marketplace, staying updated on trends is one of the most crucial aspects of maintaining and growing a successful eBay business. As the online retail environment is constantly evolving, keeping your finger on the pulse of new developments, tools, policies, and shifts in consumer behavior is essential. Without staying informed, sellers risk falling behind the competition, missing out on emerging opportunities, or inadvertently violating platform rules. To ensure you're always in the know, there are a variety of resources available to help you stay up to date on eBay trends, and it's important to leverage these to maintain your competitive edge.

One of the most valuable resources for any eBay seller is eBay's own seller tools and updates. eBay has an array of official channels where they communicate directly with their sellers about platform changes, upcoming features, and trend reports. These updates are crucial because they allow sellers to adapt their business practices before changes go live, minimizing the risk of disruption. The eBay Seller Hub is the primary platform for managing your store and monitoring its performance, but it's also an excellent resource for news and alerts. Regularly checking the Seller Hub for notifications about updates to eBay's policies, search algorithms, or product categories is an important habit for any seller aiming to stay on top of eBay trends.

In addition to the Seller Hub, eBay maintains a comprehensive Help & Contact section, which provides insights into troubleshooting issues and understanding changes in fees, policies, and other core aspects of selling on the platform. The eBay Community Forums are another invaluable resource. This is a space where sellers from around the world can connect, share their experiences, and discuss updates and trends. By participating in these forums, you can get firsthand insights into what other sellers are experiencing, how they are adapting, and what tools they're finding most effective. These forums are often the first place where eBay users share feedback on new features or issues they've encountered, making it a great spot to monitor emerging trends and challenges.

Another official eBay resource that provides trend insights is the eBay Seller Newsletter. This email newsletter is a great way to stay informed about important updates, promotions, and features being rolled out across the platform. Subscribing to the newsletter will ensure that you receive curated, timely information directly from eBay, tailored to help you succeed on the platform. Whether it's news about seasonal selling strategies, tips for improving your seller performance rating, or introductions to new tools, the eBay Seller Newsletter delivers useful information straight to your inbox.

Social media also plays a significant role in staying updated on eBay trends. eBay has active accounts on platforms like Facebook, Twitter, and Instagram, where they share real-time updates, tips, and best practices for sellers. Following eBay's social media channels is a good way to keep track of quick changes, promotions, and insights about upcoming features or policy shifts. Many eBay sellers also use social media platforms like YouTube, Facebook Groups, and LinkedIn to create communities where they discuss strategies and trends. By engaging with these groups, you'll be able to access conversations about trends, upcoming holidays, and the latest tools or resources that can help you scale your business.

In addition to eBay's official resources, there are third-party websites and tools that provide valuable insights into the latest trends. Websites dedicated to eCommerce news, like Practical eCommerce or eCommerceBytes, regularly publish articles about platform changes, market trends, and best practices. These sites often provide in-depth articles that analyze eBay's latest initiatives, trends in online shopping behavior, and even predictions about the future of eCommerce. Reading these articles will help you understand how broader trends in the retail world are impacting eBay specifically.

There are also a variety of blogs and podcasts dedicated to helping online sellers succeed. Many successful eBay sellers and eCommerce experts share their insights through blogs, podcasts, and webinars. These resources can provide valuable knowledge, ranging from new marketing techniques to strategies for scaling your business. For example, blogs like eBay's own seller blog or independent blogs like Seller Hub or The Selling Family offer tutorials, case studies, and trend analysis specifically tailored to eBay sellers. These platforms often feature guest posts from industry experts or success stories from sellers who have cracked the code on building profitable businesses on eBay.

Podcasts are another excellent source of current information for eBay sellers. There are several podcasts specifically designed for online sellers, including those focused on eBay, Amazon, and other eCommerce platforms. Listening to podcasts gives you access to industry experts who discuss not only current trends but also practical advice for improving your eBay store. Many of these podcasts feature interviews with successful sellers who share their tips on adapting to new eBay policies, utilizing new features, and exploring emerging trends. Popular eBay podcasts include "The eBay Seller Podcast" and "eCommerceFuel," where hosts provide up-to-date information on eBay's changes and the broader eCommerce landscape.

For those who prefer a more interactive approach to staying updated, attending eCommerce conferences, webinars, and virtual workshops is a great option. Many industry experts and thought leaders in the eBay community host events throughout the year, where they discuss the latest trends, platform updates, and best practices for success. These events are great for networking, learning from experienced sellers, and gaining insights from thought leaders who can help you stay ahead of the curve. eBay's own annual events, such as the eBay Open conference, are fantastic opportunities to learn from the platform's leadership team, network with other sellers, and gain insights into future changes and trends.

Additionally, there are paid tools and software that provide deep insights into eBay's trends and help you make data-driven decisions. Tools like Terapeak, which is integrated with eBay, provide detailed market research that helps sellers track trends, analyze product demand, and identify profitable opportunities. Terapeak allows you to analyze the past performance of products across eBay, enabling you to make informed decisions about which products to stock and which categories to focus on. Other software options, such as Auctiva and InkFrog, provide automated listing tools, marketing resources, and trend-tracking capabilities to help sellers optimize their stores for better performance.

Beyond the digital resources available, one of the best ways to stay updated is through networking with other sellers. Whether it's through online communities, social media, or in-person meetups, engaging with other eBay sellers allows you to exchange knowledge, learn about the latest trends, and collaborate on common challenges. Networking helps you stay grounded in what is happening in the marketplace and gives you access to the collective wisdom of experienced sellers. Whether through Facebook Groups, LinkedIn connections, or even local eCommerce events, staying connected to the broader eBay community provides invaluable insights.

Staying updated on eBay trends requires an ongoing commitment to learning and adapting to the ever-changing eCommerce landscape. By utilizing a combination of official eBay resources, third-party websites, blogs, podcasts, social media, networking opportunities, and paid tools, you can ensure that you remain informed about the latest trends and best practices. The more you engage with these resources, the better equipped you'll be to stay ahead of your competition, offer exceptional customer experiences, and grow your eBay business over time. Whether it's through keeping an eye on eBay's updates, learning from other sellers, or investing in data-driven tools, staying updated is key to long-term success in the online marketplace.

CONCLUSION

Building an eBay business from the ground up is more than just a commercial endeavor—it is a journey of transformation, learning, and empowerment. The process of becoming a successful eBay seller in today's dynamic digital marketplace is not simply about listing products and waiting for sales to roll in. It requires a deliberate blend of strategy, adaptability, dedication, and resilience. Every seller who embarks on this path is not only stepping into the world of commerce but also embracing the mindset of an entrepreneur, a problem solver, and a lifelong learner.

At its core, the process is deeply human. Behind each transaction is a person—someone who either needs what you're offering or has a problem that your product can solve. When you begin to look at your listings not just as digital storefronts but as bridges connecting real needs with real solutions, your business begins to shift from transactional to relational. This is where true value is created, and where long-term growth begins to take root.

Throughout this journey, one of the most important qualities to nurture is curiosity. The eBay platform, like the broader eCommerce landscape, is always changing. Algorithms evolve, buyer preferences shift, policies are updated, and competition grows more sophisticated. Remaining curious allows you to stay ahead. It encourages you to ask why your best-selling item suddenly declined in sales, or how a new automation tool might save you five hours a week. It pushes you to explore emerging categories, test fresh listing techniques, and refine your shipping process to provide faster delivery and lower costs. Curiosity doesn't just fuel innovation—it protects you from stagnation.

Discipline is another crucial element. Selling on eBay, especially when starting out, is not a passive income stream in the romanticized sense of the word. It demands consistency—responding to buyer messages promptly, shipping on time, staying on top of inventory, and adjusting strategies when something isn't working. The sellers who build thriving stores over the long term aren't necessarily the ones with the flashiest branding or the trendiest products. They're the ones who show up, day after day, to do the work, to tweak, to learn, and to grow.

Equally important is your ability to embrace failure without letting it define your journey. Mistakes are inevitable. Maybe you'll source a product that turns out to be a dud, or you'll miscalculate shipping costs and lose money on a batch of orders. Perhaps a buyer will leave negative feedback that feels undeserved, or you'll be hit with a return you think is unfair. These experiences, frustrating as they are, offer some of the most powerful lessons you'll learn. In many ways, they are what separate short-lived efforts from sustainable businesses. What matters is not avoiding setbacks, but how quickly and creatively you recover from them.

Success on eBay, particularly in the modern era, also hinges on your ability to evolve with your customers. Buyers today are savvier than ever. They expect clear communication, transparent policies, responsive service, and an experience that feels as personal as it is professional. Sellers who thrive are those who can adapt their language, policies, and service to meet rising expectations without compromising their own boundaries or profitability. Selling isn't about pushing products—it's about building trust. And trust, once earned, becomes the bedrock of repeat business and word-of-mouth referrals.

Another powerful realization along this path is that you don't have to do it all alone. Whether it's hiring help to handle shipping, using automation tools to streamline tasks, or joining communities of like-minded sellers to swap ideas and support each other, there is strength in collaboration. Building a business is hard work, and there will be moments when burnout threatens to creep in. Knowing when and how to delegate—even if only a few hours a week—can be the difference between a business that drains you and one that energizes you.

It's also essential to celebrate the wins—big or small. The first sale. The first month you turn a profit. The first repeat customer who messages to say how much they loved your product. These milestones may seem minor in the grand scheme of your business plan, but they carry emotional weight. They are proof that your efforts are working, that you are on the right path, and that the vision you had when you started is becoming real. Taking time to reflect on these moments reinforces your motivation and reminds you of the deeper "why" behind your hustle.

Long-term success comes not only from mastering the technical aspects of the platform but also from cultivating a deep sense of self-awareness. This includes understanding your strengths and playing to them, while also being honest about your limitations and seeking support or education where needed. It means developing the emotional intelligence to handle difficult buyers gracefully, the critical thinking to navigate uncertainty, and the patience to build something meaningful over time.

There is also something deeply rewarding about creating something from nothing. Whether you're selling vintage collectibles, handmade crafts, surplus inventory, or branded products, the act of taking a product, connecting it with a buyer, and creating a transaction that benefits both parties is inherently empowering. You are learning to turn your time, effort, and knowledge into income—something that can grow, evolve, and adapt with you.

Even more importantly, you are gaining control. Control over how you work, when you work, and what you prioritize. For many, this control is a gateway to more freedom—freedom to spend time with family, pursue passions, travel, or simply enjoy the satisfaction of being your own boss. That freedom is worth the challenges, the learning curves, and the growing pains.

As technology continues to evolve and eCommerce becomes more accessible, opportunities will continue to expand. New markets will open. Tools will become more powerful. Buyer behaviors will shift in unexpected ways. But the foundation you've built—of resilience, adaptability, curiosity, and service—will carry you through whatever changes come. If you continue to invest in learning, stay grounded in your values, and remain focused on providing real value to your customers, your eBay business can thrive for years to come.

This journey is just the beginning. Whether you go on to build a full-scale operation with multiple employees and warehouses, or you continue as a solo entrepreneur running a lean and agile online store, the skills you've developed are powerful assets. You've learned how to sell, how to manage logistics, how to analyze data, how to speak to a market—and above all, how to bet on yourself.

So keep pushing. Keep learning. Keep adapting. The digital marketplace rewards those who show up, stay sharp, and lead with service. Wherever your eBay business takes you next, the road ahead is filled with opportunity—and the best chapters may still be waiting to be written.

APPENDICES

APPENDIX A: ESSENTIAL TOOLS AND RESOURCES FOR EBAY SELLERS

Success as an eBay seller in today's rapidly evolving eCommerce environment requires more than just great products and compelling listings. To operate efficiently, scale your business, and compete in a marketplace teeming with sellers, you need the right tools and resources at your disposal. These tools range from listing software and inventory management systems to market research platforms and customer service enhancers. Leveraging them effectively can dramatically increase your productivity, minimize errors, and improve your buyer's experience—all while freeing you up to focus on growing your business. Below is a detailed list of essential tools and resources every eBay seller should consider integrating into their operations.

1. **eBay Seller Hub**
   This is the central command center for all eBay sellers. It consolidates your listings, orders, performance metrics, and marketing tools into one interface. From managing returns and buyer requests to monitoring seller standards and accessing detailed analytics, Seller Hub is your primary dashboard.

2. **Terapeak Product Research**
   Included with eBay Seller Hub, Terapeak is a powerful research tool that lets you analyze eBay marketplace data. You can study successful listings, pricing trends, seasonal demand, and competitive positioning to make more informed sourcing and listing decisions.

3. **eBay Mobile App**
   The mobile app offers functionality for sellers on the go, allowing you to create listings, manage orders, respond to messages, and print shipping labels from your phone or tablet. It's especially useful for sellers who need to remain connected while juggling multiple responsibilities.

4. **Third-Party Listing Software (e.g., InkFrog, SixBit, Wonder Lister)**
   These tools help sellers list items in bulk, sync inventory across platforms, and create custom templates that improve branding. They are crucial for time-saving and for businesses managing large volumes of SKUs.

5. **Inventory Management Tools (e.g., Sellbrite, Ecomdash, Linnworks)**
   Tracking inventory manually can lead to overselling and lost

profits. Inventory management software automates stock tracking, alerts you when it's time to reorder, and helps maintain synchronization across multiple channels if you sell beyond eBay.

6. **Shipping Tools (e.g., ShipStation, ShipRush, Pirate Ship)**
Shipping software integrates with eBay to automate label printing, rate shopping, and tracking uploads. These platforms can save you money on postage and provide a faster workflow when handling dozens or hundreds of packages per week.

7. **Accounting and Bookkeeping Tools (e.g., QuickBooks, GoDaddy Bookkeeping, Xero)**
Proper financial tracking is key to understanding your profitability and managing taxes. These tools allow you to automatically import eBay sales, reconcile bank transactions, generate profit/loss reports, and simplify quarterly or annual tax preparation.

8. **Photo Editing Tools (e.g., Canva, Adobe Lightroom, PhotoRoom)**
High-quality images are crucial for converting shoppers into buyers. These tools help you remove backgrounds, adjust lighting, and add text overlays or branding, ensuring your listings look professional and appealing.

9. **Customer Service Platforms (e.g., Zendesk, Freshdesk)**
As your business grows, responding to customer inquiries efficiently becomes more challenging. Customer service software helps organize tickets, create canned responses, and streamline communication with buyers.

10. **Automated Feedback Tools (e.g., FeedbackExpress, Bqool)**
Positive feedback influences buyer trust and conversion rates. These tools automate feedback requests, helping you maintain a high seller rating and identify negative experiences before they escalate.

11. **Dropshipping Software (e.g., AutoDS, DSM Tool, Spocket)**
If you're using dropshipping as a fulfillment model, these platforms assist in locating suppliers, syncing product details, automating orders, and updating tracking information. They minimize the need for manual coordination.

12. **Tax Compliance Tools (e.g., Avalara, TaxJar)**
Sales tax can get complicated, especially if you sell across states or internationally. These tools help calculate and file taxes accurately and ensure compliance with evolving tax regulations.

13. **eBay Community and Forums**
The eBay Community forums are a treasure trove of insights from

other sellers. You can ask questions, share tips, learn from experienced users, and keep up with platform changes.
14. **YouTube Channels and Podcasts (e.g., Daily Refinement, Rockstar Flipper, Pure Hustle Podcast)**
Consuming content from established sellers provides ongoing education and motivation. These creators often share sourcing strategies, case studies, and platform updates in an accessible, conversational format.
15. **Marketplaces and Product Sourcing Platforms (e.g., Alibaba, Faire, Wholesale Central)**
To scale, many sellers look for wholesale suppliers or new products to add to their catalog. These platforms connect you with manufacturers and distributors who can offer bulk pricing and exclusive products.
16. **Time Management Tools (e.g., Trello, Asana, Notion)**
Staying organized is critical as you juggle product sourcing, listings, customer service, and shipping. Project management apps help track tasks, set deadlines, and collaborate if you're building a team.
17. **Pricing Tools (e.g., RepricerExpress, PriceYak)**
These allow you to monitor competitors' prices and automatically adjust your own to stay competitive. Ideal for sellers in highly competitive niches or using dropshipping models.
18. **Analytics and Reporting Tools (e.g., Google Analytics, eBay Analytics, Sellerboard)**
Understanding your performance metrics helps you make smarter business decisions. These platforms let you dig into traffic sources, conversion rates, average order value, and profit margins.
19. **Email Marketing Tools (e.g., Mailchimp, Klaviyo)**
Even though eBay limits direct buyer communication, savvy sellers use email marketing off-platform to build loyalty and drive repeat sales through their own websites or social channels.
20. **AI Product Description Generators (e.g., ChatGPT, Copy.ai)**
Writing effective descriptions quickly is now easier than ever. AI tools help generate SEO-friendly, clear, and engaging copy that improves conversion while saving time.

Each of these tools and resources can play a vital role in helping you run your eBay business more smoothly, make better decisions, and stay ahead of the competition. The key is to assess your needs, test different options, and implement those that offer the most return for your time and money. As your business evolves, so will the tools you need—but starting with a strong foundation of these essentials will give you a powerful head start.

APPENDIX B: GLOSSARY OF EBAY TERMS

1. **Account Limits** – Restrictions eBay places on new or low-feedback sellers to control the number of listings they can post. These limits help ensure a quality selling experience while a seller builds credibility.

2. **Auction-Style Listing** – A format where the seller lists an item for bidding, and buyers compete by placing increasing bids until the listing ends. The highest bidder wins the item.

3. **Best Match** – eBay's default search algorithm that determines the order in which listings appear in search results. It considers factors like price, seller rating, shipping speed, item popularity, and listing quality.

4. **Best Offer** – A feature that allows buyers to negotiate a price with sellers on fixed-price listings. Sellers can accept, decline, or counter a buyer's offer.

5. **Business Policies** – Pre-set rules for shipping, payment, and returns that sellers can apply across multiple listings for consistency and easier management.

6. **Category** – The specific classification or section under which a product is listed on eBay. Proper categorization improves visibility and ensures buyers can easily find listings.

7. **Click-Through Rate (CTR)** – A performance metric that shows how often people click on a seller's listing or ad after seeing it. Higher CTR indicates effective marketing or listing appeal.

8. **eBay Buyer Protection** – A program that protects buyers from fraud or unsatisfactory transactions. It provides remedies like refunds or return support if the item is not as described or doesn't arrive.

9. **eBay Managed Payments** – eBay's payment system where it handles all transactions directly, allowing buyers to pay using various methods and ensuring sellers receive payouts directly into their bank accounts.

10. **eBay Stores** – Subscription-based seller accounts that provide storefront customization, marketing tools, and reduced fees. Stores come in different levels like Starter, Basic, Premium, and Anchor.

11. **Feedback Score** – A numerical rating based on the positive, neutral, or negative feedback received from buyers. It helps build seller reputation and buyer trust.

12. **Final Value Fee** – A commission eBay charges on the total amount of the sale (including shipping and taxes). It varies depending on the category and seller account type.

13. **Fixed-Price Listing** – A selling format where the item is sold at a set price, allowing buyers to purchase immediately without bidding.

14. Global Shipping Program (GSP) – eBay's service that simplifies international shipping. Sellers ship to a U.S. location, and eBay handles customs and delivery to the international buyer.

15. Handling Time – The time a seller takes to prepare and ship an order after receiving payment. Shorter handling times improve buyer satisfaction and can boost listing visibility.

16. Insertion Fee – The fee eBay charges for creating a listing. Sellers typically receive a number of free listings per month before insertion fees apply.

17. Invoice – A document sent to buyers summarizing the items purchased, including cost, taxes, shipping, and payment information.

18. Item Specifics – Detailed attributes like brand, size, color, and model that improve listing visibility and buyer searchability.

19. Listing – The act of posting an item for sale on eBay. A listing includes title, description, photos, price, shipping details, and more.

20. Managed Returns – eBay's system that helps streamline return requests. Sellers can set policies, issue refunds, and provide return labels all within the eBay platform.

21. PayPal – Formerly eBay's primary payment processor. While still used by some buyers, PayPal is no longer required since eBay moved to managed payments.

22. PowerSeller – A status awarded to sellers who maintain high performance in terms of sales volume, feedback, and service quality.

23. Promoted Listings – An advertising option where sellers can pay to increase the visibility of their listings in search results.

24. Resolution Center – A tool used to resolve transaction problems such as items not received, returns, or buyer-seller disputes.

25. Seller Hub – The central dashboard where sellers can manage listings, orders, marketing tools, performance metrics, and business policies.

26. Seller Level – A tiered performance ranking (Top Rated, Above Standard, or Below Standard) based on customer service, transaction defect rate, late shipment rate, and tracking upload.

27. Shipping Labels – Printable postage labels sellers can purchase directly through eBay, often at discounted rates.

28. SKU (Stock Keeping Unit) – A unique identifier assigned by the seller to manage inventory. Helps track stock, sales, and restocking needs.

29. Sniping – The act of placing a last-second bid in an auction to win an item before other bidders can respond.

30. Store Categories – Custom categories sellers create within their eBay Store to organize listings for easier navigation.

31. Title Optimization – The process of writing a compelling, keyword-rich title to improve search visibility and buyer interest.

32. Top Rated Seller – A designation for sellers who provide exceptional service, fast handling, and consistent positive feedback.

33. Tracking Number – A code assigned by the shipping carrier to monitor the movement and delivery of a package.

34. Unpaid Item Case – A process that sellers initiate when a buyer fails to pay for a won or purchased item. It can lead to cancellation and possible account penalties for the buyer.

35. Watchers – Users who bookmark or follow a listing without making an immediate purchase or bid. Can indicate interest or demand.

36. Zero Insertion Fee Listings – Free listings provided monthly by eBay. Sellers can list a set number of items without paying insertion fees, depending on their account level.

This glossary serves as a reference point to clarify unfamiliar terminology, helping sellers navigate the platform with greater ease and confidence.

APPENDIX C: COMMON MISTAKES TO AVOID AS A NEW EBAY SELLER

Starting a business on eBay can be an exciting and profitable venture. However, like any new endeavor, it can also come with its challenges. Many new eBay sellers make common mistakes that can hinder their success or even cause them to fail altogether. Being aware of these potential pitfalls and understanding how to avoid them is key to building a strong and sustainable business on the platform. In this appendix, we will discuss some of the most frequent mistakes made by new eBay sellers and offer advice on how to steer clear of them.

1. Poorly Written Listings

One of the most common mistakes made by new sellers is neglecting the importance of well-written listings. Your product description is your first opportunity to convince buyers that your product is the one they need. If your descriptions are vague, incomplete, or riddled with errors, you will lose the trust of potential buyers.

To avoid this, take the time to craft clear, detailed, and accurate descriptions. Be honest about the condition of the product, its features, and its benefits. Include high-quality images that give buyers a clear idea of what they are purchasing. Consider including measurements, color descriptions, and any relevant information that can help a buyer make an informed decision. Remember, eBay's search algorithm also looks for detailed descriptions, so the more information you provide, the better your chances of appearing in relevant searches.

2. Ignoring Shipping Costs and Policies

Shipping can be one of the most confusing and costly aspects of selling on eBay. New sellers often make the mistake of underestimating shipping costs or not offering competitive shipping options, leading to frustration for both themselves and their buyers.

To avoid this, make sure to accurately calculate the shipping cost before listing your items. Consider offering multiple shipping options to give your customers more flexibility. Additionally, try to take advantage of eBay's discounted shipping rates through partnerships with carriers like USPS, UPS, and FedEx. You should also be transparent about your shipping policies, including estimated delivery times, handling times, and any shipping restrictions. By doing this, you will prevent unexpected issues with customers, leading to smoother transactions.

3. Failing to Research Market Prices

Another critical mistake that new sellers often make is failing to research market prices before listing their products. Pricing your items too high or too low can significantly impact your sales. Setting the right price requires a thorough understanding of the competition and the market trends within your niche.

To avoid this, conduct thorough research on eBay and other online marketplaces to see what similar products are selling for. Take note of the condition, brand, and features of the items you are selling and compare them to other listings. This will help you set a competitive price that attracts buyers while still allowing you to make a reasonable profit.

4. Overlooking eBay's Seller Performance Metrics

Many new sellers focus on getting their listings live and making their first sale without paying enough attention to eBay's seller performance metrics. These metrics, including feedback ratings, shipping times, and return rates, are crucial for building trust with potential buyers. Poor performance in these areas can result in penalties, reduced visibility in search results, or even account suspension.

To avoid this mistake, take the time to familiarize yourself with eBay's seller performance standards. Aim to provide excellent customer service by shipping items promptly, accurately describing your products, and handling returns efficiently. Monitor your metrics regularly and make adjustments as needed to maintain a high level of performance.

5. Not Offering Returns

Some new eBay sellers make the mistake of not offering returns, thinking that it will save them money and hassle. However, this decision can severely limit your sales potential. Many buyers are hesitant to purchase items from sellers who don't offer return options because they want the reassurance that they can return an item if it doesn't meet their expectations.

To avoid this mistake, consider offering a return policy. Even a 30-day return window can significantly increase your credibility and boost your sales. eBay also tends to favor sellers who offer returns, which can improve your chances of being featured in search results.

6. Not Staying On Top of Customer Communication

Effective communication with your buyers is key to maintaining a good reputation on eBay. New sellers often make the mistake of ignoring or neglecting customer inquiries, which can lead to negative feedback or disputes. If a customer has a question about your product, they expect a prompt response.

To avoid this, make sure to check your eBay inbox regularly and respond to customer inquiries in a timely manner. Clear and professional communication can go a long way in preventing misunderstandings and building trust with your customers. If a customer is unhappy with their purchase, reach out to them immediately to resolve the issue. This proactive approach will help you maintain a high seller rating and build a loyal customer base.

7. Ignoring eBay's Fees

eBay charges various fees for listing and selling items, including insertion fees, final value fees, and additional charges for premium services. New sellers sometimes overlook these fees when setting their prices, leading to lower profit margins than anticipated.

To avoid this, familiarize yourself with eBay's fee structure and factor these costs into your pricing strategy. Remember to account for the cost of shipping and any other overheads when calculating your profit margins. By doing so, you can ensure that you are pricing your products correctly to make a profit while still remaining competitive.

8. Failing to Optimize Listings for Search

eBay's search engine plays a crucial role in driving traffic to your listings. New sellers often make the mistake of not optimizing their listings for eBay's search algorithm, known as "Best Match." This can result in your items being buried in search results, making it harder for buyers to find them.

To avoid this mistake, use relevant keywords in your product title, description, and item specifics. Be sure to fill in all available fields, including the brand, size, and color, as these attributes help your listings appear in more targeted searches. Additionally, high-quality photos, competitive pricing, and positive customer feedback will all contribute to better search rankings.

9. Underestimating the Importance of Customer Feedback

Feedback is one of the most powerful tools in building a strong reputation on eBay. New sellers sometimes underestimate the importance of feedback and fail to actively encourage customers to leave reviews.

Positive feedback helps establish trust with potential buyers and can boost your visibility on eBay.

To avoid this mistake, actively encourage buyers to leave feedback after completing a purchase. A simple message thanking them for their purchase and politely asking for feedback can go a long way. Remember that negative feedback can be mitigated by offering excellent customer service, responding to issues quickly, and resolving disputes fairly.

10. Not Having a Business Plan

Finally, one of the biggest mistakes that new eBay sellers make is starting their business without a clear plan. It's easy to get caught up in the excitement of listing products and making sales, but without a solid business strategy, your growth may be limited.

To avoid this mistake, take the time to create a business plan for your eBay store. Set clear goals, such as sales targets and profit margins, and develop a strategy for sourcing products, managing inventory, and scaling your business. A well-thought-out plan will help you stay focused and make informed decisions as you grow your eBay business.

Success on eBay requires more than just listing products and waiting for buyers. It involves careful planning, attention to detail, and a commitment to providing excellent customer service. By avoiding these common mistakes, you can set yourself up for long-term success and build a profitable business on eBay. Stay focused, keep learning, and adapt to changes in the marketplace, and you will be well on your way to becoming a successful eBay seller.